French Perspectives in
African Studies

French Perspectives in African Studies

A Collection of Translated Essays

EDITED WITH AN INTRODUCTION BY
PIERRE ALEXANDRE

Foreword by Daryll Forde

Published for the
INTERNATIONAL AFRICAN INSTITUTE
by the
OXFORD UNIVERSITY PRESS

LONDON   IBADAN   NAIROBI

1973

Oxford University Press, Ely House, London W. 1

GLASGOW NEW YORK TORONTO MELBOURNE WELLINGTON
CAPE TOWN IBADAN NAIROBI DAR ES SALAAM LUSAKA ADDIS ABABA
DELHI BOMBAY CALCUTTA MADRAS KARACHI LAHORE DACCA
KUALA LUMPUR SINGAPORE HONG KONG TOKYO

ISBN 0 19 724191 3

Printed in Great Britain by
Richard Clay (The Chaucer Press), Ltd., Bungay, Suffolk

Contents

III

Foreword

The preparation of this English version of a collection of studies by French Africanists arose from discussions at a special meeting on Francophone-Anglophone collaboration in African Studies which was convened by the Institute in April 1969. These included consideration of the need to make significant work published by scholars in either language more widely accessible.

While it might appear paradoxical that a need for much more extensive translation should be urged with reference to African studies, especially in the West African area, when the achievement of bilingual competence on the part of all serious scholars and research students was generally regarded as essential, it was also recognized that this was largely a question of timing and the range of dissemination of information. In Africa itself, even under favourable conditions it was thought that it would take a number of years before there was a considerable body of bilingual African students working in the African studies field, and that the same probably applied elsewhere. Meanwhile, a large amount of basic work and important lines of thought remained virtually excluded from undergraduate and even postgraduate training programmes owing to the lack of linguistic competence on the part of students and the difficulties of effective procurement of foreign books.

It was also thought that the anglophone academic world was less familiar with and made less use of francophone material than vice versa, and that this could be held a reason for concentrating in the first place on securing translations into English of French studies relating to the West African region. It was urged that the Institute itself should contribute to this effort by undertaking the publication in English of a collection of studies which would present in brief compass some of the main approaches and methods that had been developed by French Africanists since the forties.

This proposal was accepted by the Council of the Institute, and Professor Pierre Alexandre kindly consented to undertake the editorship of the volume. This, as he makes clear in his Introduction, has been no easy task. Limitations of space and the very wide range of publications to be considered raised difficult problems of selection, which called for many consultations with colleagues and subsequent discussions with those who consented to contribute studies. Professor Alexandre has also given careful consideration, in consultation wherever possible with the authors, to the translations, in order to ensure faithful and clear rendering of the original texts.

While he stresses that a small collection of studies of this kind can make no claim to be comprehensive or systematic, it will, we hope, be recognized as providing a fair conspectus of the scope and trends of African studies in France. The salient features of these are outlined and vividly commented on by Professor Alexandre in his own Introduction. The Institute is greatly indebted to him for the care and pertinacity that he has devoted to the editing of this volume. Its thanks are also due to the co-operation of the authors whose work is included in this volume and to Dr. Robert Brain for the translations, in which he has endeavoured to present as effectively as possible versions of concepts and modes of expression in the original French texts which might otherwise have been obscure to English readers.

We are also indebted to the editors and publishers of the journals in which the original French texts appeared for permission to publish these translations.

The International African Institute gratefully acknowledges the assistance provided for the translations presented in this volume by a grant from the Secrétariat d'Etat aux Affaires Etrangères, Paris, accorded with the support of the International Social Science Council. The Secrétariat d'Etat has, however, had no part in the selection of the French texts for which the International African Institute is solely responsible.

DARYLL FORDE
Director

Introduction

PIERRE ALEXANDRE

'*Africanisme*' is generally translated as 'African studies', yet I could not swear that the semantic fields of both terms are exactly co-terminal. '*Africanisme*' was coined some sixty years ago after '*Orientalisme*' which had been in use since the beginning of the nineteenth century with the meaning '*science ou étude des choses de l'Orient*'. In fact, owing to the peculiar logic of the French diplomatic service, '*Africanisme*'—probably as the 'science or study of things African'—was (still is even now) a part of '*Orientalisme*'. The most recent of French dictionaries (*Petit Robert*, Paris, 1967) ignores '*Africanisme*' but presents the '*Africaniste*' as 'a specialist in African languages and civilizations'. The latter term, even before the creation of Congrès International des Africanistes (1964) had gained official recognition in France, so to speak, with the foundation of the Société des Africanistes, whose *Journal*, now in its fortieth volume, was for long the only, and is still the main, French learned periodical exclusively devoted to African topics. In spite of this it is only since the late fifties that African studies have been officially introduced in some French universities.

At this point the non-Gallic reader must probably be reminded of an idiosyncrasy of the French higher-education system, i.e. the division between *Grandes Ecoles*,[1] which are mainly vocational, with admission by competitive examination, and universities, which are open to all and only slightly concerned with vocational training. Things African were, at first, a monopoly of the Ecole Coloniale, the Colonial service training college, and the Ecole des Langues Orientales, which coaches people for the Diplomatic Service examinations. The infiltration of African studies into academic university curricula did not begin in earnest before French colonialism was decidedly on the wane.

This does not mean that the prehistory—so to speak—of African studies, the period where those concerned were mostly colonial administrators and Christian missionaries, must be underrated. There

---

[1] Now called 'Grands établissements'; in literal translation: 'Grand establishment', a not insignificant pun . . .

were sound workers among them, as typified by the dominant figure of Governor Maurice Delafosse (1870–1927), anthropologist, linguist, and historian, a scholar of international repute, often prophetic in both his methods and his views. Nevertheless those pioneer Africanists were, on the whole, a closed group (with frequently ferocious strife between laymen and clergy), whose work had little direct impact outside their own ranks. They were still the 'explorers' or 'travellers' whose reports were theorized upon by stay-at-home professors. It must be confessed that most of them were, for evident reasons, more concerned with immediate application of their observations than with general theories. This is evidenced by the fact that most scholarly administrators put the stress of their researches on law and political institutions, while the missionaries preferred to look into religion and systems of values and beliefs. Such theoretical background as existed came mainly from P. Schmidt's *Anthropos* school with the clerics, from Comte through Durkheim and Levi-Bruhl with the laymen. The main fields of studies were anthropology (only sociology was then officially taught in France), linguistics (French universities preferred philology), and history (it was the academic historians' dogma that Africa *could not* have a history). There was no question of an African equivalent of the Ecole Française d'Extrême-Orient: the mere idea of it would have been considered a joke before 1914.

The change started between the two World Wars; there was increased interest in the social sciences in French universities, and especially in that rather queer, marginal institution, the Ecole Pratique des Hautes Etudes à la Sorbonne.[2]

Then, in the early thirties, the Ministry of Colonies endowed a chair of anthropology (French: *ethnologie*) in the Sorbonne, while the Governor General of French West Africa created the Institut Français d'Afrique Noire (IFAN) with headquarters in Dakar and local branches in the several territories.

The first holder of the chair of anthropology was Marcel Mauss. He was not an Africanist, nor even a 'real' anthropologist, in so far as he had no experience of field-work. Nevertheless he was the father of professional anthropology in France: by 1935 his first students were engaged in their initiatory field-work in various parts of the world,

[2] Founded in 1862, reputedly on an Oxbridge model, it associates research and teaching; with no regular curriculum, teaching chiefly in seminars and tutorials, it does not grant degrees, but offers subjects ignored by Universities, often on an experimental basis; sections IV, V, and VI are concerned with the social sciences and the humanities.

including Africa, starting a new trend which had taken firm roots by 1939.

In 1940 Professor Mauss was deprived of his chair by the Nazis and Vichyites. He was eventually replaced by Professor Marcel Griaule (1898–1956), the first Africanist to hold a chair in a French university: this was the end of our prehistory, and marked the start of the anthropology of today.

IFAN was probably the first all-embracing institute of African studies, dealing with both social and natural sciences as applying to the African milieu. It employed both professionals and amateurs (some of whom eventually turned professional), African as well as European, obtaining results out of proportion with its shoestring budget. One of its main functions was to ensure coordination of research and mutual information for research workers, both residents and visitors. It was to become, after 1945, the nucleus of the University of Dakar which eventually took over a large part of its former functions.

*

This collection is a partial one, in every sense of the term. Unwillingly partial, but partial just the same. There is no room here to explain in detail the methods and constraints which played a part in the final selection of texts and authors. Those authors who are represented here chose their own texts—subject to the limitations of conditions of reprinting and the space available—so that their contributions can be considered as fairly typical of their own work. But they are not representative of the whole panorama of contemporary trends among French Africanists. To begin with, all of them are, now, working in Paris: the provincial and African universities and research centres have to some extent been left out from lack of space. Even then the sample is not representative of all the trends in the Paris schools. The youngest generation, which tends to be much more radical in outlook, methods, and aims is hardly represented at all. For the more senior practitioners, the sample is fair enough as regards disciplines, but not too well balanced with respect to trends and methods. To take but one example, such a respected scholar as Professor Bastide (Afro-American ethno-psychology) very kindly agreed to step aside to make room for a younger person. Of course, Professor Bastide does not need to be introduced to specialists; yet his absence, even if it has allowed us to correct to some extent the effects of the generation gap, still results in some imbalance of the general picture. And we could quote about a dozen other obvious omissions, such as R. Mauny, E. de Dampierre, C. Tardits, P. F. Lacroix, R. Pélissier, M. Houis, H. Deschamps, to mention only a few well-known names. Exhaustiveness was, however, impossible within the assigned limits, while it is doubtful whether a purely random choice of authors and subjects would have provided a better overall view. It may well be that a purely personal and subjective choice of writers and topics would have offered a better solution than the present compromise. On the other hand it is perhaps more significant to have let the authors make their own choice, the editor being responsible only for apportioning space between the various disciplines.

As the reader will come to realize, anthropology is central in the field of Francophone African studies. Yet the table of contents shows only three pieces of straight anthropology (the French word *ethnologie* would perhaps be more apt). For, in fact, most, if not all articles are basically anthropology in combination with some other discipline. Another indication of this is the proliferation in French of compound phrases such as *ethnosociologie, ethnohistoire, ethnolinguistique*, etc. *Ethnogéographie* is hardly, if ever, used today, yet this does not prevent the geographers from having anthropological (they tend to say 'sociological') preoccupations and from working in teams with anthropologists.

As mentioned before, Marcel Griaule was the real pioneer in African anthropology and many of his students and disciples are still active in the discipline. Griaule's anthropology is not too easy to define in Anglo-Saxon terms. His approach, influenced as it was by the Durkheimian tradition, was nevertheless probably closer to American cultural anthropology than to British social anthropology (the latter found a parallel more in applied sociology as expounded by Robert Montagne and his school in North Africa and the Near East). The main concern of Griaule and his students was directed towards systems of values, beliefs, and Weltanschauung, rather than towards kinship systems and political structures. It led to meticulous, pains-taking, almost exhaustive ethnography, with an attempt to interpret the resultant data in the Africans' own terms or views. *Dieu d'eau* (*Conversations with Ogotemmêli*, London, 1965) or *Le Renard pâle* are thus Dogon ethnography rather than an ethnography of the Dogon. Or, to put it another way, it is second level ethnography—the ethnography of Dogon ethnography. Griaule's classic article on the mother's brother in the Western Sudan is quite typical in this respect, especially when compared with, for instance, that of Radcliffe-Brown. Similarly Germaine Dieterlen's description of the blacksmith caste in the same region is primarily cultural rather than structural or functional as would probably have been the case with a student of Malinowski or Radcliffe-Brown, and this is true to an only slightly lesser extent of Denise Paulme's work on age-sets and blood-pacts as compared, for instance, with Evans-Pritchard on those of the Nuer or Azande.

It is rather difficult to describe the philosophy underlying the works of this school and period. The *ethnologues*, at least in Africa, kept aloof from the sociologists, striving more or less explicitly to keep the two disciplines apart. In so far as French sociological work on Africa had been influenced—quite strongly in some cases (cf. Maunier's *Sociologie coloniale*, 1932)—by Comte's and Spencer's evolutionism, the African anthropologists reacted against this tendency which had all too often led to rather unpleasant racial stereotypes of 'primitive' or 'backward' peoples. Griaule himself fought, fiercely at times, to have African cultures recognized as real and valid ones, on a level both with Western and with 'classical' and exotic civilizations.

This kind of anti-evolutionist, possibly anti-sociological bias, resulted in a somewhat static approach, producing splendidly detailed descriptive work as far as traditional customs and modes of behaviour were concerned, but often failing to take into account phenomena of social change with the ensuing modifications or re-interpretations of customary values. The implicit ideology of the Griaulean school has been a generous universalist humanism which sought, so to speak, for proofs of the essential humanity—and hence equality—of Africans, through and beyond the originality of their cultures. Save ye first the kingdom of culture and politics and economy will be added unto you . . . Griaule himself, as a politician (he was active in the demo-christian Mouvement Republicain Populaire and a member of the Assemblée de l'Union Française), was strongly critical of the assimilationist aims and methods of the French colonial administration, yet he never confronted the existence of the colonial relationship as such. In fact he tended to ignore all manifestations of the colonial presence among his beloved Dogon, to leave it out of the otherwise meticulous picture he gave of their society.

The colonial facts of life were to be discovered only by the post-war generation with the initiative of Georges Balandier, who introduced the notion of the 'colonial situation' in 1955, a bare five years before the official demise of colonialism. This generation saw the end of the divorce between anthropology and sociology, a rapprochement which soon extended to other disciplines as well. The initiative cannot be laid exclusively at Balandier's feet. It was a result, in part, of the growth in numbers of younger French Africanist research workers, in part of a better knowledge of British and later American studies, both in anthropological theory and in African field-research. Some of Griaule's followers actively joined in this widening of aims, approaches, and methods. Yet differences are evident from a comparison, for instance, of Calame's and Alexandre's work in linguistics, the former being rather ethnological, the latter rather sociological in their contexts.

Balandier's *Sociologie actuelle de l'Afrique noire* (1955) offered a dynamic, future-oriented approach, which not only did not try to sift out the 'impure' non-ethnological modern traits but in fact consciously sought to integrate them into the description of contemporary African societies as total systems. It was an anthropology of function, much influenced by the British functional–structural school, and making no really clear-cut distinction between anthropology and sciology. Its practitioners would probably prefer to be called *ethnosociologues* rather than plain *ethnologues*, and rightly so. Culture is not, however, neglected in this approach (as it tended to be in some British works of the forties), but it is no longer analysed as an isolated or isolable phenomenon. Rather it is viewed in a dynamic, dialectic relationship with the other aspects of the total field, including politics and the economy. Scholars of this persuasion are certainly not orthodox marxists but they have read Marx whose influence, if not determinant, still remains quite perceptible in their writings. Multi-disciplinary studies become a necessity with this group, be they conducted by teams (e.g. Sautter's and Balandier–Mercier's *Atlas des terroirs africains*, associating geographers and ethno-sociologists) or by general practitioners (Alexandre on language problems and nation-building). Lifelong, intensive studies of one group *à la* Griaule tend to be replaced by a shorter term of concentrated field-work followed by still shorter trips to other regions and other tribes, offering a wider basis for theorizing. The scholars' personal involvement with one particular people is probably less deep than in the Griaulian approach, the overall concern with Africa has taken on a different orientation. It is also significant that the growth and academic installation of this school—if it can be called a school—was contemporary with the decolonization of Africa.

The most recent generation working in independent Africa, then, would be represented in this volume by Claude Meillassoux and

J. Zempleni-Rabain. The latter, as a psychologist with good anthropological training, is probably less typical of the new trend than Meillassoux, who is often categorized as an economic anthropologist. It would be more to the point to characterize him as a neo-marxian general anthropologist, since his preoccupation with economic structures derives from a rigorous application of some of Marx's social concepts, that is, to simplify somewhat unduly, on occasion, an explanation of the total structure of any society based on the study of the modes and relationships of production. As such he is typical of a new radical trend—whose exponents do not belong to the French Communist Party—including such people as E. Terray or P. P. Rey, whose views also derive from Lévi-Straussian structuralism as well as from the works of neo-marxian philosophers such as G. Althusser.

With this group the fusion of anthropology and sociology is complete. What they advocate is, in fact, a unified field theory of all the social sciences, a single, all-embracing, total Sociology. *Africanisme* then would no longer have its own theoretical *raison d'être*. It would become a local application of the general Science of Society—which would at the same time be the Science of Man. Thus would the circle be closed: we should be back at the situation which obtained at the end of the nineteenth century, only at a higher level of abstraction, with a higher power of explanation. One does not want to sound too pessimistic or old-fashioned, yet it is difficult to escape a feeling that this is still a little premature.

While there is certainly a very definite need for synthetic and comprehensive studies of Africa and Africans much—if not most—of the data are still to be collected. It is an interesting fact that many African students are going back to ethnography, a field which has been somewhat neglected since the late fifties. And a similar tendency can be observed among young African linguists, geographers, and historians: they engage in monographic studies, not because it is an easier apprenticeship (it is not) but because they are probably more aware than their European colleagues of the actual scarcity of reliable data and of the difficulty and urgency of their collection. This does not mean either that they wish to renounce communication outside the bounds of their own methodology or that they make no attempt at theoretical analyses or generalization. But they approach Africa as insiders, even while using outsiders' methods and instruments. This is likely to lead to a new type of relationship between foreign Africanists and African social scientists—an issue which is of world-wide, not just French or European, dimensions.

I

The Mother's Brother in
the Western Sudan

MARCEL GRIAULE[1]

The problem of the relationship between the maternal uncle and his sister's son has long been under discussion by sociologists and anthropologists. A considerable amount of documentation has been collected on the rites, practices, and representations which characterize this relationship, and attempts to explain and to become more deeply aware of the subject-matter are many in the literature. It would therefore seem to be of some interest to contribute to this debate, which is far from closed, some explanations provided by the people themselves on situations originating from this type of kinship.

The Sudan provides an excellent field of study, offering at first sight clear-cut examples of this institution, which among the Bambara and the Fulani, for example, manifests itself both during periods of tension on the occasion of funerals, weddings, and births, and also in the most current events of everyday life. Among the Fulani, where children live in close contact with both the father and the mother's brother, they will certainly expect a degree of attachment from the former, but it is the latter who shows tender affection on all occasions. If today a boy goes to school, his father gives him advice but will restrict his compliments and will be harsh in his criticism. The mother's brother, on the other hand, will always show great indulgence. A father, when scolding his son for unsatisfactory school results will often conclude: '. . . and now go and be comforted by your uncle.'

[1] *Marcel Griaule* (1898–1956), Dr. es L. The first field anthropologist appointed to a Chair of Ethnology at the Sorbonne (1942). Initially trained in Semitic languages, he worked first (1928) in Ethiopia and then, from 1931, in West Africa, specializing on the Dogon of Mali. Developed a method of exhaustive ethnography, working with a team of students year after year on a limited area. After the Second World War he also entered politics, being elected a Councillor of the French Union, in which capacity he played an important part in the drafting of constitutional and legal reforms in West Africa. Until his death he was the dominant figure in French African studies. The original French text of this paper was published as 'Remarques sur l'oncle utérin au Soudan', *Cahiers Internationaux de Sociologie*, xvi (1954), 35–49.

Later on the relationship undergoes a change: in spite of the uncle's continuing indulgence, the nephew will start criticizing him and making demands, most of which will be met, the most important being, among the Bambara for example, the provision of a wife. In many cases, moreover, the kind of obligation which the uncle seems to have assumed towards his nephew will be extinguished as soon as marriage takes place. Somehow compensatory to this attitude we can observe, among the same people, a classic rivalry between the father and the son, a so-called *fadena* in which substantive expression the terms *fa* 'father' and *de* 'son' could mean 'father–son rapport', 'father–son way of relating'. This term is applied to practically all kinds of rivalry, that between father and son being the prototype. Among some peoples these attitudes are even more pronounced; among the Dogon, when the death of the mother's brother is announced, his sister's sons are told by the elders on the paternal side that 'their millet is ripe!': *yu bemme illawa*. By this they mean that it is the time for them to go and 'harvest' the crops, that is the wealth of their uterine kin, wealth which has become available on the death of their uncle and which, mythically, should belong to them.

The same encouragement is given to them at the end of the mourning period, *dama*, which is celebrated several months or even years after the funeral; those who participate take the opportunity to indulge in apparent violence,[2] raiding cattle and foodstuffs which they carry off to the young men's house in their village ward. It is all eaten on the spot and shared with members of their age classes, *tonno*, who receive the plunderers with shouts of *day sõ*, which is normally shouted at hunters in order to bring them luck or to praise them for their spoils. The elders call after the young men *olu po*, 'good bush', when they see them going off to the meal, known as *niñu walu* 'the diminishing of the uncle'.

A 'diminishing of the uncle' also takes place on other occasions. Any visit which the nephew makes to his house is a pretext for levying small amounts of goods, and this is done with a great deal of furore while daring jokes and insults are directed at the uncle's wife.

Along with customs such as these we have, among the same people, rivalry between father and son and between brothers, and a marked reserve between mother and son.

---

[2] This feigned attitude parallels the actual limitations on the amount of goods taken. In 1946 the young men of a family in Dozyou Oreil (Upper Sanga) pillaged their maternal kin living in Dyamini (Lower Sanga) and their booty, considered a large one, consisted of ten measures of millet, a dozen chickens and a goat.

These classic facts, so well established that we do not need to elaborate on them here, are given an initial explanation:

'All those things, the Dogon say, which the *mangou*[3] nephew (joking relative) steals from his uncle, it is because of (his) mother: it is because of the anger (which he feels at the idea) that there has been no marriage between (his) uterine uncle and (his) mother. If (the nephew) insults his uncle's wife, it is because she has taken his mother's place. The symbolic anger he feels towards his father is because his mother did not stay (marry) with his uncle.'[4]

The focal point of interest, therefore, in these initial statements, is the non-realized union of his mother and his uterine uncle: i.e. between a brother and a sister. In fact, the ideal union, mythically speaking, is between a pair of twins whose prototype came from the egg of the world. They consider any situation in the present to be the direct consequence of the first acts of creation, which must be presented here, as succinctly as possible, if we wish to comprehend the problem.

Creation began with a seed of *Digitaria exilis* which is euphemistically known as *kize uzi*, 'the little thing', that is, in the minds of the people, the smallest of all things.[5] This tiny grain was the prefiguration of a limitless world: it contained, in particular, a central kernel made of a tablet bearing signs which, after being dispersed in outer space, fell on mankind thereby making people conscious of themselves.[6]

The interior of this egg-seed was divided into two placentas which prefigured the worlds of heaven and earth and each contained a pair of twins of both sexes, Nommo, direct emanations of the creator Amma. While Amma is unique, his perfect unity is only realized in the association of two complementary creatures, male and female in

[3] The word *mangou* is used here to explain the nephew's attitude to his uncle and recalls that of his 'joking partner'. This over-simple translation is used here for convenience only. Cf. my article 'Alliance cathartique', *Africa*, xviii, 4 (October 1948).

[4] Ledu woniñi mon māgugo kede woy guyā. wozogo wona sabde. wogŏ woniñugo wo na belle yagi yolugo kine ban dige. wo niñu yana woduyozogo wo na dŏy dāga dige. wo de le kine banu le wo aduno sone wona wo niñu mon toyoluga.

[5] This euphemism is used mostly by totemic priests for whom this grain is strictly tabooed.

[6] The metaphysical part of creation will not be treated here. We shall deal only with that mythical part which concerns beings whose situation and sentiments are prototypes for those of mankind today. The Dogon system of astronomy will also be omitted along with a detailed description of twinship which we shall mention only briefly. For signs, cf. M. Griaule and G. Dieterlen, *Signes graphiques soudanais* (L'Homme: Cah. Ethnol. Géog. et Ling., no. 3), 1951.

each case. In one of these parts the male did not wait the correct amount of time to be formed but sprang out prematurely, disappearing into space, taking with him some grains of *Digitaria exilis* and a piece of his own placenta.

He wanted to create his own world, a replica, before its time, of the one which, until then, had only a potential existence and which was to develop normally.[7]

He made a rough shape of the earth with the things he brought with him but since he had been separated from his female twin he climbed back into the egg in order to try and find that part of the placenta where she was. However Amma stepped in then and dispersed the contents of the egg and the creature went back down again, incomplete, to begin his ever fruitless quest for his twin, Yasigi, whom Amma handed to the other pair of Nommo.

However by procreating in his own placenta which had become the earth and was the avatar of his genitrix, he created—into obscurity, dryness, and the absence of time—single creatures who were incomplete like himself. At the same time he himself took the form of an animal called Yurugu (*Vulpes pallida*).

Henceforth everything in the world below became impure, as the result of incest which had been prefigured by Yurugu's fruitless return into the egg from which he had been born.

In order to remedy the drawbacks of this situation, Amma sent the couple of Nommo to earth accompanied by blacksmiths and four couples who were to be the second generation. They occupied a huge ark which bore a whole new world which with light, moisture, and time, took over from the earlier world. Nevertheless, the latter did not disappear; order and disorder coexisted, one being necessary to the other, a situation which revealed itself in the ceaseless struggle between Nommo and Yurugu, in which the latter is for ever vanquished.

This brief outline of the considerable myth developed by the Dogon will suffice to enable us to follow the inquiries into their representations of kinship and their attitudes to these.

The Dogon joint family forms an exogamous group which is patrilocal and patrilineal. As far as marriage is concerned they

[7] Here, as far as the Dogon are concerned, we are presenting a summary and necessarily clumsy picture of these events. This person is the avatar of an internal vibration of the egg, which once it pierced the sheath joined the external world. It was therefore normal for him to come out first, and it was in the creator's plan. What was abnormal was his theft which caused disorder, a feature equally essential to creation.

practise a form of generalized exchange, the preferred spouse being the daughter of the mother's brother.[8]

However, this situation and similar practices are the basic structure supporting complex patterns, varying according to the reciprocal position of the agnatic and uterine kin, or between spouses or again between generations as in the case of uncle and uterine nephew. Thus for each individual the uterine group represents feminity and maternity. Whatever his age he calls all the women of his maternal family 'mother', even small girls. This group's patron is the Nommo pair, first expression of the embryo which was to become a universe based on the principle of twinness.

On the opposite side, the agnatic group represents masculinity and paternity, being the guarantor of Amma the creator. In this case, Amma-creator and the created Nommo-universe are equivalent, the universe being nothing more than a replica of Amma, as are also the two groups which unite in order that life may continue.[9] The non-paired couple Yurugu and Yasigi do not appear.

Seen from another angle, the two lines merge at the level of *ego*'s grandfathers, who are Amma and bifurcate on the level of genitors: the father and his sister are the pair of reorganizing Nommo, and the mother and her brother are the other couple from the egg, Yurugu and Yasigi. In other words, it means that agnatic kin are images of those beings in that part of the egg where all events took place in an orderly fashion, other kinsfolk, on the other hand, correspond to that part where disorder reigned and where the generations became muddled.

Indeed the norms, at the beginning of creation, involved twinship parity on the one hand, and union between a brother and a sister belonging to the same pair of twins on the other. The twins who were born of this union, and who also married, had as their father the twin brother of their mother; later, as a result of the incest prohibition, he became the uterine uncle. Let us provisionally content ourselves with looking at this mythical rule and its projection into the real world

[8] Cf. M. Griaule and G. Dieterlen, 'The Dogon' in *African Worlds*, ed. Daryll Forde, London, 1954; also G. Dieterlen, 'Parenté et mariage chez les Dogon', *Africa*, xxvi, 2 (April 1956).

[9] We could almost say that we are dealing with the subordination of the creator to his work. This idea, at all events, is expressed in a phrase, *Amma gunnono* ('captive of God' or 'God captive'). Cf. M. Griaule and G. Dieterlen, 'Signes graphiques soudanais', p. 22, fig. 41. See also fig. 43, ibid. *Amma koho* ('water-drawer of God' or 'God water-drawer') which shows the creator in his role as a drawer of water, that is, bearer of life to the world or in his role as master of a water-drawer.

where marriages between brothers and sisters are, in fact, prohibited.[10]
Ego today has his mother's husband for a father and not his mother's
brother. The husband is therefore a foreign element who, if we refer
back to the mythical rule, has unduly taken the part of the genitrix's
brother; and he, for his part, has married a woman from outside who,
in return, has usurped the place of her husband's sister, i.e. *ego*'s
mother.

Ego's aggressiveness will therefore be exercised against the wife of
his uterine uncle, because she is an usurper, against his uncle's
property, the possession of which he has been denied and also against
his father whose presence is out of place. On the practical level he
raids his uncle's goods, insults his wife and lives in a relationship of
tension with his father, a relationship known as *na ginu baba* 'competition[11] of the mother's house' which is reflected in special kinds of
joking.

Two facts remain to be explained, however. On the one hand the
mother's brother must not only endure his nephew plundering his
goods but he must also give one of his daughters in marriage to him;
moreover, the shouting sessions between the nephew and his aunt by
marriage basically involve their supposed but ridiculed marriage and
any theft which he commits in her house is mythically equivalent to
having sexual intercourse with her. These thefts are not given their
full meaning unless they take place in the presence of the woman
concerned and are accompanied by joking directed at her, the most
frequent of which involves the remark 'my wife!' to which she
replies 'my husband!'

All this takes place as though *ego* were symbolically substituting
himself for his uncle and as if incest would only be avoided if he were
to marry a woman borne by his aunt and who would play her role. Here
we are confronted with a more complex reaction than the one so far
envisaged, a reaction whose motivation is well understood by
knowledgeable Dogon. They find a precedent for it in the adventures
of Yurugu, who sprang too early from the egg of the world.

Yurugu did indeed jump into space carrying a piece of the nurtur-
ing placenta along with him, that is part of his mother. He also considered that this organ was his own property, part of his own person,
so much so that he identified himself with his genitrix, in fact the

[10] We are not concerned here with tracing the origin of the incest prohibition as
far as native thought is concerned. This institution is explained by a quite different
method involving the division of cultivated fields and the clavicular contents. Cf.
G. Dieterlen, ibid., note 7.
[11] *Baba* means 'competition, rivalry' and also 'respect'.

matrix of the world, and deemed himself to be on the same level as her from the point of view of the generations.

As a result, today, every male considering himself from the point of view of the maternal line, that is in relation to the part of the egg where the pair Yurugu–Yasigi were conceived, likens himself to Yurugu. It is because of this fact that he unconsciously feels that symbolically he belongs to his mother's generation and is detached from the actual generation to which he belongs. This is a situation which is a replica of Yurugu's own when he was deprived of that part of the placenta containing his twin or proper wife, and taking the part which was his own[12] and representing his mother, had intercourse with her, legitimately according to him but incestuously according to the others. This feeling has the effect, in the first place, of reinforcing the subject's attitude of hostility towards members of the generation which, in fact, precedes him: the father, the uterine uncle, and his wife are all held responsible by him for this kind of *diminutio capitis*. However, this is not the most important aspect: according to him he is of the same substance and generation as his mother and he assimilates himself to a male twin of his genitrix, and the mythical rule of the union of a paired couple proposes him as her ideal husband. Therefore as the 'pseudo-brother' of his genitrix he should occupy the place of his uterine uncle, the designated husband of this woman. It is this person, i.e. the monopolizer of both his personality and his mythically possible wife, who has to put up with his reactions, much more than his father, a kind of supernumerary stranger figure who has merely deprived him of a wife.

However, since incest with the mother is impossible he falls back on somebody who is, in a way, his mother's shadow, that is his uncle's wife, a woman who is, incidentally, sexually tabooed. The difficulty is resolved by means of insults and thefts which constitute both a taking possession (which causes impurity since it is simulating incest) and a catharsis.

The nephew, indeed, through his insults and joking, is ridding himself of his anger (*kinu ban* 'red heart') and bringing peace by making his matrilateral kin laugh. Moreover, the theft of an animal or some food is sufficient to represent the totality of wealth. Symbolically, therefore, he has stolen the whole avuncular patrimony and also taken his sought-after wife.

On the one hand, however, the product of the theft, the material

[12] It is to be understood that these parts formed a single placenta, which was paired with that containing the Nommo couple.

projection of a fictive incest contains all the impurity of the actual act; on the other hand, it contains all the impurities which have been contracted previously, on every occasion, by the goods involved. Finally the nephew's action recalls that of Yurugu when he steals the seed from the egg of the world, a theft which led to the intervention of Nommo. It was he, indeed, who brought back the seed on Amma's order and devoted himself to searching everywhere, thus extending his rule. Stealing ritually involves the intervention of the Reorganizer: that is he has to put everything in order again by means of a purificatory rite. It is also through reference to this intervention that a seizure of another type takes place at a time when agnates steal from matrilateral kin in order to celebrate the birth of twin calves. This is an exceptional event and is attributed to the reorganizing Nommo. The district concerned and also the neighbouring ones become the theatre for comings and goings which, sometimes, last several weeks. Everyone capable of walking and talking makes for his mother's natal compound in order to take the news and receive a gift in return. In former times, only the women were asked, and they handed over cowries. Today, all members of the group join together and usually give money. As for the old men who are incapable of walking, they must be content with visiting kinsfolk who are married in their village or watching out for those who are coming to the market.

But since, on the one hand, everyone is related to a matrilateral lineage and is also, in return, the matrilateral kinsman of other groups of people, the money received at the end of the long trek must, in the end, be handed over the next time to those who come begging with the announcement of a similar piece of news.

They hand over the same amount they had received; and since they also had expenses on the journey it means that a loss was made on the whole transaction. As for the man who does not put himself out to visit his kin, he is the loser since he has to give without receiving. The whole process thing keeps money circulating.[13]

In this case matrilateral kin is assimilated to Yurugu, and the agnates, as Nommo's representatives, force them to celebrate, through gifts, an event which marks his adversary's power.

We can therefore see that in certain cases the nephew, in so far as he is a member of the agnatic group, acts in quite the opposite way. Instead of playing the role of thief and trying to commit incest he is now Nommo's representative, the promoter of twin births which constitute a challenge to the single nature of Yurugu. However, if we

[13] Cf. *Dieu d'eau*, p. 235.

return to the nephew's action at his uncle's, we see that it is manifested, as far as incest is concerned, in other ways than by scabrous words and spectacular thefts. When he marries the uncle's daughter, *ego* marries a replica of his affinally related aunt. The latter, as we pointed out, is herself a substitute for *ego*'s mother. Here we are faced with an imitation of the mythical incestuous act which at the same time, nevertheless, is made fun of. Indeed, the marriage is actually licit and any kind of satisfaction which Yurugu might derive from this act is nothing but a mere decoy and mockery.

Marrying a cousin of the same generation who implicitly represents an older generation involves a symmetrical correspondence and also a palliative: while an uncle is not able to dispose of his sister's sons he can dispose of her daughters, which he does by selling them to his younger brothers. In this situation the uterine niece represents her own genitrix. The younger brothers take possession, in this way, through successive assimilations of a replica of their own sister. Therefore, through this oblique action, two different generations are placed on the same level; this time it is the woman, younger in fact, who finds herself at the disposal of a generation which is actually older, while in cousin marriage, i.e. between two persons who are really members of the same generation, it is through successive correspondences that the wife is fictively substituted for the mother of her husband. This means that in return for providing a daughter for the agnatic group of the nephew, a compensation of equal value is handed over to the matrilateral kin in the form of a sister of the beneficiary.

This direct compensation in the form of women is also carried out, in a sense, with other goods. The nephew's plundering is paralleled by the role played by matrilateral kinsfolk when the agnates are mourning a dead person; it takes the form of an attack on the cortège when it returns from the mortuary shelter bearing the shroud. Their violent intention is to take the piece of cloth away from them. It is a symbol of the dead man and of his resurrection and they will only hand it back if they are given a goat.

The uncle has another chance of recouping his losses in goods, losses which, if the rule were applied strictly, would be total. Every object which the thief touches should, in fact, belong to him; he only needs to mention the name of an object in the compound for them to lose all their strength and become impure.[14] As a result, a man's

[14] Impurity for the Dogon is less the result of contact with a human body, miasma or moral filth than an emptiness provoked in one's life force. Cf. G. Dieterlen, 'Mécanisme de l'impureté chez les Dogon', *J. Soc. Africanistes*, xvii (1947), 81–90.

patrimony could theoretically be reduced to nothing every time his nephew pays him a visit. Such inconvenience is avoided, on the one hand, by partial thefts which are meant to represent a total spoliation; but it can also be reduced to a large extent by a precautionary measure whereby the uncle absorbs the whole body of plunderers in the person of his eldest nephew.

An eldest son may, in fact, be brought up by his maternal grandfather, which means his maternal uncles and their wives and more particularly by the elder uncle. In such circumstances he becomes the spoilt child and bullies his aunts. His power reflects, among others, the power of his clavicles, a power which varies according to whether he is in relation with his agnates or his uterine kin: instead of the usual eight seeds he has sixteen as far as the group who brings him up is concerned. Consequently he is all-powerful and acts constantly as the *mangou*, the purifying allied agent,[15] more particularly with regard to those elements of property which, thanks to his very presence, recover again their purity which they might have lost through the breaking of a taboo. In fact, the excess of seed, i.e. life force, which the nephew possesses, replenishes, as they arise, the voids caused by the pollution of goods. In return the nephew's clavicular contents are reconstituted by the absorption of food and other substances which are taken from the patrimony he has thus protected.

These goods, therefore, are constantly in a state of increase and fructification; one of the aims of this institution is to provide an advantage for the matrilateral kin's property over that of the agnates through the acts and qualifications of the nephew who, in fact, given the patrilineal rule, belongs to the other group. This derives from the fact that the nephew, theoretically, has more to gain from his mother's brothers than from his father; and it is a way of showing the state of unfriendly rivalry which exists between him and his father.

Of course, by means of a permutating reciprocity, the agnatic group also bring up their own sisters' sons and consequently achieve constant equality.

This convenient, balanced situation does not last for long; it will soon be disturbed by the fact that the nephew grows up, becomes the

---

[15] Cf. M. Griaule, 'L'alliance cathartique', *Africa* xviii, 4 (October 1948). At the time of writing the clavicular contents had not yet been revealed by the old blind Innekouzou, priestess of Amma in Upper Sanga. The deposit to which we allude in this article is only the clavicular seeds. On these seeds, see G. Dieterlen, 'Les correspondances cosmo-biologiques chez les Soudanais', *Journal de Psychologie normale et pathologique* (July–Sept. 1950).

husband of one of the daughters of his maternal uncle and achieves the highest development of his personality and power which will bring him wealth whether from outside or inside. Just as the Yurugu, by virtue of his status as husband and son, plunders all the riches contained in the great womb, so does the nephew, pseudo-son of the couple uncle–aunt and pseudo-husband of his aunt, possesses all powers and especially 'good fortune'. Consequently if things were allowed to remain as they were, there would be a rupture in the established equilibrium, leading to the excessive enrichment of one and the progressive diminishment and stagnation of the others.

This is the reason why, once he is married, that is, once he is established',[16] the guest is exposed to slight but persistent pressure in order to encourage him to leave the matrilateral group; the latter has the right to act in this way in so far as the period of subjection of their nephew ends with marriage. Indeed, the sister's son, even when he quits the family which brought him up, retains throughout his lifetime the prestige of a beneficient power with which he was credited. For this reason the Arou tribe would never allow any person brought up among matrilateral kin to succeed to the chiefship.

The Arou chief, Hogon, chosen when young, becomes in a way the representative of the whole Dogon people; he thus differs from other chiefs who exercise authority over a limited region and are chosen because they are the eldest among their group. A man who like the uterine nephew would enter into great power by his very situation, would reign too long and would acquire too much wealth and power, would cause excessive prejudice to the prosperity of the people and to the political balance.

For the same reasons the Hogon of Arou is hedged in by strict taboos concerning his kinship. As the supreme authority he is considered to be the representative of all the mythical entities; all ritual situations which he is called to face are the replica of events which took place at the beginning of the world. The Hogon is the image of Yurugu, in particular; he is the prototype of the pilfering nephew, and it is in order to prevent any exaggeration of his power that he is not chosen from among the first-born who have been brought up by matrilateral kinsfolk, i.e. among those who represent, *par excellence*, this mythical figure.

Like Yurugu the Hogon is supposed to have intercourse with his

---

[16] The essential feature of this 'establishment' is the receipt of the usufruct of a field from his agnates. Cf. G. Dieterlen's article cited in note 8.

mother.[17] Therefore, as soon as he accedes to power, he is separated from her. However, he keeps in touch with her and feeds her, acting through the intermediary of his sisters who are, at the same time, his daughters since he is his mother's pseudo-husband and his wives, because they are like the twins whom, according to the myth, he should have married. Similar prohibitions apply to the Hogon's eldest son: he is his father's replica and, also, the pseudo-husband of his own mother, i.e. the Hogon's wife.

We find therefore that, to a very large extent, kinship takes into account the mythical situation, particularly as far as Yurugu is concerned. It is because he is a symbol of Yurugu that the supreme chief is separated from his mother and from his eldest son; the nephew who insults his kin is also Yurugu, his thefts are not only permissible but are actually encouraged by older agnates who egg him on, with the cry *yurugu yoy ya* 'Go! Get inside like Yurugu!' and congratulate him on his return.

It would therefore seem that this mythical person Yurugu is taken seriously and worshipped in the same way as the other actors in those first scenes of world creation. He is, indeed, often evoked and represented, but this is only to ridicule him all the more, to reveal the vanity of his efforts in his perpetual search for his twin sister and to show the reprobation which his intercourse with his mother provoked. Incest interdictions, like those positive actions which tend to approach it without, in fact, reaching the state, are replicas of those actions which he failed to bring off or which, though successful, brought shame with them, resulting in a continual demonstration of his impotence.

We have already seen that, along with those actual institutions which involved *ego* and his matrilateral kin, there was a corresponding state of moral tension between *ego* and his father; this is partly explained by the fact that his physiological father is a kind of stranger compared to the mother's brother who is his mythical father. What we might call the metaphysics of mythology uses a different approach.

In the infinitely small beginning symbolized by the seed of *Digitaria exilis*,[18] seven internal vibrations developed in the kernel, represented by seven segments of ever-increasing size which spread

---

[17] *Aru ogono dago año yurugule wo nale bana kalegin wo*, 'the Hogon of Aru, chosen young, it is as if this is finished between Yurugu and his mother'. Meaning: the situation of the Hogon in relation to his mother is comparable to that between Yurugu and his own mother.

[18] See above, p. 13.

out into a fan of 360°.[19] The ends of each segment together formed a spiral representing the starting-point of an extending movement which was to be continued in the external world as the work of creation because the end of the seventh segment touched the envelope and opened a necessary passage. Through this gap there came out, among other things, an extension of the seventh segment which, in some kind of way, represented an eighth vibration which grew out of its predecessor.

If we look at the symbolism involved in this figuration we find first, in these unequal traits, the delineation of a human silhouette. The first and the sixth are legs, the second and the fifth the arms, the third and the fourth the head and the seventh the genitals, placed between the sixth and the first. This silhouette, in its geometrical aspect, represents man as the 'seed of the world' *aduno dene*. In its numerological aspect it brings back to memory the fact that human microcosm is conceived as an ideal pair of number 4 (female symbol) and 3 (male symbol) in a procreating situation which is represented by the ejection of the eighth segment, an extension of the seventh, which is the genitals.

However, this eighth segment already lies outside the group formed by the first seven, it marks the beginning of another series of seven and its quality of being a beginning also marks its incompleteness. Because of this it is identified with Yurugu, i.e. with the most incomplete creature of all. We can therefore expect a most demanding attitude on the part of the offspring towards his genitors and more particularly towards his male genitor: indeed, as the positions of the segments indicate, the one representing the male genitals is that which, in these particular circumstances, sends off a detached part of itself.

This mythical and metaphysical way of representing the reciprocal primordial situations between father and son makes present-day attitudes intelligible to a knowledgeable Dogon. The son bears a grudge against his father for his initial incompleteness. He also blames him for the part his father played in the situation which led to his not being an integral product of his mother nor wholly derived from the root *du*, maternal, and from this alone. There would be a palliative for this if he were the son of his mother and his mother's brother, i.e. of two parents belonging to the same root. However, even in this case he would hold it against his genitor for procreating again and presenting him with brothers like himself. The son, in fact,

---

[19] See the figure in my *Connaissance de l'homme noir*, Rencontres internationales de Genève, Geneva, 1951, and in 'The Dogon', *African Worlds*, p. 83.

considers that during sexual intercourse his father introduces into his
mother seed which is identical to that which gave birth to him. The
father, therefore, is dismissing the earlier product as nought since he
is desirous of creating another.

The hostility which has been provoked in this manner reaches beyond
the genitor to affect the product of these fresh unions, his younger
brothers. On the other hand all younger brothers eventually come
under the authority of their elders, specially under the authority of the
first-born who assumes the status of their father once he dies. Towards
their future patriarch they therefore show early feelings of mistrust.

These attitudes are reinforced by competition in the sphere of
marriage: ideally *ego* would like to marry all his maternal uncle's
daughters who actually become, if the rule is followed,[20] the wives of
his brothers.

Symmetrically, according to the myth of the primordial couple, he
is the ideal spouse of his sisters; however, in theory, these are supposed to marry their cousins who become his brothers-in-law. There
is, however, subtle compensation on this level; the following is an
example: under her tongue, behind the frenum, the sister places a
seed of *onugo*,[21] keeping it there for weeks until a cavity is formed
in the tongue. When the seed thus adheres to the tongue it is then
offered in a phylactery to her favourite brother when he goes off to
war. This seed is a symbol of the brother's genitals and it has pene-
trated the flesh of the sister, thereby realizing the act of the primordial pair of twins.

Moreover, unions between *ego*'s brothers and sisters-in-law and
between his sisters and brothers-in-law (although they derive from
the same process as *ego*'s own marriage to his cousin) provoke
hostility on the part of *ego* which is known by the kin term *gala*. This
word, from the root of the same formation meaning 'to overstep the
bounds' shows how *ego* feels towards these kinsfolk. The term alludes
to the 'inordinateness' of Yurugu having intercourse with his mother.
In other words, *ego* abandoning the role of Yurugu which led him
into this marriage with his uncle's daughter takes up the position of
Nommo, scorner of the incestuous act, considering the other couples
as symbols of Yurugu and his genitrix. His role is expressed by special
joking whereby he pretends to separate the two spouses whose union,
in his eyes, is incestuous.

[20] The system of generalized exchange practically upsets all these rules.
[21] *Zizyphus mauritania* Lam or *Z. jujuba* Lam. Years ago we met women with
this incysted seed. I have not made recent inquiries into this practice.

In his extended family a Dogon finds only a limited group of persons from whom he can expect whole-hearted sympathy, if at all. Indeed, the agnates, who so far, in our account, seem to have escaped *ego*'s vigilant hostility, are in fact all included in the paternal image.

As for *ego*'s wife, for whom he has competed, she is a sort of makeshift wife who provides only incomplete satisfaction. If he had married his twin sister instead, according to the rule of the myth, the arrangement of things would not be better taken care of. Indeed, a union of such perfection, according to the Dogon, would first result in a disequilibrium in the household due to the excessive authority which his wife would wield; and also in the family at large by excess of good fortune of ideal spouses.

If *ego* were, in fact, to marry his mother, thereby following the disorderly mythical example, he would pay for it by provoking a general upheaval in society. As it happens, although the Dogon is not able to satisfy his eternal but illicit longing to marry his mother or his mythically permissible but prohibited desire to marry his sister, he nevertheless has a very wide choice of spouses since this society practises generalized exchange. But this compensation is poorly tailored to suit the Dogon personality and does not do anything to prevent his being in an almost constant state of competition with all his relatives. Unconsciously[22] he considers his father an intruder, his mother an unavowed twin sister, his mother's brother a provider of wives and goods and a miser, and his mother's brother's wife an unobtainable spouse, the object of his insults, his brothers as his rivals, and his sisters as his unreachable wives; the marriages of his brothers and sisters-in-law as well as of his sisters and brothers-in-law he deems illegal. The Dogon, in theory, stands alone against all.

In fact the atmosphere is less tense than the present study might lead one to believe. Insults, joking, claims, and real thefts reveal feelings which are only half feigned and of which the deeper roots reach down into what we, in the Western world, would call the unconscious. These practices have the advantage of providing a catharsis and are also proof that this African society, and we have only given one of many examples here, has been able to canalize and regulate those tensions and strains which are inherent in family life.

[22] It should be made clear that the practices and situations described here are seen from the point of view of Dogon 'scholars'. Ordinary adults are more or less informed on these matters, younger people much less; all the young people are concerned with is to exercise, with energy and good humour, their right to snatch, joke, insult, and make recriminations in their relations with certain groups of people.

B

Stylistic Study of a
Dogon Text

GENEVIÈVE CALAME-GRIAULE[1]

The text presented in this study[1a] would seem to deserve the title of poetry, either by reference to extrinsic criteria (rhythmic declamation) or intrinsic ones (stylistic modes). It has a religious and incantatory character, common in Dogon poetry, belonging in effect to a genre known as praise-poems (*tíge*); it would equally well qualify as a 'prayer' (*aŋa sɔ*: 'word of the mouth'), the two genres being linked in so far as prayers, on the one hand, always have a poetic form, and, on the other, very often contain fragments of praise poems.[2] This text bears the title of 'Praise-poem of Death' (*yìmu tíge*) and describes the journey of the 'soul'[3] after death. Its recital during the course of a funeral ceremony is intended to help the soul overcome the obstacles it may meet on the way. The text we present here is part of a much longer one which includes, in particular, an enumeration of all the places the deceased visited during his lifetime. However, in the form given here, identical to that published by Solange de Ganay[4], it constitutes an ensemble which can be analysed satisfactorily.

The text has an initiatory value; in order to provide a commentary on it in depth we should require a complete understanding of Dogon culture. However, it may be of interest to attempt an initial analysis

[1] *Geneviève Calame-Griaule* (b. 1924), Dr. es L., Sorbonne. Senior Research Fellow of the French National Centre for Scientific Research (CNRS). Lecturer at Sorbonne Nouvelle University (Paris III). First trained in classics and then in Arabic, she joined her father's research team among the Dogon. Currently engaged in ethnolinguistic research in West Africa. The original French text of this paper was published as 'Essai d'étude stylistique d'un texte dogon', *Journal of West African Languages*, iv, 1 (1967), 15–24.

[1a] Contributed to the Fifth West African Linguistic Conference, Accra, 1965.

[2] On the question of praise-poems, see S. de Ganay, *Les Devises des Dogon*, and on the relationship between prayers and praise-poems, see my study *Ethnologie et Langage*, chapters IV and V (third part).

[3] We use this word here for convenience sake and do not wish to go into any detail concerning the spiritual principles involved in the idea of self.

[4] op. cit., p. 73. Another version of this text has been published by G. Dieterlen (*Les Ames des Dogon*, p. 105). We compare these two texts below.

from a formal point of view to see if we can bring out the intentions of its poetic message; for this reason we shall attempt to decipher the methods used in order to 'pass on' this message to the listeners, remembering while doing so that the 'listeners' are of different kinds: the living, who are present at the funeral, the dead man himself (the principal person involved) and the spirit forces evoked.

Here is Solange de Ganay's version of this text, with revised orthography.[5]

THE DOGON TEXT

1 mana tằ / tằ pínela // áma uy tɛ̀mɛmo ///
2 yìmu ódu / ódu tà:nu gì ///
3 ódu lògoro tò // áma uy kúno ///
4 yìmunɛ ódu-nɛ // ìdu gulɔ́ yò gì ///
5 uy gálamɛlɛ gì ///
6 pùlɔ yà:na // ɛ́m kɔrɔ̀ /uy óbo ///
7 yìmunɛ ódu-nɛ // éɲe yò gì ///
8 íne gálamɛlɛ gì ///
9 yà:na pὲy // púnu sàru / uy óbo ///
10 sá nì: / ýaũ kíde // mìɲu nì:/ ýaũ kíde ///
11 nà: nì: // áma/ sὲgɛ uo-nɛ yàɲa///
12 gunoi ná: teí // áma uy sùŋono///
13 mὲnu bílu níɲu // áma uy sùŋono ///
14 válu bílu níɲu // áma uy sùŋono///
15 ínu bílu níɲu// áma uy sùŋono///
16 áma /// ùɲu uo / tàma kúno///

Literal translation

1 kneader door / door un-closed // Amma thee should make-find ///
2 dead-man road / road three they-say ///
3 road middle is / Amma thee shall put ///
4 dead-man road-upon // dog young there-is they-say ///
5 thee makes-not-pass they-say ///
6 Fulani woman // milk calabash / thee give

[5] For a description of the Dogon phonological system, see the Introduction to my *Dictionnaire Dogon* (*Dialecte tɔrɔ*). There is a concise table in *Ethnologie et Langage*, op. cit., p. 18.

7 dead-man road-upon // cock there-is they-say ///
8 nobody makes-not-pass they say ///
9 old woman // flour ground / thee give ///
10 *sá* oil/fire thing // shea butter / fire thing ///
11 cow oil // Amma / bone thy-on rub ///
12 easy (?) cow degrees // Amma thee make-come-down ///
13 copper ladder luck // Amma thee make-come-down ///
14 silver ladder luck // Amma thee make-come-down ///
15 iron ladder luck // Amma thee make-come-down ///
16 Amma // bed thy / cool put ///

English translation

1 The door of the kneader, the open door, let Amma make you find it.
2 The roads of the dead [are] three roads, they say.
3 On the middle road let Amma place you.
4 On the road of the dead there is a young dog, they say.
5 He will not let you through, they say.
6 A Fulani woman [will] give you a calabash of milk.
7 On the road of the dead there is a cock, they say.
8 Allowing nobody to pass, they say.
9 An old woman [will] give you ground flour.
10 The *sá*[6] oil [is] a thing of fire, the shea butter [is] a thing of fire
11 With the cow butter let Amma anoint your bones.
12 The easy steps [as for] a cow, let Amma make you come down them.
13 [If] the ladder of copper [is your] luck, let Amma make you come
   down it.
14 [If] the ladder of silver [is your] luck, let Amma make you come
   down it.
15 [If] the ladder of iron [is your] luck, let Amma make you come
   down it.
16 May Amma make your bed cool.

As far as the 'lines' of the text are concerned we have followed the
treatment used by S. de Ganay because this way of dividing up the poem
corresponds to an articulatory reality: each of the lines (numbered

[6] *Lannea acida.*

from 1 to 16) corresponds to a releasing of breath, after which the speaker pauses (this is marked here by three oblique dashes). Within each line we have marked the main breaks, by two oblique bars and sometimes a secondary break, by a single bar. Each of these utterances forms a well-defined syntactic group, ending with a verbal form (excepting line 10, which is, as we shall see, no accident).

The immediately obvious meaning of the text leads to a provisional division of the poem into the following sections:

a (line 1) Aim of the dead man's voyage: he is returning to the womb of the God creator, Amma, the 'kneader' of the world.
b (lines 2–9) The dead man's course, the obstacles he finds on the way and their initiatory negotiation.
c (lines 10–11) The different types of oil used in anointing the body.
d (lines 12–15) The 'coming down' of the soul by an easy way.
e (line 16) The wish that he should arrive safely, and lie on a cool bed.

In the course of our analysis it should be remembered that we are dealing with a text which is essentially incantatory in character and that its precise aim is to facilitate the passage of the dead man into the other world, by helping him triumph over the hazards which lie in wait for him on the way. Corresponding to these aims we have special poetic techniques, which we shall attempt to analyse from several angles: phonematic, morphological, and syntactic, and finally from the point of view of images and symbols.[7]

I PHONOLOGICAL LEVEL

In order to work out the distribution of phonemes in their stylistic aspect we should ideally require a computer in order to achieve a systematic study. However, apart from the fact that it would be necessary to extend our analysis to cover a large number of similar messages in order to be able to draw any valid conclusions, the interpretation of numerical results of this kind does not seem to have led to any convincing results so far. Nevertheless, an attempt ought to be made. Since we lack the material means to undertake an analysis of this nature, we have restricted ourselves to those comments which may be drawn from an empirical, though scrupulous, examination of the text; this will provide us with an opportunity to offer an hypothesis concerning the stylistic significance of the facts.

[7] These different levels of analysis were suggested by T. A. Sebeok's study 'Decoding a text: levels and aspects in a Cheremis Sonnet'.

CONSONANTS[8]

Only the nasal series is well represented in all positions, throughout the whole text. The apical consonant /t/ is repeated insistently in the first three lines, but after line 3 it seems to make way for initial /g/ and /k/'s which in turn fade into the background to make way for the sibiliant /s/, which returns as an initial in each line after line 9. The semi-vowel /y/ is frequently in an initial position—particularly when it is associated with a nasal—in the first two-thirds of the poem, although it drops out after line 11.

It would appear, then that, apart from the nasal series, we find in this text small 'constellations' of phonemes which dominate certain groups of lines and then disappear to make way for others. We shall see below what kind of conclusions may be derived from this.

VOWELS

The distribution of vowels in the text is less clearly marked, vowels being always very abundant, given the structure of Dogon roots (CVC'V, VCV, CV, or V). Nevertheless we can point to a greater frequency of phoneme /a/ in lines 1, 11, and 16 and also to its complete absence in lines 4 and 7. In the body of the text the sonorities are sometimes in /o-u/, sometimes in /i-e/. From line 13 onwards, all the vowels appear together and in a balanced fashion.

We have attempted to summarize these facts in the following diagrams:

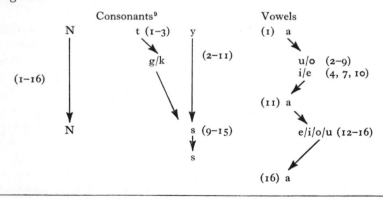

---

[8] We are primarily concerned with initial consonants, the initial syllable being most commonly accented (we have only noted the tone of the accented syllable).

[9] We have used N to denote all the nasals.

Let us now see if a particular semantic content may be associated with these phonemes. As far as the initial consonants are concerned it seems that they are to be found in certain important words which give a particular flavour to different passages in the text. Initial /t/ is concerned primarily with the word *tǎ* 'door': it is essential for the dead man to find this door. On the other hand the initials in /g/k/ seem to become more numerous as the obstacles along the road become more numerous: the most important word in this passage, according to us, is *gálamɛlɛ*, 'not let through'. When they make way for initials in /s/, the important idea becomes the concept of the 'coming down' (*sùgo*); here, in fact, it is a question of facilitating the descent of the soul (we shall see the significance of this when we come to discuss the symbols involved). As for /y/, which is primarily associated with a nasal, it is effectively associated with the word *yìmu*, 'death'. It no longer appears once the obstacles have been overcome and the dead man, as we shall see, is resuscitated. While nasals are found throughout the text, it is because they are found in two of the most important words, which are found, moreover, in a kind of basic opposition: *áma*—'God' and *yìmu*—'death'.

A look at the positioning of the vowels is no less rewarding. /a/ seems to be linked with the triumph of the divinity (*áma*). When the powers of death (i.e. the obstacles) seem to be overcoming, /a/ is absent and the dominants are /i-e/ (*yìmu*) or /o-u/ (*odu*, road). In the last part of the text all the vowels are balanced in each line, giving them a kind of harmony: complex /i-u/ at the beginning of the line, /a/ in the middle, /o-u/ at the end. The last line is constructed with the paralls /a-u/—/a-u/.

The positioning of the phonemes is certainly not something which has been left to chance. Small 'constellations' of identical phonemes cluster around words which we might call 'key-words' and which emphasize the basic meaning of a passage. More important than this, the absence of a phoneme seems to be as significant as its presence. In line 7 the meaning would seem to have required *éɲe ána*, since according to informants' comments the animal concerned is a 'cock'; *éɲe* by itself simply means 'a hen', although it is also the generic term for 'fowl'. The use of the less precise term here seems to be intentional.

Apart from the general distribution of phonemes, which we can accept as being unconsciously structured, we also note that the phonemes are organized in associative or contrasting groups,

according to well-known stylistic procedures. Nearly all the lines
provide examples:

l. 1   alliteration *t . . . t . . . t . . .*
l. 2   assonance (four words together with a final *-u*); correspon-
          dence *yi-* . . . *gi.*
l. 3   assonance in *-o.*
l. 4   internal rhyme (*-nɛ* . . .*-nɛ*).
l. 5   alliteration *g-* . . . *g-* . . .
l. 9   alliteration in *p-* . . .
l. 11   alliteration in *n-* . . .
l. 12–15 repetition of the final *-u.*
l. 16   association *áma/tàma.*

Apart from these facts concerning individual lines, we also have
correspondences between several consecutive lines, where sonorities
can be linked together: *yà:na* (9), *yáũ* . . . *yáũ* (10), *yàɲa* (11), and
also *níɲu* (13, 14, 15) continuing into *uɲu* (16).

We can see by this that there is a large variety of methods used at
the second level of articulation in order to endow this text with poetic
colour.

2 MORPHOLOGY AND SYNTAX

On this level the striking fact is a considerable simplification in
comparison with the norms of current speech. The verbal forms are
injunctives corresponding to the so-called 'bare' forms of the
verbo-nominal radical (*tɛ̀mɛmo, kúno, yàɲa, sùɲono*) or very simple
fixed forms (*gi*, 'they say'; *yò*, 'there is') or forms which have been
simplified and reduced to the bare forms of the radicals: *óbo-[dɔ]*,
'will give'. The only two complex verbal forms are *pínela* in line 1
and *gálamɛlɛ* in lines 5 and 8; their negative character is essential;
they serve to contrast 'the door which is not closed', in other words
open, with the symbolic animals which 'will not let through', in
other words 'close', the way. The compactness of *gálamɛlɛ* stresses
even more this idea of obstacle.

Certain nominal forms are also simplified: *màɲa*, a radical form,
for *màɲanɛ*, an agent-noun meaning 'kneader' in line 1; *yìmu* for
yìmunɛ meaning the dead man in line 2 (although in line 4 we have
the complete form because of the stylistic effect produced by the
internal rhyme *yìmunɛ ódu-nɛ*), etc.

The monemes are not only simplified in form; some of them, necessary in any correct 'prose' expression, are simply suppressed: examples include the copulative *vɔ̀*, 'is', in lines 2 and 13–15; the demonstrative-relative *-gɔ* (lines 1, 3). Functional monemes are not expressed unless they are absolutely necessary to convey the meaning: *-nɛ*, 'in' is found three time (lines 4, 7, 11); it is left out in line 3 where the usual way of speech, if it were not poetical, would be: *áma ódu lògoro tò-gɔ-nɛ uy kúno*.

We find therefore a tendency towards simplification plus the juxtaposition of nominals and verbal forms, as reduced in shape as possible, with all the monemes used gaining in expressive value as a result.

Words chosen in this way are not distributed haphazardly. In the very way they are organized we once again find the means of expressing a poetic message. Various methods are used: words are repeated, either within a single line (*tằ . . . tằ* in line 1) or linking up different lines (*ódu* in lines 2, 3, 4, 7, *galamɛlɛ* in lines 5 and 8, etc.; the arrangement of hiatuses (lines 1 and 2); an absolutely parallel construction of certain lines (lines 4 and 7, 5 and 8, 6 and 9, 13, 14 and 15); finely worked out patterning of line endings, which are all composed of verbal forms apart from line 10: we have in fact regular patterns *gì/kúno/gì/gì/óbo/gì/óbo*, then, following on from the pivot formed by lines 10 and 11, we have a succession of four *sùŋono* which form a kind of 'litany'; lines 1 and 16 are linked through the forms *tɛ̀mɛmo* and *kúno*.

From a syntactical point of view we should notice that the canonical construction of Dogon sentences (which are normally ordered: subject—[circumstantial complement]—object—verb) is retained in lines 6, 9, and 16. In lines 2 and 10 we have a construction which would have been regular (subject-predicate) if the copula *vɔ̀* (or the actualizer *-i*) had not been left out. Elsewhere the 'prose' construction is upset by various practices: the object (lines 1 and 11), the circumstantial complement (lines 3, 4, 7, and 12) put at the beginning of the line. In lines 13, 14, 15, the phrases have been rendered extremely elliptical by dropping the particle of subordination *-ye* ('if').

Lines 10 and 11 should be considered separately since they provide an example of a construction totally different from that of the rest of the poem. First they are syntactically linked in a very elliptical fashion through the fact that line 10 ends with a nominal form (*kíde*) and not with a verbal form as in all the other lines (*i*, the actualizer, necessary in prose, has been left out here and we are left with simply the nominal subject–predicate construction). Line 11 ends correctly with a verbal form like the others, but it is a form which is the only one to have the vowel /a/. The construction of line 10 involves the parallels: subject–predicate / subject–predicate; no other construction of this kind is found elsewhere in the text. The parallelism is absolute since the two subjects and the two predicates are formed by the same determinative syntagms, only the name of the plant changing in the second half of the line. As for line 11, it uses the complement *nà: ni:*, 'cow oil', which changes the two-term opposition (*sá* oil and shea-butter) into a three-term opposition. In fact, however, this new element brings out a more profound opposition between the two vegetable oils, 'things of fire', and the cow butter, animal fat and (although this is implicit) 'thing of life'. In fact these two lines provide the poem's pivot; as has often been observed in poetry[10] a change in construction marks the passage from one term of the opposition to the other and opens the way for the development of the poem's crucial idea.

We shall grasp this more clearly by studying the symbols in the text. We should point out at once, however, that a change occurs in the tone and rhythm of the poem after what we have called the pivotal passage of lines 10–11.

RHYTHM

In fact, until we reach these pivotal lines, the others, while offering clear-cut parallelisms and connections in rhythmic construction, which we have already mentioned (lines 4 and 7, 5 and 8, 6 and 9 among others), present a large variety of breaks. The main break is found in different positions and may even be accompanied by secondary ones. In lines 5 and 8 there is no break at all; their 'compact' nature may be interpreted as a means of making one feel that the road of the dead man is 'barred'. We then have a series of descriptive lines whose irregular and rhythmic character tends to evoke those difficulties which the soul has to overcome on the way of death.

After lines 10 and 11, the change in both rhythm and construction is complete. Four consecutive lines of an absolutely identical syntactic and rhythmic construction make use of the same words and the

[10] Cf., for example, R. Jakobson and C. Lévi-Strauss, ' "Les Chats" de Charles Baudelaire', p. 19: 'This passage operates through a couplet, which, for a brief moment and by an accumulation of semantic and formal procedures, draws the readers into a doubly unreal universe.'

same sonorities and form what we have already called a 'litany'. This is the real incantation, which is expected to act upon the antagonistic forces in a concrete fashion. The stubborn repetition of the same elements, which differ from one another in the most subtle way, is aimed at facilitating the 'coming down' of the soul once it has overcome the hurdles. The symbolic idea expressed by this descent is that of the resurrection. We shall now see how—through the passage of our two pivot-lines—the passage from death to life is achieved.

4 IMAGES AND SYMBOLS

Here we have the appearance of oppositions which remind us, through words, of the symbolic values of the realities being expressed. We shall briefly review the more important of these oppositions.

As a contrast to the notion of the 'open door', which appears in the first line, we soon have the hazards which 'do not let him through'. The evocation of this difficult road is then set against (lines 12–15) that of an easy descent by ladders. In contraposition to the two animals (males according to informants' comments), which try to stop the dead man passing, we have two female human images which neutralize them by the use of talismans. After the vegetable oils, prepared with the aid of fire,[11] we have cow butter, an animal product obtained without the aid of any intermediary: the idea of coolness inherent in cow butter is implicit here and offers a contrast with the 'things of fire'; this is taken up again in the last line ('let Amma make your bed cool').

The cow, moreover, is a very common image of maternal femininity and fertility; she should therefore be classed with those female images which contrast with the male animals. Finally, in the last part of the poem, the idea of 'descent' seems to predominate; the opposite notion of 'climbing', which might be thought to provide a contrast with this, is not expressed. It seems, however, that it may be implicit in the concept of 'death' itself; in fact there are Dogon locutions such as 'to go up on to the terrace', which is a euphemism used when the Hogon, the religious chief, dies; we might also consider the symbolic meaning of the terrace where the masks dance during funerals and which represent the sky, the 'seat' of Amma where the dead man must return. It seems clear that in Dogon ideas, at least on a subconscious level, death is a kind of 'climbing', a symbolic image

---

[11] On the making of these oils, cf. G. Dieterlen and G. Calame-Griaule, 'L'Alimentation dogon', pp. 74 and 81.

which is possibly connected with the steep and difficult nature of the cliff paths.

We may now summarize these different oppositions:

open door	obstacles
easy descent	difficult road
human beings	animals
femininity	[masculinity]
freshness	fire
cow butter	vegetable oil
coming down	[climbing]
life (fertility)	death

The positioning of the words which express these oppositions in our text does not seem to have been chosen haphazardly. In fact if we consider the distribution of terms of opposition in relation to the major break in each line we see that it well-nigh corresponds to the distribution indicated in the above columns. Before the caesura we find the open door (a feminine symbol), female entities (women and cow), therefore life and fertility; after it come animals, masculinity (symbolized by the figure three), and fire. As far as the vegetable oils are concerned—opposed to the cow butter—we might perhaps consider them as being opposed among themselves: the oil of *lannea acida* is feminine and reserved for the female toilet, while shea butter oil involves a male symbolism. We are, however, unable to accord an absolute value to this criterion of distribution; symbols relative to femininity and life, such as the calabash and the idea of coolness, are found on the 'right-hand side' of the text, along with male symbols, a fact which can hardly be justified. On the other hand it may be that the word expressing the idea of 'death' appears on the left-hand side, with femininity, because womanhood is an ambivalent concept among the Dogon—harbinger of death and life.[12] As for Amma, the God Creator, his name is to be found scattered throughout the text, since according to the Dogon he is 'neither man nor woman' and hence is above all oppositions.

Therefore we find, generally, the male/female opposition associated with the death/life opposition, with the fire/coolness duality being one of the common images of the latter; we are also aware that this grouping of oppositions plays a fundamental role in Dogon culture. When dealing with an unwritten text we can hardly speak of

[12] On the ambivalence of women in Dogon culture, cf. in particular our study *Ethnologie et Langage*, vol. III, chap. II.

the opposition right/left. However it must be admitted that the opposition right/left, an important corollary of the opposition male/female, is replaced in such a case by contrasts between the beginnings and endings of vocal utterances which we have called 'lines', the boundaries of which are marked by syntactical and rhythmic breaks. Although, as we have seen, this does not involve absolutely systematic procedures, it does seem to be worthy of comment.

An esoteric explanation of the text under consideration[13] has been proffered by Dogon informants as follows: The dead man has to return to the womb of his creator, the 'kneader'; the young dog and the cock which try to stop the way are avatars of the Fox, a mythical character, who incarnates all the negative forces of the world;[14] these two animals' aspects (a young dog and a grown cock) symbolize the different ages of life. The two women (a young one and an old one), who provide the dead man with talismans (in the form of white food, images of fertility and purity) to enable him to overcome the hurdles, are expressions of Nommo, the Fox's twin brother who represents fertility and life. The cow is the 'mother' and her evocation brings up the idea of resurrection, since the 'cool bed' desired by the dead man represents the waters of the womb. Thus the dead man is trying to return to his mother's womb, to seek out once again his foetal state in order to be 'reborn', according to Dogon belief, by imparting some of his life force to his new descendants.

A ladder is always a symbol of passing from one level to another. The different metals also have their symbolic value: copper in particular is a 'wet' metal—attributed to Nommo—and its therapeutic virtues are well known; it works in favour of life, hence resurrection. In this way we find that all the symbols in this text are organized around one central theme, which is the passage between death and life. It is really this 'passage' which comes out even in the structure of the text. The transmutation takes place by means of the cow butter, a 'cool thing' which is contrasted to the 'thing of fire', the fire being death. By anointing the dead man's bones with butter, Amma brings him back to life by providing him with renewed suppleness in his joints. The word *sɛ̀gɛ* (bone, skeleton) appears to be a key word in the text, around which the notion of this passage is centred. In fact it is this word which appears precisely at the end of our two pivot-lines, where is found the basic oppositions of fire/coolness, that is death/life. These two lines, in which we have located the quintessence

[13] Information from G. Dieterlen.
[14] Cf. M. Griaule and G. Dieterlen, *Le Renard pâle*.

of poetic style, really contain the crucial idea of the poem. What the
dead man is really after is not merely to overcome the obstacles on
his path, but to achieve resurrection. In order to show this the poem
makes use of an array of stylistic methods which operates on all levels
of language. Incantation does not only depend on repetition, but on
a harmonious synthesis of all those elements involved in a fundamental opposition. It is precisely because these poetic procedures are
linked to the means of expression provided by a given language, that
they become untranslatable.

ADDENDUM

A version of this text, differing a little from this one, has been published by Germaine Dieterlen (*Les Ames des Dogons*, p. 105). It may
be of interest to compare these two variants.

G. Dieterlen's version is part of a longer text which includes an
enumeration of the places visited by the dead man and ends with an
invocation to him, begging him not to bring harm to those who survive him. Nevertheless our text is easily singled out from among these
different parts. Apparently the informant who provided the text knew
it imperfectly; the poetic structure comes out much less clearly. We
still have more or less the same lines and groups of lines, although
they are presented in a different order which means that the opposition of the two parts (death and resurrection), linked by the pivot-
lines, disappears; these are in fact relegated to the end of the text.
As for the desire for a 'cool bed' we now find it at the beginning, a
fact which no longer warrants our final explanation of the expression
of a resurrection through a return to the maternal womb. The order
of certain details has also been upset; the cock appears before the
young dog, the old woman before the young one. The evocation of
the three roads of death is missing, along with the silver ladder, while
the other two ladders are placed in one and the same line, thus completely destroying the 'litany' effect. We give here a translation of this
version, the Dogon text being more or less the same.[15]

1 Amma created you, Amma has taken you back, go with him.
2 May Amma give you a cool bed.
3 On the big road is a cock who will stop your way.

[15] There are some exceptions however. Thus the expression *nà: ǹ:*, 'cow oil',
which forms a striking parallel with *sá ǹ:* and *mìɲu ǹ:*, in the preceding line, is
replaced by the banal expression *náɲa tè*, 'cow butter'.

4 An old woman will give you millet flour.
5 On the road of death there is a young dog.
6 He lets no one pass.
7 A Fulani woman will give you a calabash of milk.
8 May Amma let you come down by easy degrees like a cow.
9 There is a copper ladder, there is an iron ladder.
10 May Amma make you come down the good ladder.
11 May Amma let you find the kneader's door open.
12 The shea butter is a thing of fire, the *sà* oil is a thing of fire.
13 You shall be able to anoint your bones with cow butter.

It would seem that this text has undergone a degree of impoverishment in passing from one informant to the next.

BIBLIOGRAPHY

Calame-Griaule, G. 1965. *Ethnologie et Langage. La parole chez les Dogon*. Paris, Gallimard.
——— 1968. *Dictionnaire Dogon* (Dialecte tɔrɔ). Paris, Klinksieck.
de Ganay, S. 1941. *Les Devises des Dogons*. (Travaux et Mémoires de l'Institut d'Ethnologie de l'Université de Paris, vol. xli.)
Dieterlen, G. 1941. *Les Ames des Dogon*. (Travaux et Mémoires de l'Institut d'Ethnologie de l'Université de Paris, vol. xl.)
Dieterlen, G. and Calame-Griaule, G. 1960. 'L'alimentation dogon', *Cahiers d'Etudes Africaines*, 3 (October).
Griaule, M. and Dieterlen, G. 1965. *Le Renard pâle*. (Travaux et Mémoires de l'Institut d'Ethnologie de l'Université de Paris, vol. lxxii.)
Jakobson, R. and Lévi-Strauss, C. 1962. '"Les Chats" de Charles Baudelaire', *L'Homme, Revue Française d'Anthropologie*, vol. ii (January–April).
Sebeok, T. A. 1960. 'Decoding a text: levels and aspects in a Cheremis Sonnet', in *Style in Language*. New York–London, The Technology Press, M.I.T., and J. Wiley and Sons.

A Contribution to the Study of Blacksmiths

in West Africa

G. DIETERLEN[1]

Almost everywhere in Africa south of the Sahara, where anthropological inquiries have been carried out and the results published, scholars have considered one or other of the aspects associated with the working of the smithy; it is a subject which has always attracted attention, particularly since it is hedged in by taboos and special technical precautions. The same applies to the smith himself, his general status and daily activities presenting specific features which place him apart from other categories of workers.

In West Africa blacksmiths constitute endogamous social groups. They are independent, quasi-international in character—a blacksmith is 'at home' wherever he goes; as long as there is a forge he can set up in business anywhere he pleases, anywhere he is needed.[1a] They live in a symbiotic relationship with those people for whom they work, people whose own basic occupations are different—whether they are farmers, fishermen, or pastoralists. All require tools and weapons for use in hunting—and formerly in war—and they observe, vis-à-vis the blacksmith, special forms of behaviour which share common elements. Each tribe—in a manner of speaking—finds itself confronted with its own blacksmith group, a group which, meanwhile, plays a very important role in its social and religious organization.

In an article dedicated to Marcel Griaule, on 'Le Symbolisme du

---

[1] *Germaine Dieterlen* (b. 1903), Dr. es L., Sorbonne. A Director of Research at the National Centre for Scientific Research (CNRS) and Director of Studies at the Ecole Pratique des Hautes Etudes, Section V, Religious Science. Joined the Griaule Mission in 1937; since when she has pursued field research mainly among the Dogon and Bambara over many years. In addition to her own work on Bambara religion and Dogon myths she is revising for publication earlier researches undertaken jointly with M. Griaule (see *Le Renard pâle*, vol. 1 (Paris, 1965). The original French text of this paper was published as 'Contribution à l'étude des forgerons en Afrique Occidentale', *Annuaire de l'E.P.H.E.*, v, 73 (1965–6), 1–28.

[1a] There are exceptions of course; some blacksmiths are attached to special chiefs, special peoples, special areas. This very complex problem will require an exhaustive comparative study.

Forgeron en Afrique',[2] Luc de Heusch brought together for purposes of analysis, observations collected by several field-workers, along with those from his own area, the Kasai. He compared—or rather singled out—divergent opinions which were found in these different studies, including in his analysis materials from the Dogon on the symbolism of the smithy and the role of the mythical blacksmith, published in *Dieu d'Eau*.[3] He also stressed the fact that the ambivalent nature of the blacksmith's status meant that any interpretation was very difficult —he criticized in particular the work of P. Clément,[4] noting the various attitudes of different ethnic groups towards the blacksmith. These included, specially, those 'positive' valuations of the work of the smithy—the blacksmith as 'master of the fire', a mythical solar hero, 'endowed with a quasi-royal, and at all events, privileged status' (p. 62); as well as the 'negative' valuations—the blacksmith makes weapons, hence he has a 'great responsibility for the spilling of blood' (p. 66) and is dangerous since he possesses magical powers; in sum, he is both 'feared and honoured, both respected and despised' (p. 65).

Much information has been collected since the publication of *Dieu d'Eau* which sheds light, not only on Dogon blacksmiths, but on others as well, which is presented in outline here.[5] On the one hand this will involve complementary material on the myth of the blacksmith or rather on the 'history' of the mythical blacksmith, which was begun in this publication; on the other hand we shall comment on some of those representations relative to the data concerned and to the smithy and present a picture of the special rites which are performed by the blacksmith.

In order to do this we must first outline the cosmogony which the Dogon have elaborated, a cosmogony which subtends the social and religious organization of this people. The Universe as a whole issued from an infinite smallness, created by the 'word' (*so*) of a single god, Amma; this is symbolized today on Earth, by both the fonio seed (*digitaria exilis*, Dogon, *põ*) and the egg of the mud-fish (*Clarias senegalensis*, Dogon, *anagonno*), and in space by a satellite of Sirius, the

[2] Luc de Heusch, *Reflets du Monde*, no. 10 (July 1956), p. 57–70.

[3] M. Griaule, *Dieu d'Eau, Entretiens avec Ogotemmêli* (Paris, Éditions du Chêne, 1948).

[4] P. Clément, 'Le forgeron en Afrique Noire, quelques attitudes du groupe à son égard'. *Revue de Géographie humaine et d'Ethnologie, no. 2* (April–June 1948).

[5] M. Griaule and G. Dieterlen, *Le Renard pâle*, vol. I, *Le Mythe Cosmogonique*, no. 1. Travaux et Mémoires de l'Institut d'Ethnologie, vol. lxxii (Paris, 1965). Names and statuses of our Dogon informants and blacksmiths who worked with us on our inquiries, carried out up till 1965, are to be found on pp. 10 and 11 of this work.

star Digitaria (põ tolo). This infinite smallness developed and formed a vast womb, called the 'egg of the world' (aduno talu) which was divided into twin parts and contained two placentas which eventually gave birth to two couples, pairs of mixed twins, living and animated beings, prototypes of man, who possessed the creative Word. These beings had the form of a fish (mud-fish). They are likened to human foetuses in the waters of the womb. From one half of this egg one of the male twins was born prematurely, and, in order to gain possession of the nascent universe for himself, he rebelled against his creator and, tearing off a piece of his placenta, which had formed a kind of ark, he climbed down into empty space on it. The torn-off piece of placenta became earth, our Earth, our planet; he went inside it in order to look for his twin sister, since, without her, he was powerless to realize any of his ambitions for domination. Walking in every direction he made five rows of twelve holes in the still wet and bloody soil; in this way he set out the first 'field' of the future, with its sixty plots. When his searches on Earth came to nought he went back up into the Sky; but Amma had given his twin to the pair in the other half of the egg so that he should not get hold of her and put the rest of the placenta out of his reach by turning it into a Sun—that is, into burning fire.

The rebel then stole eight seeds of cereal treated by Amma, including fonio (põ), the seed of the world, and went down to Earth again; he sowed them in the north-eastern hole of the field he had set out. Seven of these were taken away from him, but the humidity of the placenta, which was not yet entirely dried out, caused the fonio seed to germinate and become red (põ banu) and impure.

The premature intervention on the part of this audacious creature, the incest he had committed by penetrating his own placenta, that is the womb of his 'mother', and, above all, his theft and planting of the fonio seed—'sperm' of his father Amma—permanently disturbed the order of creation. Incomplete and impure, Ogo was transformed into an animal, the pale fox, yurugu (Vulpes pallida); he brought with him to Earth his own impurity, making it dry and sterile.

In order to remedy this situation Amma had one of the twins in the other half of the egg castrated and then offered in sacrifice to heaven. Thus this twin shed both his blood and 'the seeds on his clavicles' (man's future food) for purifying to please the Universe. He was given the name of Nommo, which literally means 'to give drink'. Nommo's body, apart from his arms, was cut in sixty pieces and one by one they were thrown into space at the four cardinal points; some of them fell to the earth and were transformed into plants, symbols of the purification wrought by this sacrifice.

Amma then put together the victim's vital organs (except for his genitals and the sperm they contained which he set aside) and brought him back to life by refashioning him from the stuff of his own placenta. Sacrificed in the form of a fish-foetus, Nommo was resuscitated as a human couple—a man and a woman. Still using the material from the placenta of the sacrificial victim, Amma then created four pairs of mixed twins, who were the ancestors of mankind, the 'sons', *unum*, of Nommo, who is considered to be their 'father', *ba*. Then he sent down to the Earth of the Fox a rectangular ark (*koro*) which bore the resuscitated male Nommo, 'master of the verb, the sky and the waters'. To him was confided the care of the Universe, along with the other four mixed couples, his 'children' created from the same placenta, the ancestors of all human beings. The ark, a pure, second Earth, was designed to fit on top of the old one; it contained all the animals, minerals and plants created by Amma, which were to multiply and occupy the whole planet. The descent of this structure coincided with the appearance of solar light and was followed by the first fall of rain, the sperm of Nommo which had been put aside after he had been sacrificed.

Born from the unions of the ancestors in the ark, mankind grew apace and life became organized on Earth; the constituent, complementary parts of this organization included: on the one hand drought, sterility, disorder, impurity, and death—the sphere of the Fox; and on the other fertility, order, purity, and life—the sphere of Nommo.

This period of organization lasted for the first five generations of the four lineages which issued from Nommo and the eight mythical ancestors. It included, in particular, the sharing out of farmland, the setting up of marriage rules, the acquisition of technical skills, etc.

Although he possessed the divine Word, the Fox, a single being, was incapable of achieving his wished-for domination: he was fated to pass his time vainly pursuing his lost twin sister, Yasigi, who was at the same time his 'female soul'. Nommo's role, as instructor to the Universe, and especially as absolute lord of the sky-atmosphere, of the waters, of 'souls', and of fertility, was to limit the disorderly activities of the Fox. To do this he divided up all the constituent elements of the Universe and placed them into categories, keeping them under his constant control; then he regulated their relationships which were marked off by taboos. This is how the twenty-two main families of categories became known as the 'twenty-two teeth of Nommo', through which the reorganizing 'words' passed, while two complementary families represented him with his predecessor, the Fox. However, while the activities of the latter continued, Nommo brought about several stages of progressive reorganization through a series of techniques which he revealed to mankind and which constituted a perpetual reordering: among these—and most important of all—we find agriculture, the basic occupation; although it was invented by the Fox, it was developed by men under the guidance of Nommo. The cultivation of the soil purified the Earth which became fertile and helped the human race to proliferate: men became 'as many as the fonio' from which the whole Universe had been created.

This summarizes the main lines of the myth of the creation of the world. In order to bring out the biological status of the blacksmith we shall have to look at certain sequences in the myth in greater detail. In fact, the blacksmith is considered by the Dogon to be Nommo's twin, and he is always associated in their minds with the stages of the latter's sacrifice and resurrection.

(a) Before the sacrifice Amma divides into two the victim's four 'body souls' (which bear witness for the four 'elements'), in order to form, at a later date, the four 'sex souls'. From this time on all living beings will be provided with these two series of principles, essential for reproduction.

(b) He then cuts off the umbilical cord, at the same time castrating his victim, empties the testicles of their contents, and puts away the sperm apart from the emptied sex organs.

(c) The Fox tries to steal Nommo's seed and his 'sex souls' in order to place them in his own genitals; he is circumcised by the scarificator who takes them away from him: part of his blood runs away on to the victim's placenta.

(d) Amma then sacrifices Nommo, divides his body into pieces and throws them 'out of the sky' in order to purify space and Earth, the home of the Fox.

(e) He resuscitates Nommo in the form of a human couple using the stuff of his own placenta from which he had separated him when cutting the umbilical cord.

(f) He then creates man's eight ancestors, 'sons' of the victim, still with the stuff remaining from the placenta.

(g) Finally he also creates other human beings, who will be deemed to possess a different biological status. To do this he uses material from Nommo's placenta, using the parts where the blood from the victim or from the Fox had fallen on to it.

Yasigui, 'twin sister' of the Fox, was created from the part of the placenta on which blood from the Fox's genitals had dripped. The griot and his twin sister were made from those parts where the blood from the throat of the sacrificed Nommo had fallen. The blacksmith (and his twin) were made from the umbilical cord of the victim and the blood which came from the blood of the castrated genitals and the cord.

It is said: 'The *ḍemme na*, the "big sack", twin of the slaughtered Nommo, has come down; he represents Nommo [who has been] slaughtered for purification'.[6] Blacksmiths, *ḍemme na*, are sometimes called *sérem*, Nommo's 'witnesses'. Twinness finds expression in a phrase linking them through the blood which formed them: 'Nommo and the blacksmith are of red blood, like a resplendent ball.'[7] They also say: 'Nommo and the blacksmith are twins; both are red like copper; at his forge, the heat of the fire and the charcoal have blackened the smith.'[8] This is the reason for the popular beliefs that they are able to transform themselves at will into all sorts of living beings, animals and plants, as Nommo himself does. The blacksmith is the 'twin' par excellence, a fact which is attested by the different versions which explain the origin of his spiritual powers.[9]

Not only are the origins and creation of the smith treated in detail in the Dogon myth but we also have information on the invention of his tools, materials, and craft methods.[10] We shall begin by summarizing those relevant sequences of the myth concerned and which to an even greater extent stress the intimate association between the work of the 'master of the forge' and the purificatory sacrifice and the

---

[6] *ḍemme-na nǫmmǫ sẹmi ḍįnẹ sugá; nǫmmǫ ḍolu-go yala.*

[7] *nǫmmǫ-le irinẹ-le illì banu gunnu-gin ere ere bẹ̃.* This is said before the rainy season when the blacksmith is hammering out the iron, red from the fire. The Dogon distinguish the *ḍemma na*, 'blacksmith by birth', who is a member of a caste and works in the Northern Yatenga among the different tribes of this region (Dogon, Kouroumba, Mossi and Fulani), and the *irū*, an individual who is Dogon-born, but who has learnt the smith's skills and therefore 'become a blacksmith'. The latter leads the same way of life and has the same privileges as the *ḍemme-na* and receives a similar initiation.

[8] *nǫmmǫ-le irinẹ-le dìne ū be; bẹllẹy mẹnnu-gin bani* bé; *irinẹ dubǫ dubǫgu dubǫ-gǫ-dẹ yaū uzu-le kile-lẹ dega ḍemme.*

[9] *Le Renard pâle*, vol. I, no. 1, p. 376.

[10] The data which follow are published in Part 2 of Volume I of *Le Renard pâle*.

reordering of the universe. We shall then present those geographical representations which are associated with the myth and which serve as a basis for rituals which are found both inside and outside Dogon territory. We shall also mention data concerning the 'international' status of the West African blacksmith.

1. As we have seen, the fonio which the Fox sowed germinated in his placenta and came out red and impure. In order to destroy this 'red fonio' (põ banu) and prevent it transmitting its impurity all over the Earth, the god Amma, at the time of the resurrection, threw on to the soil 'the blood of the heart' of the victim, rolled in a ball which immediately blazed up. The 'blood' became the anvil: like a flaming mass, a 'ball of burning' fire, it fell, 'upside down', making a vast pit in the Earth as it did so. It struck the impure fonio, but the plant grew up again spreading around the anvil; since this was an instrument of purification it was unable to remain any longer in this soiled place; it rose up again from the hollow it had made in the ground and imbedded itself right side up in a place outside, to the south, where it became deeply imbedded in the ground; the protruding part was later used by the blacksmith when he set up his first forge. Today, whenever the blacksmith 'plants' his anvil (dẹnẹ pegu) in a shelter he acts out this part of the myth in which the anvil imbeds itself in another place after raising itself up out of the hole. The hollow which was left became filled with water from the first rains and the põ banu, which was sprinkled around it, germinated and ripened.

When Amma threw down to Earth the 'blood of the heart-anvil' he also threw down the 'blood of the spleen' which turned into a metallic lump, sagala, which the blacksmith then used before he learnt to extract iron from minerals inside the Earth. The Dogon distinguish two types of sagala; one, 'a black one', is the blood of the internal part of the spleen, which they say remained enclosed inside after death and became dark; and the 'white one', likened to the blood of the 'spleen's skin'. They say: 'Amma sacrified Nommo, then brought him back to life again. At that moment he sent down the anvil: the world roared. Amma, when he resuscitated Nommo, made the world roar by sending the anvil. Amma sent the anvil on to the Fox's põ field. The anvil, falling down, made a hole, which became a pool: the tõnõ of the forge represents this. The põ whirled about and spread around this hole in the ground, around the edges of the pool; the põ ripened. The anvil Amma sent down from the sky made the pool; it jumped up (and) set itself up in the place of the valu hole. That is where the blacksmith began to 'set up' his first forge. The *sagala* came from out of the sky, following the anvil when it came down.'[11] The blacksmith prayed to Amma, the morning before he began his work, saying: 'Amma, accept my morning greetings, Amma, who sacrificed Nommo in the sky, has sent down to earth part of his heart which has been transformed into an anvil, a part of his spleen which he sent down and has been transformed into a *sagala*; after that the forge was forged. Amma, give me this day.'[12]

2. After the descent to the Earth of the ark containing almost all the beings Amma had created in the sky, including the male Nommo, who had been resurrected, and the eight ancestors of mankind, his 'sons', the blacksmith came down in turn—but in a special way. 'The creation of the blacksmith from the blood of the castration is recalled in the events following the descent of the ark. The blacksmith received the penis and the emptied testicles of the victim, which contained, however, the 'four elements' *kizę nay*. He also received the amputated 'arm' emptied of its marrow and formed into a lump which contained sixteen cereal seeds. After the descent of the ark Amma ordered the blacksmith to come down first—as a twin—using the sexual parts as his support: he put his two arms in the testicles, his legs around the penis. These elements changed once they reached the earth: the penis became the blast-pipe and the testicles the bellows of the forge. The blacksmith came down to Earth accompanied by his female twin. Thanks to the presence of the four elements he could extract iron and work it. He brought with him the cereal seeds contained in his hammer, planning to cultivate them: the souls of the latter were momentarily placed into an iron hoe. When speaking of the smith it is said: 'Of Nommo (from whom he had received) his share of *kikinu* (souls), (Amma) having taken the sperm from the sacrificed Nommo, gave it to him, placed him in his empty testicles, entered inside there himself and went down to Earth. He was changed into

---

[11] *amma nǫmmǫ sema, onunę omo bilęmę vo do. varu dęnę kolle ti: ganna ninnu. amma nǫmmǫ ǫmǫ-gǫ bilęmę vo-da ganna ninnema dęňε ti. dęňę polo ǫ nǫmmǫ yulugu pŏ minnę-nę tiya. dęňę vo suga bunno togulu, ǫ gǫ bi: dugǫ ginu tŏňo yo-go tozey. pŏ ginnigili bunnǫ togulo ǫ ginę, pŏ ille. dęňę alagala gǫa amma suňoni ǫ tāñana. dęňę kilia valu bunno gani-nę sibi. dubǫ polo dęmme na-ne kono tolo. sagala alagala goa, dęňę-le dimmia sugi.* The *tŏňo* is a grinding stone in which the blacksmith keeps water for tempering the iron. The roan antelope *valu*, is associated with certain mythical facts concerning the blacksmith which are beyond the scope of this article.

[12] *amma aga na yaba, amma alagala-ne nǫmmǫ uǫ semi kinne-donno gamma minnę-le suňuni dęňę bilęmi, kinne-lara gamma minnę-le suňuna sagala bilęmi; dubǫ kǫ-le duboni, amma denu mui obo.*

a man. His name, it is said: in the "big sack" [that is, he who came down inside the testicles called the "big sack"].'[13]

Along with his twin sister, the blacksmith also came down with the resuscitated Nommo female twin, Yasa. As he came down he stole part of the sun, that is a burning piece of the remains of the Fox's placenta.[14] The smith used this solar fire to light his forge fire, thereby emphasizing that his power paralleled, if it did not equal, that of his 'twin', Nommo, who fights victoriously against the fomenters of disorder. He arrived at a spot on the Earth where he found a piece of *sagala* which he used to fashion the first iron implement. Accompanied everywhere by the two women, he made a lengthy perambulation which brought him to the place where the anvil had impaled itself and here he set up his anvil. The sperm of the sacrificial victim was in part made up of water which Amma had sent to Earth in the form of rain, in order to bring about germination of the seeds. This water filled up the hole made by the anvil and it became a pool; when the Fox approached to drink, Amma threw down from the sky one of the mineral elements of the contents of the victim's genitals, a 'rain axe', *anagulo*, in order to chase him away. The blacksmith turned this celestial stone into his working stool.

The craftsman was now in possession of all his basic materials, all of celestial origin: his stool, anvil, hammer, ore, bellows and blasting pipe, fire. Helped by Yasa—he amputated one of her arms in order to make his hammer and a hand for a pair of pincers—he lit the fire and forged the first farm tool, in order to help mankind to whom he had handed over the seed corn which Amma had placed in his care and which he had brought down from the sky in Nommo's hammer-arm.

The annual ceremony performed before the sowing of the crops involves a blood sacrifice on the anvil. The chief blacksmith, who officiates, says: 'In the olden days, at the beginning, he collected pieces of *sagala* and put them into the fire; all the pieces stuck together; he hit with the hammer, tempered in water, and rubbed with earth; afterwards he placed it in the fire, (then) reddened it in the fire. He took it out and hammered it again. The matrix of the *sagala* burst; the iron formed a ball (ingot).'[15]

---

[13] *nǫmmǫ kikinu gammala nǫmmǫ sęmí dęnę yabo vo obi, dǫlǫ kǫlǫ-nę kunnā vo ya yoā minnę-nę sugā inne bilemā. boy-gǫ dęmme na-nę g̃i.* Le Renard pâle, vol. I, no. 1, p. 378.

[14] Cf. above, p. 42.

[15] *vo tolozę sagala gunni mona yam kunna; be uǫi daniya; syenu-le laga, di-ne kunna, olu-gǫ minne para; yam-le kunni, oñu yam banięmęze. gona lagavoze. sagala bozo kilięze; inu gunnu-gǫ monyay.*

A Contribution to the Study of Blacksmiths in West Africa 49

After several incidents, occasioned by the activities of the Fox, Yasa, the twin of the resurrected Nommo took on her earlier form of a fish and, like the latter, went into the pool to stay there for ever; the pool became the 'sacred pool' of the smiths.

Masters of fire, the blacksmith had been given the power to extract minerals (*banu minne*) from the soil, smelting it and transforming it; the result of this process is also known as *sagala*, and the matrix is called the 'excrement of the *sagala*' (*sagala bozo*).

Endowed with the capacity to make arms and tools, vital to man, the smith now became a 'master of knowledge'. He carried out circumcision and excision rites on the ancestors of mankind in order to render them fit for marriage and also to prepare them to receive the 'word', that is learning.

The doings of the Fox—his struggles against established order—led to a number of serious incidents. Among these, in particular, was the appearance of death on Earth. Such incidents continued until the commemoration of the revelation of the 'Word', sixty years afterwards at the time of the celebration of the Sigi: learning was transmitted to young people by the blacksmith who survived the death of the eight primordial ancestors. The myth finishes with his death and the celebration of his funeral, sixty-six years after his 'descent' to Earth.

Events pertaining to the mythical smith, and their consequences, are symbolically re-enacted whenever a new smithy or a temporarily deserted shelter are built or repaired.

As we have seen, the 'planting of the anvil' recalls, for the Dogon, the imbedding of a blazing lump from the sky into the ground for the second time, after its initial impact:[16] the anvil is then consecrated by a blood sacrifice. At the top of his furnace the smith fashions a small hollow into which he pours a mash of boiled cereals after an offering has been made to the anvil. He places a small iron hook (*gobo*) inside it. The small hollow represents the excavation wrought by the fall of the anvil, and the iron hook is the germinating *põ*. Beside the forge there is a flat grind-stone (*tõño*) which is always kept full of water: this is the hollow, filled by the rain water, which became a 'pool'.

In the morning before he begins work every day, the blacksmith knocks on the anvil three times with his hammer. The three blows have a precise meaning: the first is in the form of an apology to Nommo's twin, Yasa—that is he honours her and tells her his working

[16] See above, p. 46.

programme for the day; the second is a 'greeting' to the antelope, *valu*. After this he says: 'Amma, receive my morning greetings; we had a good night, and let Amma give us a good day.'[17]

Furthermore the oldest of the smiths in a territorial group keeps a shrine in his dwelling which has three major features:

1. A mud mound made of 'red clay' 'of the pool' (*nange*)— obtained from deep pits in the earth on the banks of rivers. It must be red because Nommo's organs—that is the anvil and the celestial mineral—were red from the sacrificial blood. Imbedded in the clay is a piece of *sagala*, not the kind extracted from the earth, but the kind which has 'fallen from the sky'.[18] Underneath the mound, the smith has traced with boiled cereals four spots in the four cardinal directions since 'the *sagala* is available to blacksmiths all over the Earth'.

2. A wooden statue of a one-armed woman representing Yasa, Nommo's twin; the other arm, cut off by the smith to make his hammer, is missing.

3. A mask of the roan antelope (*valu*) which commemorates the role of this animal and certain actions of the Fox.[19]

An annual ceremony involving all the smiths of a region takes place every year before the sowing period; blood sacrifices are performed on these shrines and the resurrected Nommo and his twin sister, Yasa, are invoked.

These sequences in this 'history of the creation of the world' elaborated by the Dogon, reveal a certain number of themes about the smith and throw some light on the 'positive' and 'negative' valuations of his social status.

1. The smith is essentially a 'twin', like all the first living creatures who were created by God. He shares their privileges and their powers —in particular a certain intangibility—and also their 'sacred' character. It is for this reason that he is able to invoke Amma when he prays for rain—the sperm of the sacrificed Nommo, his 'twin', whose sexual attributes he manipulates in his forge.

Like Nommo, he is able to change himself, at will, into all kinds of

[17] *amma na yaba, yoy si ęsu bęmaze; amma denu si ęsu emmi obo. yoy si* refers to the period from twilight to dawn, and *denu*, the period between the rising and the setting of the sun.
[18] This is a mineral of sidereal origin, probably a fragment of a meteorite.
[19] These two objects were shown at the exhibition, *Le Masque*, held at the Musée Guimet (in collaboration with the Section des Sciences Religieuses de l'E.P.H.E.) in 1959. See exhibition catalogue, no. 108, p. 116.

beings: that is why he inspires fear, people believing that he can take on any animal form he wishes.

2. He is also essentially a member of the 'fathers'' generation, *ba*; whatever his age set he is ontologically considered to belong to the same class as the members of the oldest generation. Owing to his special nature and his status, the smith is 'seated' beside the chief village or regional priest during communal ceremonies. One of his functions consists of forging or carving from wood those sacred objects, attributes, and emblems of power which priests and chiefs require. These duties are all hedged in by special taboos. For example, he must use wood or charcoal which has come from a special tree, metal from a particular place; he must observe a certain number of strict precautions, etc. . . .

3. From the biological point of view his veins contain 'mixed blood', made up partially of 'sacrificial' blood. Because of this duality, Dogon who are not smiths will not mix blood with them in marriage; blacksmiths form a kind of endogamous caste. For the Dogon, breaking the taboo harms the blacksmith more than it would his consort, whatever the latter's origins.[20]

4. Materials and tools used by the smith are symbols of the organs and limbs of a sacrificed person; one who has passed through the extreme stage of impurity, Death—who was then resurrected—a fact which implies a triumph over the impurity involved in the loss of life. The smith works with both the 'pure' and the 'impure'. His status will ever remain associated—on a cosmic plane—both with a break-down in an earlier established order, as well as the organization and functioning of a 'new' world.

5. The 'sacrificial' blood which flows in the veins of all blacksmiths comes from the umbilical cord of a sacrificial victim, and also from his sexual attributes which are considered to be the most 'vital' aspects of a person. Work in the forge is, in fact, assimilated to the sexual act: the fire receives the air which comes from the bellows-testicles passing through the pipe-penis, allowing the iron to be moulded by hammering, and giving form to the desired object. Thus the smith's work is similar to the process of procreation. The taboos which are respected both outside and inside the forge are to a great extent due to this assimilation. At the same time this almost

[20] Fulani and blacksmiths—who share kinship through a joking relationship—
—observe the same taboo. However when a Fulani chief reached the peak of his powers, he broke this taboo and married a woman from a blacksmith caste; this act, which seems to have served to enhance his power, was considered beneficial for the whole group.

daily—and at least permanent—reminder of these facts, places the
smith outside the norm. The sexual act generates life, it is true, but
it also involves the risk of impurity (it is generally proscribed before
most religious rites). Sex has ambivalent characteristics which are
also found in the activities of the smith.

6. Comparable representations are also associated with one of the
smith's social roles: he performs circumcisions. This means that he
can cut the sexual attributes of circumcised boys—because he himself
is made of the 'blood' which came from a comparable operation. For
this reason he may—at least in this case—cause the blood of others to
run with impunity. From one point of view circumcision is assimilated to a sacrifice presided over by the smith.[21] And the results of his
activities are similar to those changes wrought on the materials he
extracts and handles in the forge: circumcision changes a child into
a man (vir) in the full meaning of the word. At the same time, the
smith simulates a second cutting of the umbilical cord (represented
by a little stick placed on the penis): the circumcised boy, at this time,
is definitively taken away from his mother and made to enter the
'society' of men.[22] From now on he is deemed capable of gradually
receiving traditional instruction, an education which is initiated by the
blacksmith who operated on his body.

7. While he has no specific role to play in the formal education of
the young people by their elders, the blacksmith is, among the Dogon
and elsewhere,[23] one of the masters of initiatory knowledge. This fact
is emphasized in the last episodes of the myth; it is the blacksmith
who, before his death, transmits the 'word' to the younger generations at the second Sigi.[24] The smith still plays an eminent role
during the Sigi, those ceremonies which commemorate the 'renewal
of the world' and take place every sixty years. They begin—as we

[21] We know that those precautions which hunters and warriors take (wearing
amulets and charms, strictly observing specific taboos) are in order to protect
their lives during hunting and fighting; but they are also to protect them at a
later date from the avenging life force of the game or enemy they have killed, a life
force which has been freed from the body at the moment of death and 'runs out'
with the spilt blood. In the case of sacrifice, the spiritual principles and life force
of the victim are controlled and safeguarded against, and therefore are not capable
of attacking the officiant or any of the participants.

[22] Le Renard pâle, vol. I, no. 1, p. 257.

[23] Among the Bambara, the blacksmith circumciser is most frequently the head of
the Komo, the first male institution into which members of a grade of circumcised
boys are introduced at the end of their seclusion period. In this role he gives the
young people their first instruction. Unfortunately we have no space here to dwell on
the role of the smith among the Bambara, the Malinke, etc.

[24] Cf. supra, p. 49.

shall see later—in a village where a masterly representation of the fall of the anvil is to be found.

The second part of this essay will be devoted to geographical representations of certain episodes involving the mythical blacksmith. When the Dogon settled in the land they came to after migrating from their original homelands, buildings, caves, rock shelters, standing stones, cave paintings all multiplied throughout the country. They had both initiatory and ritual objectives. All of them are connected with different sequences in the myth, whose main outlines have been sketched above. They also interpreted those accidental territorial landmarks they found and made them fit into this system of representations. However, most of them, in Dogon territory, are simply reproductions of others which can be found over a large region of West Africa. This gives them an international character: they are well known by knowledgeable men and women of various tribes we have studied: Malinke, Sarakole, Bambara, Bozo, for example, whose cosmology and religion have much in common with those of the Dogon.[25] To give an example: a stone table, an image of the ark, which supported the resurrected male Nommo and man's eight ancestors, was set up near Sanga; it is a replica of a similar table found on the top of Mount Gourao at Lake Debo—the place where Dogon myth places the arrival of the ark on the earth.[26] In the same way the course of the Gona, a wet-season river, which runs along the cliff plateau, represents the Niger; a certain number of 'water-holes' are the scenes of purificatory rites similar to those carried out at certain points along the latter river.[27]

Events relating to the fall of the anvil, the descent of the blacksmith and the 'rain axe' (which became his stool) are the objects of comparable geographical representations.

According to explicit accounts given to us by informants (and this should be valid for all West African blacksmiths) it was the burning mass of 'heart's blood', from the sacrificed Nommo, turned into the anvil, which hollowed out the crater of Lake Bosumtwi in Ghana, which they call the 'pool of the descended anvil' (*dęnę sugu bunnǫ ǫ*).

[25] The Fulani also 'integrated' the courses of the rivers Senegal and Niger into the representations found in their traditional beliefs after their arrival in West Africa. Cf. A. Hampaté Ba and G. Dieterlen, *Koumen, Texte initiatique des pasteurs Peul* (Mouton et Cie, Paris, 1960), pp. 26 ff.

[26] M. Griaule et G. Dieterlen, *Le Renard pâle*, vol. I, no. 1, loc. cit., p. 458.

[27] G. Dieterlen, 'Mythe et organisation sociale au Soudan français'. *J. Soc. Africanistes*, xxv (1955), 42, n. 4.

To the south of this crater is the spot where it afterwards 'imbedded itself in the ground' after raising itself up out of the first hole. The blacksmith came down from the sky in Mande country; he picked up a piece of celestial *sagala*—'blood of Nommo's spleen', left this region for the edges of the crater which had become filled with water, and set up his first forge where the anvil had landed, thus performing a peregrination which has been interpreted as a repetition, on Earth, of the 'way of the blood' which spilled from Nommo when he was sacrificed in the sky, 'as if he were going back to his place of origin'. It was here, on the slopes of this lake that the 'rain axe' fell down, the axe which chased away the Fox when he came to drink; and it was the stone which the blacksmith used as his seat after using it to purify the land and the water. 'The Fox arrived to drink water from the pool. Amma threw the "rain axe" at the top of his head; the Fox jumped up and ran away. The blacksmith came, the "rain axe" became his seat; and a purificatory rite (a sacrifice) was made with a goat. Each year a purificatory sacrifice is made there because it is not known if the Fox may not have come to drink during the night.'[28]

The Dogon recall these facts in various places inside their own territory. On the southern flank of the Yougo massif a huge hole has been dug out to represent the crater which became a 'pool', that is a lake. This is at Yougo Dogorou, a village perched almost on the summit of the massif and right over this excavation, where the Sigi ceremonies which occur every sixty years take place: here above the cave where the masks and various ritual objects are kept, there is a natural vertical rock of huge proportions which represents the anvil.

At Arou near Ibi, where the most important Dogon religious chief lives—he once also had political powers—special places have been fitted out in and around this official's house. In the courtyard there is a large circular excavation which represents the lake. Opposite his dwelling, on a slope which dominates the courtyard, beside a shrine consecrated to the creator Amma, a vertical block of stone has been set up to represent the anvil.[29] The death of this chief is announced by fixing a flaming torch of straw on to the top of it—'as the anvil appeared when it came down'. In the Sanga area, three caves have been fitted out as shrines; in one of them the descent of the blacksmith

---

[28] *nǫmmǫ ǫ-nę yurugu di nō dua. amma anagulǫ ku nǫmǫne tiya; yurugu kiliay. ḍemmę na-ne suga, anagulǫ dōy uǫmǫ bi; uguru ene-le kunni. anakuzu vuęzę uguri-nu yurugu digę di no yueabe innemo.*

[29] Called *sǫrǫ dummo* or 'rock which projects'.

A Contribution to the Study of Blacksmiths in West Africa 55

is symbolized; in the second there are representations of the 'heavenly events' associated with the fall of the anvil; the third, which is very big, opens on to a valley in which there is the 'pool'; inside an arrangement of stone blocks includes representations of the anvil, the blacksmith's seat, his tomb, etc.; and very many schematic paintings (and also some masks) are found on the ceiling and recall events caused by the revolt of the Fox.

Lake Bosumtwi, situated about 31 kilometres to the south-east of Kumasi in Ghana, is circular in form, and occupies the bottom of a crater; its sheer sides are covered with luxuriant vegetation.[30] A certain number of hamlets have been built by fishermen around the shores of the lake, and there are others further up, on different levels of the surrounding slopes. Fishing still seems to be the only resource of these small ethnic groups, but it is a fruitful occupation; women dry the fish brought back by the men. The lake has no connection with the neighbouring network of large rivers. It is only fed by short streams and temporary rivulets and by rainwater. Its shape, plus the appearance of the crater's slopes, have attracted the attention of scholars interested in its geological origins.

Rattray in his celebrated work on the Ashanti[31] devotes a long study to Lake Bosumtwi. He describes the lake and its banks, the hamlets clustering around it, the fishing crafts, the tools and techniques of the fishermen. He also discusses representations involving the lake; he records the local myth of the 'spirit' which is supposed to inhabit it and to whom the inhabitants of the lake offer regular sacrifices; and he provides a list of taboos which the latter observe in relation to their own system of belief. The etymology of the 'sacred lake' of the Ashanti is suggestive: 'The name and "strong names" (*mmerane* is the

---

[30] We have taken the geographical particulars concerning this lake from a catalogue published by Th. Monod, *Contribution à l'établissement d'une liste d'accidents circulaires d'origine météoritique (reconnue, possible ou supposée), cryptoexplosive, etc. ... les charactéristiques géographiques du lac.* Catalogues et Documents de l'Université de Dakar. No. XVIII, Institut Français d'Afrique Noire (Dakar, 1965), pp. 9 and 10. 'Lake Bosumtwi is about 20 miles (32 kilometres) south-east of Kumasi, Ashanti, Ghana, at 6°30′N–1°25′W. The altitude of the lake is about 100 metres (311 (Junner) or 340 (Maclaren) feet); the diameter of the lake is about 5 miles (eight kilometres), that of the crater about 6½ miles (10.4 kilometres) (7 miles = 11.3 kilometres) E.W. to 9 miles = 14.5 kilometres N.S.; the crater: = 450 feet (137 metres) to + 1,500 feet (456 metres) (Junner), 900 feet (274 metres) to 1,200 feet (365 metres) (Maclaren); highest point: + 1,800 feet (548 m) at the Beposo Mine; depth of lake 240 feet (73 metres).' The author then gives a list of those men of science who have visited the lake, the crater and its surrounding.
[31] Capt. R. S. Rattray, *Ashanti* (Oxford, Clarendon Press, 1923), 349 pp., 143 ill., maps.

Ashanti word for the latter) of this so-called "Sacred Lake" are as follows and practically constitute a title: Akwasi Bosomtwe Akowuakra (. . .) *Bosomtwe*. This word is derived from *obosom* (God) and *Twe*: the latter is here a name for the supposed anthropomorphic lake spirit . . .'[32]

An annual sacrifice is offered on a sacred stone situated in the village of Abrodwum: Rattray describes this ceremony, which he attended himself, in some detail; an initial offering (a white fowl) is followed by the immolation of another fowl, also white, which is thrown into the lake. When the victim has sunk, Rattray emphasizes that: 'The spirit of the lake had accepted the offering.'[33] He also records a series of ceremonies which take place when the colour and the appearance of the lake make it clear that an out-of-the-ordinary phenomenon is about to occur (they do occur frequently enough, although irregularly), as a result of the abundance of decomposed organic matter which is found at the bottom.[34] This putrefaction brings a considerable number of dead fish to the surface, all at once, a fact which the fishermen attribute to the work of the 'spirit' of the lake. On this occasion, and after the Ashanti king—who will send a representative—has been forewarned at Kumasi, sacrifices of white hens are made on the 'sacred stone' of Abrodwum and also in the lake, sacrifices which are similar to ones described earlier; then a cow is slaughtered; finally a dog, in honour of 'the mother of Twe' who is supposed to live at the mouth of the river Aberewa, which enters the lake in the south-east by the village of Apeu.[35] Thus the 'spirit' which haunts the lake and which, according to the myth mentioned by Rattray, manifested itself in the guise of a man, had a 'mother' who also lived in or along the shores of the lake.

We have quoted certain passages from Rattray's work in order to stress the fact that the 'sacred Ashanti lake', both for these peoples, as well as for the Dogon and the blacksmiths, is a source of supernatural power and that it is the object of a cult. Rattray makes no allusion to the smith; but in the list of taboos there are primary ones which forbid the use of metal or its presence near the lake: '1. Iron hooks of any description, or any kind of lure or live fishing . . .; 5. Brass or metal pans (only wooden ones must be used).'[36] No informa-

---

[32] Rattray loc. cit., p. 55. [33] Rattray, loc. cit., p. 60.
[34] Rattray, loc. cit., Appendix D. Letter from the geologist T. Robertson to the author, p. 76. The author of this letter writes of the results of soundings he made in the lake.
[35] Rattray, loc. cit., p. 61. [36] Rattray, loc. cit., pp. 61–2.

tion concerning these prescriptions was collected, but they are directly related to the cult and traditional lore.

As far as our Dogon informants are concerned, and also for any blacksmith—who has lived for a long time in Ghana, particularly in Kumasi and at a hamlet situated to the north of the lake[37]—the 'sacred stone' of Abrodwum is the symbol of the 'rain axe' which was thrown down from the sky to chase away the Fox, and which afterwards became the mythical smith's stool. Several of them have more than once attended the annual sacrifice described by Rattray, and freely gave their own account. Having slit the throats of the white sacrificial victims, the person in charge of the sacrifice, appointed by the chief of Asamang village, 'master of the lake' and officiant in charge of the cult, throws a mash of boiled cereals on to the stone and then performs the same libation in the centre of the lake.[38] This is a purificatory sacrifice performed because 'one never knows, whether, during the past year, the Fox may not have come down to the bank to drink'. It is said that this rite is comparable, both in aim and content, to those carried out regularly in certain localities found near deep water-holes along the course of the Niger—or along the Gona, the Dogon 'Niger' at Sanga—and also in certain pools, such as that of Dya.[39] 'All the pools where purificatory rites are performed are replicas of the Dya pool—home of the resuscitated male Nommo— or of Lake Bosumtwi—home of his twin.' The latter is the 'sacred lake of the blacksmiths'; when our informant was there the taboo involving the ban on the presence of metal was still strictly enforced.

Furthermore, in Kumasi town, set up at the top of one of the hills on which the town is built, we find a kind of iron stake, deeply imbedded in the ground. It is placed in the centre of a large oval plaque

[37] Our blacksmith informant worked for nine years in Ghana; several of our Dogon informants have stayed in Kumasi and in Accra and also know the lake.

[38] This pap is made of a special variety of finger millet (*yu pilu* in Dogon) cultivated in a small field maintained for ritual purposes at Asamang, where the religious chief, the 'master of the lake' lives. This information (which will have to be verified on the spot) should be compared with results of inquiries carried out in Accra where the priests of Gā fishermen, in Jamestown quarter, cultivate a field, which we saw, whose crops are kept as offerings to be made in their shrines and on the banks of the 'sacred lagoon' (cf. G. Dieterlen, 'Mythe et organisation sociale en Afrique Occidentale', *J. Soc. Africanistes*, xxix, 1 (1959), p. 136). If these facts are confirmed for Bosumtwe we should then be dealing, as at Accra, with the cultivation of a grain which was imported for ritual ends and plays no part in local foodstuff production. In 1965 the chief of Asamang, Nana Adsei Twum, carried out a sacrifice of a white ram on the Abrodwum stone, on the 23 or 24 August.

[39] Cf. G. Dieterlen, *Mythe et organisation sociale au Soudan français*, pp. 51 ff; *Mythe et organisation sociale en Afrique Occidentale*, p. 126; M. Griaule and G. Dieterlen, *Le Renard pâle*, vol. I, no. 1, p. 462.

C

of the same metal which must have been covered with earth; it has now deteriorated. This stake is found quite near the tombs of the Ashanti kings which were built at the end of the last century by the British administration in the garden of the present Nkwame Nkrumah Hospital. Following popular beliefs, the object is shown to foreign visitors and described as a kind of regalia: it is called 'Osei Tutu's sword';[40] it was placed here as a symbol of his power, and of that of his descendants, over the whole territory which they ruled. However, for those instructed in traditional matters—and for all our informants —this object which they call the *kumasi dẹ̀nẹ̀*, is, in this royal city, a replica and a symbol of the anvil 'imbedded in place' after its ejection from the first hollow it first made.[41] 'The anvil,' they say, 'is like the *pegu* shrine.'[42] The iron plaque, in the centre of which it stands, re-produces the universe—that is the sky and the earth 'which had first of all been separated because of the Fox's carryings on, and then been united again by the effects of the sacrifice of Nommo and both of them had then been placed under his control'. At a certain distance from this stake there stood, in 1963, a *ficus* of a great height (*Ficus glumosa*) under which, in the past, invalids undergoing traditional healing had to be brought; in many West African tribes the ficus is considered to be a 'purificatory tree' and is planted for ritual purposes.[43]

If possible, before the rite admitting them to their duties, Dogon postulants to the priesthood should go to Kumasi in order to make their vows in front of this symbol of the 'anvil'[44]. Blacksmiths, during their apprenticeship and their initiation, should do the same and also pay a visit to the sacred lake.

All this information will have to be studied intensively with our

[40] Nana Osei Tutu, first Ashanti king at Kumasi, reigned from 1700 to 1730 (Eva L. R. Meyerowitz, *Akan Traditions of Origin*, Appendix IV (London, Faber and Faber, 1950), p. 139).

[41] During our first stay in Kumasi, one of our Dogon informants who had come with us, said, of his own accord, as we stood in front of the stake: 'It is an anvil.' Later inquiries, made among the blacksmiths and our Sanga collaborators, con-firmed this early statement

[42] Literally, 'to plant'; a Dogon shrine which is generally erected in the bush, near a tree. It sometimes includes an anthropomorphic male figurine with an iron hook knocked into its vertex. The aim of the shrine is to 'settle' and 'protect' local groups in the name of Nommo (M. Griaule and G. Dieterlen, *Le Renard pâle*, vol. I, no. 1, p. 317).

[43] See in particular G. Dieterlen, 'Classification des végétaux chez les Dogon', *J. Soc. Africanistes*, xxii (1952), 145. In 1965, when I was passing through Kumasi again, this ficus had died and been replaced by another, planted a little distance away.

[44] One of our informants, Yébéné, now deceased, actually made this pilgrimage.

informants, and also considered in the light of material from the Malinke, Bambara, Sarakole, and Bozo of Mali, people whose social and religious structures are so very close to those of the Dogon, as well as that from other tribes of Africa south of the Sahara. Further research will also have to be undertaken among the blacksmiths who live among each of these peoples. It should be of interest to compare, for example, the representations involving the fall of the anvil among the Dogon and the Ashanti—from the point of view of political and religious authority—along with observations relative to the symbolism of one of the palace monuments found in Logone Birni, in Chad: the *guti*, now destroyed, was built originally in the image of a primordial anvil which fell from the sky into its initial position, that is 'with its point facing the sky'. According to the myth, the first Sao blacksmith brought back the object in order to set it up in the soil and use it. The *guti* 'illustrated the myth of origin of metallurgy'.[45]

Furthermore, other research should also be undertaken in Ghana, at Kumasi and at Lake Bosumtwi. Many publications have been devoted to the flora and fauna, the climatic and geological features of the lake and region. But no research has been carried out into the social and religious organization of these lacustrian fishermen, since the appearance of Rattray's work.[46]

As we have already pointed out this crater has been the object of geological and mineralogical studies for several decades.[47] Three hypotheses have been suggested by these specialists: the lake may have been formed from volcanic activity, tectonic movements, or the impact of a meteorite. A long article by A. F. J. Smith, published in 1962, 'The Origin of Lake Bosumtwi and some other problematic structures'[48] has been devoted to this question. The author examines the different possible answers as to the formation of the crater, summarizing various articles by students who have carried out geological studies in the region and at the lake and concludes in the

[45] A. and J.-P. Lebeuf, 'Monuments symboliques du Palais royal de Logone-Birni', *J. Soc. Africanistes*, xxv (Paris, 1955), 25–34.
[46] This was confirmed for us by inquiries at the University of Ghana; we wish to take this opportunity of thanking these scholars for providing publications and documents for us; and also Th. Monod, J. L. Tournier, and T. Grjebine (of the Laboratoire des Faibles Radioactivités du C.N.R.S.) who have shown an interest in the various problems involving the lake's origin.
[47] Th. Monod in the article quoted above gives a list of the specialists concerned and the dates of their visits.
[48] *Ghana Journal of Science*, Vol. 2 (1 October 1962), published by the Ghana Science Association, Government Printing Department, Accra, Ghana.

following manner: 'There is insufficient evidence for either a volcanic or a meteorological origin for the Bosumtwi depression in Ghana to accept either of them as proven . . . The geology of the area around Lake Bosumtwi is still imperfectly known and a detailed mapping on a large scale and careful analysis of the structures of the rocks in and around the depression is necessary.[49]

Since the appearance of this article several specialists have carried out research in the field, collecting samples of vitrified stone near the rivers Ata and Buonim. An analysis of these materials was made at the same time as tectites, collected previously in the Ivory Coast by Th. Monod, were examined. A study by W. Gentner, H. J. Lippolt, and O. Muller, 'Das Kalium-Argon-Alter des Bosumtwi Kraters in Ghana und die chemische Beschaffenheit seiner Gläser',[50] provides the results. The vitrified samples collected near the lake are of the same age and chemical composition as the tectites from the Ivory Coast. The lake is found in a region of pre-Cambrian rocks; the formation of the crater, which came much later, must have taken place during the recent tertiary, perhaps at the level of the Middle Pleistocene. The study of the samples allows the formations to be dated at 1·3 ± 0·3 ten years. The results of the analysis of the 'rare elements' in these various samples confirm the original relation between the vitreous minerals at Bosumtwi and the Ivory Coast tectites, a relation which was established by potassium–argon dating. In both cases a gigantic natural event is held to be the common cause, probably the fall of a meteorite. ('In beiden Fällen dürfte ein ähnlich grossartiges Naturereignis, wahrscheinlich ein Meteoriteneinschlag, also Ursache anzusehen sein.')[51]

The authors have announced that they intend to bring out a detailed study in co-operation with Professor Th. Monod, to whom they owe the discovery of the vitrified rocks, as well as to publish a full geological and mineralogical description.

Information collected from the Dogon and their blacksmiths concerning representations of the lake must, as we emphasized earlier, be corroborated by further studies to be carried out among various other tribes as well as among the Ashanti and related people in Ghana. At the same time the geological origins of the lake should receive further attention. Nevertheless it seems to us that it would be of

[49] Loc. cit., pp. 194 and 195.
[50] *Zeitschrift für Naturforschung.* Band 19a, Heft 1, 1964. Verlag der Zeitschrift für Naturforschung, Tübingen.
[51] Loc. cit., p. 153.

great interest to compare the hypotheses presented about the crater's formation through a meteorite and our informants' statements. All of them, without exception, attribute its origin to the impact of a burning, metallic mass of huge dimensions, 'which came from the sky'. Later on, if the meteorite origin of the lake is verified and the date of its formation becomes known more exactly, the problem will then have to be faced as to how such a fact, of such an ancient origin, could have been observed[52] and its memory preserved and transmitted in the traditions of West African peoples.

Postscript: January–December 1969. Inquiries carried out by specialists in Ghana have resulted in proof that the formation of this lake was caused by the fall of a gigantic meteorite.

[52] We could envisage the hypothesis of an *a posteriori* interpretation of the lake's origin by analogy with the results of falls of smaller meteorites, which the people concerned have collected and used. Mme B. Appia has brought together details on the probable use of meteorites as anvils among certain blacksmiths in the Foutah Djallon region.

Symbolic Monuments of the Logone-Birni

Royal Palace (Northern Cameroons)

ANNIE and JEAN-PAUL LEBEUF[1]

In an earlier article[1a] we gave a brief explanation of the conceptions which lay behind the erection by the Lagouané[2] of their capital, Logone Birni, on the left bank of the Logone. An image of the world, the town is divided into two parts: Halaka (north) and Alagué (south),[3] separated by a median zone, *mzaɡə* ('boundary'), where we find the king's residence, *ralme*.[4] Within the precincts of the Palace, a microcosm in itself (Figure 1), there were at one time[5] two structures, the *tukuri* and the *guti*, both remarkable for their symbolism. These two monuments were erected for an essentially religious purpose, and

[1] *Jean-Paul Lebeuf* (b. 1907), Dr. es L., Sorbonne. Research Director, National Centre for Scientific Research (CNRS); Head of the Chadian Institute for Social Sciences (INTSH) and of the Laboratory of Camerounian and Chadian Archaeology and Ethnology (CNRS). Lecturer at the René Descartes University (Paris V). Has been engaged in field research in Chad, Northern Cameroun, Mali, Central African Republic, and Congo (Bra.) since 1936, specializing in ethno-archaeology. *Annie Masson Detourbet Lebeuf* (b. 1921), Dr. es L., Sorbonne. Senior Research Fellow of the National Centre for Scientific Research (CNRS); Head of the Protohistory department at the Chadian Institute for Social Sciences, and Lecturer at the René Descartes University (Paris V). Field research since 1947 in Chad, Northern Cameroun, Katanga and Congo (Bra.). The original French text of this paper was published as 'Monuments symboliques du palais royal de Logone-Birni (Nord Cameroun)', *J. Soc. Africanistes*, xxv (1955), 25–34.

[1a] cf. Masson Detourbet, 'Croyances relatives à l'organisation politique du royaume lagouané (Nord-Cameroun)', *J. Soc. Africanistes*, xxiii (1953), 7–34.

[2] Name which the Kotoko living in the Logone Kingdom give themselves.

[3] This orientation has no relationship with our own cardinal points: in Lagouané thinking, East, *rsevəni*, and West, *maze*, are associated with Halaka and Alagué respectively. At Logone Birni the Halaka zone of the town corresponds to the lower waters of the river and Alagué to the upper waters.

[4] In Lagouané literally: *ra*, dwelling, palace, *me*, an abbreviation of *miarre*, sovereign, *l* being a liaison consonant. Barth, who writes *hálaka* and *álage*, links these terms with *kalogo* and *aroga*, from the Nubian and Berber (H. Barth, *Central-afrikanische Vokabularien*, Gotha, 1863, 2 vols.); J. Lukas, following Nachtigal, gives *álage* and *hálaka* as Lagouané words, i.e. of a language belonging to the Chad–Hamitic group (J. Lukas, *Die Logone-Sprache in Zentralen Süden* (Leipzig, 1936)).

[5] The dimensions of this palace having been reduced, the *guti* ruins, still clearly visible, now lie outside the palace walls.

considerations of a practical nature played no part in their construction. Each illustrates a myth, associating them thus with the origin of the world and establishing them as guarantors of universal order.

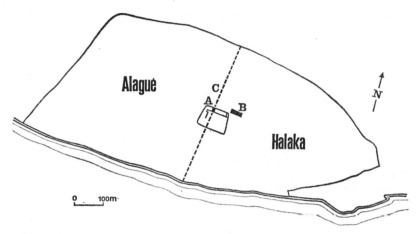

1 The palace and monuments in the town. A, *tukuri*; B, *guti*; C, boundary (*mzəgə*).

THE TUKURI

The *tukuri* (literally 'full' or 'homogeneous')[6] is found inside the dwelling area of Marouf III Adouma[7] opposite the entrance, *ngul vəni* (literally 'womb of the house) which opens towards the East;[8] it divides into two parts the vast courtyard lying along the entire length of the northern front of the surrounding wall.

It is made up of two symmetrical parallelepipedical earthen blocks (height: 5·5 metres; width: 4 metres; total length: 6·5 metres), the *gwamahə tukuri* (literally 'full rooms'), separated by a narrow passage,

[6] The word *tukuri* also implies a notion of hereditary strength; in the minds of the Lagouané, certain family groups, such as those ruling the Mandara, as well as animals such as the lion, the horse, some fish including the *tum*, a fish resembling a roach (according to Sultan Marouf), have *tukuri* bones, that is to say that they are different from normal bones and are likened to cast metal which gives them a supernatural strength. The word should be compared with the Hausa *tukuri* which, according to Abraham, means both a 'large mound' and a 'forced labourer' (R. C. Abraham, *Dictionary of the Hausa Language* (Hertford, 1949)).

[7] He has ruled in Logone Birni since 1939.

[8] This was the only door to be found in these walls until the reign of Marouf II who had a second one made (*turli*: literally 'breach') in the south wall, along the 'boundary' opposite the river.

or *darba*,[9] about a metre wide, which connects the part reserved for the Šaḥwa (*gəlrose a Šaḥwa*, literally court for [the] guardian [of the palace]) with that of the *rəli kelembia* (literally, 'child porters'[10]) (Figures 2 and 3).

A superstructure, now in ruins, is all that remains of the two living-rooms (*kal gwamahə*: literally, *kal* 'above' and *gwahamə*, room), where the rulers live after their enthroning ceremony for a variable length of time and also during Ramadan. Although the regalia, which were once kept there, disappeared during the early years of this century—during Rabeh's conquest of the country—the king still stays there for temporary periods during ritual occasions: Sultan Youssouf II lived there for six years and his son Marouf III for one year.[11] Towards the South, the *tukuri* is supported by a construction in which there is a staircase giving access to the two upper rooms, and towards the North it joins the outer palace wall.

These two rooms crown the earthen structures and the passage which together constitute the *tukuri*: one is a bedroom, *gwamahə* (2·10 m. by 4 m.) and the other a connecting vestibule, *bakəli* (3 m. by 4 m.), on to which the outer staircase opens; the first corresponds to the northern block and the *tukuri* passage, the second to the southern block. There are three windows to the bedroom, two opening on to the two parts of the Šaḥwa courtyard and the third on to the outer view from the palace, while the vestibule has four windows, in pairs, which overlook the courtyard. The staircase (five steps), enclosed in a special structure, is made entirely of earth, like the walls (Figure 4). As in all Kotoko dwellings, the openings, inner doorways and windows were kept closed with straw mats, and the inner walls were covered with fine ochre-coloured cement, without any 'ornamentation' or symbolic patterning. The superstructure of this edifice, in good condition but already inaccessible in 1952, lay in ruins under a collapsed roof in 1955; although Marouf III has never lived in these rooms after the year following his accession (1939), he is intending to restore them shortly.

[9] Literally, passage. In classical Arabic *darb*, road, way, route, street (*dérib* means road: Derendinger, *Vocabulaire pratique du dialecte centre-africain* (Paris, 1923), p. 45; *darb*, roadway, G. J. Lethem, *Colloquial Arabic, Shuwa dialect of Bornu, Nigeria and of the region of Lake Chad* (London, 1920), pp. 416, 477), according to M. Rodinson, whom we wish to take the opportunity to thank for checking the various, locally employed Arabic terms used in this article.

[10] The *rəli kelembia* form a section of the young royal bodyguard; cf. A. Masson Detourbet, '*Croyances relatives . . .*' op. cit.

[11] cf. J.-P. Lebeuf, *Les Souverains de Logone Birni* (Nord-Cameroun). Et. Camerounaises, nos. 47–48 (mars-juin, 1955), pp. 3–8.

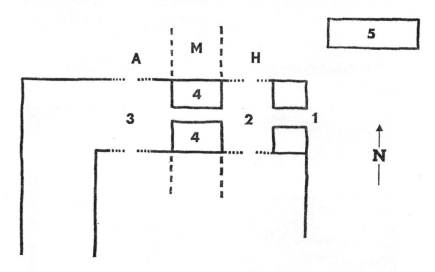

2 The *tukuri* in the palace (plan): A, Alagué; H, Halaka; M, *mzəgə* (boundary); 1, the palace vestibule (*ngulveni*); 2, palace guardian's court-yard (*golrose a Šahwa*); 3, child porters' courtyard (*rəli kelembia*); 4, *gwamahə tukuri*; 5, *guti*.

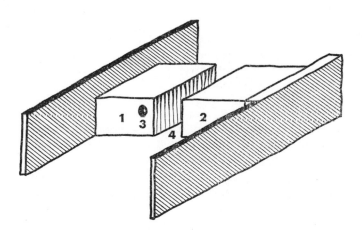

3 The *tukuri* in the palace (view); 1, northern section of the *tukuri* repre-senting the primordial male twin; 2, southern section of the *tukuri* repre-senting the primordial female twin; 3, calabashes embedded in the masonry and representing the male twin's genitalia; 4, passage (*darba*).

The building of this edifice is attributed to the first inhabitants of the region, the Sao, who are supposed to have erected it after they built the town walls. Like the *guti*, which we shall discuss below, and all

GROUND FLOOR · · · 1st STOREY

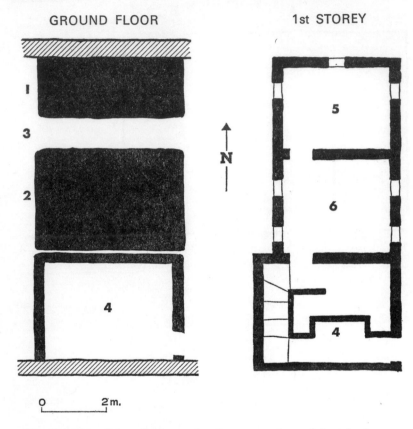

4 Detailed plan of the *tukuri*: 1 and 2, the two sections of the *tukuri* proper; 3, passageway; 4, room giving access to the upstairs part of the monument; 5, the king's room; 6, the vestibule.

Kotoko buildings, the *tukuri* is made of earth, mixed with small pebbles, chopped straw, fish bones, and all kinds of rubble without any large-stone support. Unlike the town walls, the foundations of which reveal the remains of human beings who were buried alive there,[12] the

[12] cf. in particular, M. Griaule and J.-P. Lebeuf, 'Fouilles dans la région du Tchad', *J. Soc. Africanistes*, xxi, (1951), 6; J.-P. Lebeuf and A. Masson Detourbet, *La Civilisation du Tchad*, 1 vol. (Paris, 1950), pp. 44–56.

tukuri contains no skeletal remains. Talismans in pots—perhaps royal treasure—have been found buried in it, perhaps following the Kotoko custom whereby wealth was buried in places known only to the owners (the men entrusted with this task were subsequently decapitated). Anybody entering or leaving the building must cross the *tukuri* passageway, and nobody except the sovereign may stay in the upstairs rooms.

The orientation of the building is strictly fixed and determines the setting up of the *mzɔgɔ* boundary in the town, between the two spatial regions. This bipartition is emphasized by the fact that there are only two visible sides, one facing the Halaka and the other the Alagué; of the other two, as we mentioned above, one is attached to the wall surrounding the palace and the other to that which divides off the different dwelling-rooms in the royal residence.

The manner of building the *tukuri*, along with its quadrilateral form, likens it to the earth which, according to Sao notions [13] was a solid mass without any cracks before the creation of the human race; it was *tukuri*. Its division into two elements reveals the world's duality. In fact, the two *gwamahɔ tukuri* are the supports of the two primordial twins, ancestors of the human race: the northern block represents man, and the other represents woman. At the southwestern angle of the male *gwamahɔ* two calabashes, set into the masonry flush with the walls, symbolize the male genitalia. The passage way is compared to the woman's womb, source of life for the human race; it is also an essential link between the two fundamental principles, the male and the female, the North and the South, the right and the left, permitting constant exchange between these principles to be established and thus ensuring an equilibrium in the palace, the town, and the world. Lastly, this edifice is the sovereign's *gamu* (family founder, origin, primordial ancestor),[14] and he lives there in order to become impregnated with the strength of his ancestors.

THE GUTI

Unlike the former construction, the *guti* is in ruins today; it is said that it collapsed several generations ago; the first European travellers to come to Logone-Birni (Denham and then Barth) do not mention

---

[13] While some Kotoko believe the world to be round and flat, it is always represented as a square, in accordance with early Sao ideas.
[14] The wall enclosing the town is also called *gamu*.

it.[15] A vast mound, 2 metres high, 45 metres long, and 15 metres wide, is to be found behind the north-eastern angle of the present palace walls and marks the position of this monument which a number of informants have described and sketched for us.

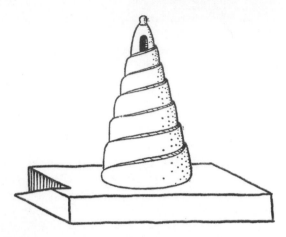

5 A reconstruction of the *guti*, showing the two access ramps rising up leftwards and the door of the room which opens to face on to the Alagué (from a sketch provided by a Kotoko informant).

Built, like the *tukuri*, of sun-baked mud, it was constructed in two sections: a large quadrilateral pedestal, similar to parts of the *tukuri* (the *guti* properly speaking) served as a base for a tower, shaped like a sugar loaf; the *sǫr* (literally tower, column)[16] (Figure 5).

Its orientation was strictly determined. The four sides of the house faced the principal spatial directions. A stairway of several steps (six or eight according to the majority of informants), built in along its west side, gave access to the top of this earth platform and to the tower which rose up in its centre. The latter, wider at its base than at

[15] cf. H. Barth, *Travels and Discoveries in North and Central Africa*, London, 1847; Denham (D.), *Narrative of Travels and Discoveries in Northern and Central Africa*, London, 1826. Nevertheless, one notices the tip of a monument, which can be none other than the *guti*, in a photograph ('Fantasia at Logone-Birni', third plate, top, between pages 126 and 127), taken by Olive MacLeod and which appeared in 1912 (*Chiefs and Cities of Central Africa*, Edinburgh and London, 1 vol.).

[16] *sǫr* recalls the Kanuri *sóro*, which according to Lukas (op. cit.) is the word for a rectangular room, and also Hausa (Kano) *sóró*, which according to Abraham (op. cit.) refers to constructions made entirely of earth (round house with a domed roof, or square house with flat terraced roof and ground floor); Rodinson points out that the Arabic for 'wall or town walls' is *súr*. The Lagouané say it is a Kanuri word.

its summit, was topped by a round room *ka na sǫr* (literally 'head of [the] tower'), built along the lines of Mousgoum[17] houses, and the domed roof was capped by a pottery *ska (l)* (Figure 6). It opened on to the Alagué by means of a small oval door and contained a throne

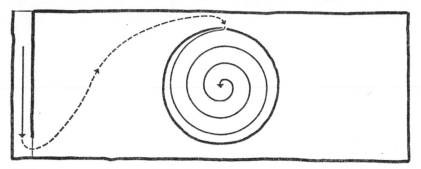

6 Reconstruction of the plan of the *guti*, showing the direction taken by the king when he climbed the monument.

zǝgakǝ which resembled a large stool; the top was made of *sakal* rope[18] and the frame of *abana* wood.[19] The sculpted feet represented the four officials: the Iba, the Mra Zina (or Zina Ma), the Šaḥwa, and one of the Ngaramané who, while the king was being presented to his subjects during one of the great public ceremonies at the door of the palace, sat at each of the four corners of another throne, the *degǝl*, made of *abana* and thongs (from the hide of a bull, which had been sacrificed after it had procreated) against which they leant, either their left shoulder (Ngaramané, Mra Zina) or their right (Šarḥwa, Iba).[20]

[17] Tradition attributes the founding of Logone-Birni to an initial group of men, the Sao, who, once they had disappeared, were replaced by the Mousgoum.

[18] Similar to the kind used for making fishing nets.

[19] Arabic *yukan* or *juhan*, *Diospyros mespiliformis* (Hochst) according to Professor Pellegrin whom we thank for this information.

[20] This ritual replaced an earlier one: in the distant past the throne, *degǝl*, made without any feet, was placed on the backs of four crouching officials. The flesh of the bull, whose hide had been used to make the *degǝl*, was shared among the same notables, the mother and the eldest of the sovereign's younger sisters, the *olendǝma*, who ruled over the daughters of former kings and whose star is referred to by the Arab term *jabah*. The word in question is doubtless *ǧabhaᵗ*, that is properly 'the brow'; this word does in fact serve to designate various stars, for example *ǧabhaᵗ al aqrab*, the 'Scorpion's brow' which is the star we know as ω of the Scorpion. However, more especially and more absolutely *al-ǧabhaᵗ*, the brow, refers to one of the lunar houses, the tenth which goes from Leo 29° to Virgo 10° (L. Massignon, *Annuaire du Monde musulman*, second edition, Paris 1925, p. 12). It includes the stars α, γ, δ, and η of Leo, the star δ of Leo being called specially *al-ǧabhaᵗ*, that is 'the

One reached the top of this tower by means of a spiral ramp *h(u)run* (literally 'snail') which began at the Halaka[21] side of the base and which wound leftwards round its axis. The edifice as a whole represented the Foukoula myth, Foukoula being the first Sao blacksmith the constructions being a representation of the primordial anvil.

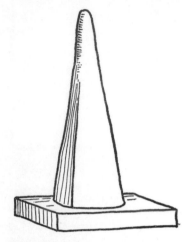

7 The anvil in its original position after falling on Foukoula's house.

Shortly after the founding of the town, a man named Foukoula (literally *fu*, 'fire' and *kula*, a vast stretch of water,[22] asked permission to settle here and did so at a spot known as *zagara*, situated at Alagué, in the foreigner's district. He was a fisherman like most of the inhabitants. One night God (*Malwa*) caused a gigantic anvil, *gamu*, to fall on the top of his house (Figure 7). It came down in a spiral

---

lion's brow' according to Rodinson. It is not possible, in the present state of our inquiries, to specify the star involved here, since the Kotoko have always been very reserved concerning relationships which link certain human beings with the stars, and this question is still under examination. Compare the position, at the foot of the throne, of the head of the Logone-Birni army (where he bears the title of Mra Zina), during the course of this ceremony and that of the same official at Goulfeil (where he is called the Mé Galgué) during the placing of the muslin on the new chief. As defenders of the Kingdom they are both to be found on the right side of their lord (cf. M. Griaule and J.-P. Lebeuf, *Fouilles* . . . op. cit., pp. 14–15, and fig. 158, p. 25).

[21] The number of times this spiral ramp encircled the construction was not specified by our informants.

[22] Lake Chad is *kula*, while the sea, now known to some Kotoko, is called *bahar* (Arabic) which is also used to designate those stretches of water known more generally by the Lagouané as *lɔrɔmi bahar* (literally: watercourse, in lagouané, then in arabic); the sea referred to in the myths is called *am itu* (literally: black water, hence the idea of the sea of obscurity, and as an extension, obscurity, according to Barth, *Vocabularien* . . . op. cit.).

movement[23] with the point turned skywards. Without waiting for any divine orders Foukoula turned the anvil around, knotted a band of cotton to it, and used it for divinatory purposes, proceeding as had been revealed to him in a dream and embedding it in the earth. His actions brought disorder to the world: men saw their stature and strength diminishing and death appeared on the earth.

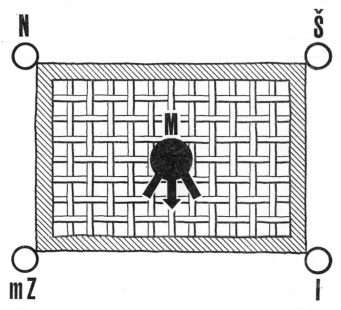

8 The Miarre on the *degəl* throne, surrounded by the four officials. N, one of the Ngaramané; Š, the Šahwa; I, the Iba; mZ, the Mra Zina.

It was in order to re-establish normal relations with the celestial powers that one of the first Logone-Birni kings built this edifice in the image of the anvil which had fallen from the sky and in its original position. He was the only one who was allowed to cross the threshold of the door into the small room which was set up at the top of the *sǫr*. He made a solemn ascent once a year, the day of the Millet Festival, in November. His successors did likewise up until the time of the country's islamization, when this ritual was placed on the day following the Feast of the Sheep (*mledə—mulud* in Arabic). He was taken there dressed in his grandest robes. After sitting on the *degəl* throne (Figure 8) in front of the *tukuri*, he was carried on the same throne to

[23] This spiral movement is called *kulkwata dətal*, the way of light: literally *kulkwata*, the path which turns (*kul*), from the verb turn, and *dətal*, light.

the foot of the *guti*. He mounted the platform accompanied by the Iba, the Mra Lagouané, and the Mraraa who remained there while he climbed to the top of the tower alone. When he reached the circular chamber he bowed towards the four major spatial directions, then meditated for a while on the throne. No one apart from the king might climb the upper ramp, except the Melima, his horn-player, who in wartime was authorized to climb there, whatever the time of year, in order to warn the people.

This solemn ascension of the Miarre to the top of the monument had the effect of re-establishing order in the universe, an order which had been upset by the mistake made by the first blacksmith; and it also ensured the regular passing of the seasons. The steps and ramp were so constructed that the ascent was made on the left-hand side and the descent consequently on the right-hand side; in the minds of the Kotoko and their ancestors, this meant that disorder was succeeded by order, thanks to the contact with the celestial powers being once more ensured by this ascent and descent and by the prayers offered up by the Miarré, i.e. by the earthly world.

The symbolism of this monument is even more complex. It had a phallic significance and symbolized the union of the earth and sky, the parallelepipedical base having the same significance as the *tukuri* which it had replaced, or duplicated, at a certain point in the past. As an image of the primordial anvil, the *guti* illustrated the myth of the origin of metallurgy, and it also marked the appearance of death on Earth, as a result of the error made by the first blacksmith; further, the annual ascent of the king up a spiral path, symbolizing the progress of light on the first day of the harvest, was associated with the agricultural cycle and fertility.

The monument has collapsed and its ruins now only serve as a stand for the people when they come to admire their Chief. There is no longer any ritual associated with it; but the Kotoko, although Moslems, none the less remain loyal to the past. Today the Miarré, surrounded by his remaining dignitaries, still solemnly retraces the way of light every Friday in a procession which passes through the town.

Blood Pacts, Age Classes and Castes

in Black Africa

DENISE PAULME[1]

Many African societies know and practise blood-brotherhood of the kind mentioned by Herodotus with reference to the Scythians.[1a] The authors who describe the concluding of these pacts are often recording their own personal experiences. Having mixed his blood with that of a native chief and pronounced the imprecatory formulae, sometimes licking his partner's incision or sharing a dish of food mixed with their respective blood, the narrator was then assured of complete protection throughout the territory under the control of his blood brother. The ease with which a total stranger found himself benefiting from such an apparently close tie surprised more than a few. Against his will, and despite his repugnance towards the ceremony, Stanley was obliged to undergo it several times in order to be allowed to continue his journey.

The initial aim of the pact was to procure mutual assistance. Apart from the usual obligations of hospitality, this included unconditional help in times of need, in legal disputes or difficulties with hierarchical superiors, attendance at funerals, vengeance in case of murder, plus multiple obligations which varied according to particular instances. To what extent are blood brothers assimilated as real brothers? This is the usual connection which is often suggested by the actors themselves; nevertheless the local languages normally have a special term for this pact and for the persons bound by it. The use of the word 'brother' in the expression 'blood brother' has resulted in some

[1] *Denise Paulme* (b. 1909), Dr. en Droit, Paris. Director of Studies at the Ecole Pratique des Hautes Etudes, Section VI, Social Sciences. Began field research among the Dogon under the direction of Marcel Griaule in 1935; later turned her attention to Guinea (Kissi 1945–9, Baga 1954) and from 1958 to the Ivory Coast (Bete, Atié, Nzema). A general anthropologist, her more recent interests have been in oral literature and its social context. The original French text of this paper was published as 'Pactes de sang, classes d'âge et castes en Afrique noire', *Archives Européennes de Sociologie*, ix (1968), 12–33.
[1a] An entire work has been devoted to blood-brotherhood: Tegnaeus (H.) *Blood Brothers* (New York, 1952).

misunderstanding. As recently as 1920 Lindblom, speaking of the Akamba, writes that 'this tie seems to be as binding and to have the same consequences as the natural tie, which it probably imitates. The children of the two contracting parties consider themselves, and are considered by others, to be brothers and sisters and may not marry. Two men, who are bound by such a tie, are under the obligation to help one another. If one of the blood brothers is implicated in a legal dispute or if he is accused of some crime or other, the other will give evidence on his behalf, even if he has important private business he should be dealing with.' [2]

The fact that obligations engendered by these pacts are coloured by those of kinship, and that the partner is treated like a 'brother', in no way implies that he undergoes a change of status or is merged with the other's clan or lineage. Following after Frazer and Westermarck, Professor Evans-Pritchard takes up the problem of the exact nature of the engagement; he stresses the magical aspect of the ritual and the importance of the curse which is brought down on the person who breaks his word: 'It is a typical magical mechanism . . . The blood is not simply a vehicle for the spell or conditional curse. The blood itself is the "medicine", the material element in the magical complex, and it becomes such through association with spell and rite.' [3] The Azande *bakure* is not a brother substitute; while he may be required to look after his partner's widow and children, he has no right to inherit from the dead man.

The myth of origin of the blood pact often alludes to a situation of mortal peril from which one of the partners saves the other: one day Diallo and Diakute of Mali were fleeing from the enemy: Diallo revived the flagging strength of his companion by giving him a piece of his own flesh to eat.[4] I myself have referred to this kind of 'services rendered' in an earlier work and sought to compare blood pacts with alliances engendered by the exchange of women: the giving of a sister or daughter in marriage—along with those children who will be born to her—is a means of assuring the survival of your ally's lineage; in the same way the blood pact enables you to save the life of another by giving him a part of yourself.[5] Both these arrangements

[2] Lindblom (G.), *The Akamba* (Upsala, 1920).
[3] Evans-Pritchard (E. E.), 'Zande blood brotherhood', *Africa*, vi (1933), 369–401. We have quoted from his *Essays in Social Anthropology* (London, 1962), pp. 131–61.
[4] Labouret (H.), 'La parenté à plaisanterie en Afrique occidentale', *Africa*, ii (1929), 252.
[5] Paulme (D.), 'Parenté à plaisanterie et alliance par le sang', *Africa*, xii (1939), 433–44.

put an end to hostilities between groups and provide an opportunity for concluding an honourable peace. Professor Fortes also mentions a blood pact in the myth of origin of Tallensi society: the ancestor of a group of immigrants and the ancestor of the first occupants of the land mixed their blood and bound themselves, along with their descendants, to a permanent peace—'a unique instance of blood brotherhood which is not practised in Taleland today'.[6] Among the Bete of south-western Ivory Coast villages were once upon a time in a state of constant hostility with their neighbours: when the fighting was over a girl was handed over in marriage to replace every person killed on either side. At least this is what I was told in 1958 by my informants. Referring to the same region, Thomann, who first visited there sixty years earlier, mentions a ceremony of blood exchange during peace talks, where each man makes an incision with his knife and licks his partner's wound.[7]

Behaviour towards the wives of one's new associate varies according to the degree by which the blood pact links the contracting partners as if they were real brothers or as affines related through women. In Dahomey blood brothers must respect the wives of their partners 'as their own mother'. Among the Zande a man refrains from making sexual advances to the wives of his *bakure*: he could ask for a daughter's hand in marriage if she were not already married, and his partner might not refuse him any more than he might refuse the gift of a spear or any other object he owned, if he were asked for it; blood brothers were obliged to dig their partners' graves, although this task was primarily the responsibility of affines: 'What is an essential duty for relatives-in-law is more in the nature of an act of courtesy and good faith for blood brothers.'[8] Among the Wagogo and also the Banyamwezi, blood brothers may not approach their partners' wives. On the other hand, among the Banyankole, the Haya, and the Lunda, a man places his wife at his 'brother's disposal when the latter comes to spend the night with him'.[9]

We find the same kind of divergences in attitudes towards a partner's sisters; marriage is sometimes prohibited, sometimes preferred. And in relations between the children of the two parties, in places they may be treated as brothers and sisters or parallel cousins, while in others they are preferential spouses.

[6] Fortes (M.), *The Dynamics of Clanship among the Tallensi* (London, 1940), p. 22.

[7] Paulme (D.), *Une société de Côte d'Ivoire, hier et aujourdhui: Les Bété* (Paris/ The Hague, 1962), p. 132.

[8] Evans-Pritchard (E. E.), op. cit., p. 150.   [9] Tegnaeus (H.), op. cit., *passim*.

In fact partners in a blood pact fulfil obligations similar to those due to brothers or brothers-in-law, but they should not be confused with either. A blood brother was a 'supplementary ally who could be relied upon to assist a man in conjunction with his kin and relatives-in-law on those occasions when the solidarity and relationship by blood (as we would say) and by marriage were most in evidence'.[10]

They are neither brothers-in-law, nor are they brothers: the insults exchanged between partners in these pacts show this sufficiently: 'The pattern of behaviour between blood brothers is one of intimacy and equality.'[11]

'Equality' is the keyword here: within the family there is no equality; instead relations between real brothers are always in terms of an elder—that is superior—and a younger brother. In external relations lineages present a united front, a block; within the lineage the elder brother claims his rights and expects mute obedience from his juniors. During meals the youngest never helps himself first; and it is up to him to take the empty plates back to the kitchen and bring back a basin of clean water which he offers to his brother in order that he may wash his hands. Elder sisters look after their younger brothers and sisters, washing them, dressing them, and keeping an eye on them while their mother is busy with her household chores. Kinship terminology may ignore the division of the sexes, merging brothers and sisters under the same term, but it always distinguishes elder and younger siblings by the use of different terms of address. A younger brother takes care not to surpass his brother in anything, since this would be showing disrespect; these obligations are taken to such lengths that it sometimes happens that a youth will fail his examinations, of his own free will more or less, so as not to give umbrage to an elder brother who is not too bright. Nor is equality more in evidence in relations between affines, where wife-givers, in a tribal milieu, usually take precedence over wife-takers; a wife's lineage may make all kinds of demands on the husband. Even the death of his parents-in-law does not free the African son-in-law from his obligations and he must show the same respect and make the same contributions— particularly during the mourning period—to the new family head and all of his wife's elder brothers.

Unlike these hierarchical relations, blood pacts engender relations in which obligations are mutual: I expect the same services from my

[10] Op. cit., p. 149.
[11] Evans-Pritchard (E. E.), op. cit., p. 151. See also Beidelman (T. O.), 'The blood-covenant and the concept of blood in Ukaguru', *Africa*, xxxiii (1963), 321–42.

partner as those I am prepared to render to him. If he borrows a gun or a piece of cloth from me today, I can behave in exactly the same way to him tomorrow. Each keeps count of the number of times he has helped his blood brother and the settling of accounts must be more or less equally balanced; if one is generous, the other must also be generous; if he is mean, the other will be mean. The bond's reciprocity engenders its own sanctions: if I am deaf to my partner's call for help, the few drops of his blood which I have consumed will cause my death, because it is charged by a curse which will act if one of the partners breaks his word.

Kinship, affinity, blood pacts—in each case solidarity is the rule. A blood brother, however, is often held to be a closer relation than a real brother; he is the only person to whom you may confide a secret without any fear that he will divulge it.

In the overwhelming majority of cases the new engagement is contracted outside the family and it is this which allows a person to escape, to some extent, from the sometimes stifling hold of kinship ties. A new line of action is open to him. For this reason the institution may not be looked very kindly upon by the established authorities. Among the Chagga, only group pacts were allowed, any bonds between individuals being considered contrary to the interests of the respective families, since the parties to such pacts freed themselves to some degree from their group solidarity. Here pacts were made in secret, in an atmosphere of guilt; the most common motive among these pastoralists was keeping secret a herd of cattle and its natural increase; if the guilty persons were discovered the chief confiscated the beasts, appropriating them to his own use.[12] Among the Lango if the clans of two partners came to hear of the existence of such a pact they would order it to be dissolved; a small grass hut was erected and the two men were pushed inside and the opening closed behind them; each man then made a hole in the wall, climbing out on opposite sides.[13] In Dahomey these pacts often sealed a conspiracy or an association of criminals who stressed the magical aspects of the rites and called down the most terrible punishments on any of their number who betrayed their cause.[14] By leaguing itself with the power of black magic, the pact becomes a threat to society.

[12] Gutmann (B.), *Das Recht der Dschagga* (Leipzig, 1926), pp. 254 seq. Raum (J.), 'Blut und Speichelbunde bei den Wadschaga', *Archiv fur Religionwissenschaft*, x (1907), pp. 292 sqq.
[13] Hayley (T. T. S.), *The Anatomy of Lango Religion and Groups* (Cambridge, 1947), pp. 105 seq.
[14] Hazoumé (P.), *Le pacte de sang au Dahomey* (Paris, 1937), pp. 40 seq.

Blood pacts are originally the work of two individuals who commit themselves, sometimes extending it to include their descendants. In Africa there is another institution which involves similar obligations of mutual assistance and solidarity: relations engendered within an age set are also established on a footing of complete equality; the whole group of initiates are united by close bonds, based on a model other than that of the family: 'It is only this period of circumcision which can turn a disparate group into a coherent whole, a class of persons within which it is incumbent on everyone to show friendship, confidence and assistance in all spheres of social and private life.'[15]

The crystallization of these groups of children, symbolized by a tribal initiation ceremony, brings about a less rigid adherence to family ties as well as a broadening of the sphere of social relations which till then had been expressed solely in terms of kinship.[16] Activities within the family stress age differences; age sets, on the contrary, insist on parity between members: when they are directed to perform a task in the interest of the community all take part and share the same efforts; if a collection is made for a celebration, for example, everyone must contribute; if there is a fight between equivalent age sets in neighbouring villages, each must receive his share of the blows dealt out and endured. A Fulani of Fouta-Djalon considers his *yirde* friend as his closest adviser, his most discreet confidant: 'Whatever your status in the village or canton, your age-mate in the *yirde* always speaks to you in the same friendly way they have been used to since childhood.'[17]

Among the Malinke, 'boys who have undergone circumcision and girls who have been excised during the same year belong to two parallel groups bearing the same name, *fla-nse*, which are clubs whose members have a similar relationship as twins, *fula-ni* or *fla-ni*. They are called either by this term or by the phrase *de-nn'ŏřŏ*: "children-same": as proof of their unity and solidarity.'[18] The idea of two being present in one individual, the notion of twinness, is one of the major pivots of African thinking. The Dogon use this idea to express relations which, in fact, are very different: husbands and wives are twins, a man's shadow is his twin; so is his placenta; even in commercial exchanges the partners as well as the goods exchanged are

---

[15] Dieterlen (G.), *Essai sur la religion bambara* (Paris, 1951), p. 179.
[16] Eisenstadt (S. N.), *From Generation to Generation* (London, 1956).
[17] Balde (S.), 'Les associations d'âge chez les Foulbé du Fouta Djallon', *Bull. IFAN*, i (1939), 105–6.
[18] Labouret (H.), *Les Manding et leur langue* (Paris, 1934), p. 96.

called 'twins'.[19] Rich and poor, children of aristocrats and descendants of slaves—all circumcised males who have gone through initiation ordeals together, an experience everywhere likened to a social birth, are also, in a way, twins. Two family heads who belong to the same age set will always come to each other's support: if they are members of the village council they back up each other in debates and defend the same point of view.

The role assigned to age sets varies from society to society. In a general way, in the absence of centralized power, their importance seems to be in inverse proportion to that of lineages, and is all the greater when the corporate solidarity of lineages is weaker and their range, both spatially and temporally, restricted.

Among the lagoon-dwellers of the Ivory Coast where age classes are highly developed, the grouping of dwellings formerly expressed the existence of age sets, not clans and lineages, which in this case are matrilineal; the three wards of an Atié village correspond to the three recognized grades: young men, warriors, and 'mature men'. As soon as a set was formed it took over the lower section of the village, which was reserved for the 'children', building their houses on plots left by their elders. The upper sections belonged to the 'warriors' and the central one to the 'mature men' who exercised political power and acted as guardians of the village. Within each grade there were different subsidiary grades to which brothers belonged, according to their age ranking.[20] The mutual confidence which exists between members of a single sub-set is very strong indeed, any temptation to commit adultery with the wife of a co-member being wisely thwarted by the threat of a very high fine. (In the same way partners to a blood pact must respect each other's wives unless access is authorized as a matter of course; this is according to a different kind of reasoning, although the premises are basically similar.) This solidarity has survived the shift to an urban milieu and when a man in Abidjan goes on a journey he asks his age-mates who are settled in the town to look after his household, and spy on his wife if he suspects her of infidelity. The mutual aid due to members of the same set works against the interests of proximate sets, with whom relations are constantly hostile, the younger ones trying to compete with their elders, and the latter attempting to delay the hour of their political effacement. The same thing is also reflected in the lineage: a youth

[19] Griaule (M.), *Dieu d'eau* (Paris, 1948).
[20] Paulme (D.), 'Première approche des Atié', *Cahiers d'études africaines*, vi, 21 (1966), 86–120.

will counteract tyrannical whims of his lineage head by using the support of public opinion as represented by his age-mates, sometimes even calling for the leader of the age set to remonstrate with the lineage head. If an elder feels he has been offended by a lack of respect shown to him by a nephew or a great nephew, the head of the latter's age set acts as a go-between, presenting the young man's excuses and the inevitable 'gift'. Impatient of any authority which they consider tyrannical, young men frequently accuse an old man of causing an accident or an illness which has afflicted them; his malefi-cence is seen as a sign of his resentment. The misfortune of one is a misfortune for the whole age set and all become involved. If one of them falls ill the leader of his set must be immediately informed; he assigns two members the task of taking turns to stay with the patient; they never leave his bedside, call in a doctor at the lineage's expense, and carry out his instructions; they may even forbid members of his family to come near the sick man if poisoning or witchcraft is sus-pected.

Among the same riverain peoples living along the Ivory Coast lagoons, age sets formerly had an important political role—the affairs of the villages, particularly external relations, were not left to village councils of elders, but to officials of the third grade in the age hierarchy: that of the 'mature men'; the immediately lower grade was that of the 'warriors' whose main role is self-explanatory.[21]

The role of the institution becomes less clear-cut where the same patrilineal clans are found throughout the territory, forming an overall structure which embraces the whole society and provides people with the assurance of finding, in every town and village, kinsmen who will receive you as a son or a brother; in this case age sets played a role which was confined to the villages and mainly concerned adolescents: the last set to be formed constituted a reservoir of labour force for work of collective interest, such as road repairs or clearing the village head's fields; the leader of the age set represented it in councils of elders, and the opinions and wishes of the younger men were never ignored. Mutual aid and solidarity were the rule between members of an age set, the former, in particular, working to the disadvantage of family groups: both the family and a person's age set contributed, in different ways, to his marriage

---

[21] We are only able to present an outline of this organization here; it was an organization which varied from society to society, often from village to village and each had its own method of regulating the division of labour between village heads, lineage heads, and officials of the age grades. Cf. Paulme (D.), ed. *Classes et associations d'âge en Afrique de l'Ouest* (Paris: Plon, 1971).

expenses. A young man, who had previously been under the control of his father and the family patriarch, was given land by his lineage head for his exclusive use and he farmed it as he wished in order to meet the requirements of his personal household. In return he assumed new responsibilities with regard to his lineage and his chief. In earlier times his age-mates would have accompanied him to his future father-in-law's farms in order to clear them or harvest them; they would help to repair or build the young couple's dwelling, hastening in this way the setting up of the new household. It is often the same age-mates who come to collect the young bride and provide her with a merry cortège as she makes her way to her new home. If need be—when a girl's parents keep turning a deaf ear and refuse to let their daughter move away from home, even though the greater part of the marriage payments have been handed over—they will pretend to elope with her. The young men hide near the pool or well, where the women come to get water, capture the betrothed girl and carry her off to her husband's village; her companions protest, pretending to pursue them amidst shouting and laughter. The parents-in-law, faced with this *fait accompli*, soon give in.

Everywhere a man will suggest a collective enterprise to his age-mates. In former times young Wolof men would 'steal' a field from its owner by going out, unbeknown to him, and clearing or harvesting his farms; when the man was confronted with this he had to provide them with a feast and presents if he did not wish to lose face in the eyes of the whole village.[22] The same kind of thing still goes on except that now it is only after discussing the nature of the work required, and the reward expected, that the age group goes ahead with the business. Nowadays, due to economic changes, the nature of enterprises has changed: today a young man may suggest to the others that they all buy a 'bush taxi' in order to provide transport for travellers, or a lorry, the driver going into town to buy goods, which the wives sell retail in markets around the village. Sometimes an individual simply asks his age-mates for financial help; his project is looked into carefully and if the consensus of feeling is favourable he will be advanced the necessary capital from a common fund.

Age sets thus appear to complement the functions of kinship and affinity; the relationships between these three institutions bring out those elements of opposition which, through confrontation, contribute to the solidarity of the overall structure. In-laws may impoverish the

---

[22] Ames (D.), 'Wolof cooperative work groups', in Bascom (W. A.) and Herskovits (M. J.), *Continuity and Change in African Cultures* (Chicago, 1959), p. 229.

lineage through their excessive demands: but since they are providing
children they are also contributing to the well-being of the whole; age
sets may weaken lineage cohesion, by encouraging young men to
throw off ties which bind them to their kinsfolk and also their in-laws
and kinsfolk; but by grouping together adolescents they provide a
strong element of unity at village level and even at a higher political
level.[23]

Where there is some degree of centralized power, the integration
brought about by age organization has sometimes provided a means of
recruiting for the army: in Bambara military organization units were
formed on the basis of the *fla-to*. Monteil mentions that the king of
Segou used to preside over the circumcision of his slaves who were
operated on at the same time as his own children: 'When the *fama*
took part in an important affair, he liked to arrange and preside over
the circumcision of the young captives and also had several of his
numerous progeny take part.'[24] This was a means of securing the
devotion of his subjects by honouring them with his presence when
they were initiated into the adult world and also by associating them,
through the ceremony itself, with some of his own children. Age sets
functioned as military units and provided a means of assimilating the
conquered into the society of their conquerors.

Blood pacts and age sets entail comparable obligations; in both
cases the individuals involved are placed on a footing of equality,
which is not found in family relationships. From my blood brother I
expect the same kind of services I can demand from my age-mate. In
both cases, equally, reciprocity is direct; in kinship relations it is
always indirect (although 'total' in the sense that it involves the whole
society) since a man's younger brother owes him the same respect
that he owes to his own elder brother and since a man's son-in-law will
one day provide him with the same services which he is giving his
father-in-law today.

The fact remains, however, that a pact is a voluntary contract,
while an age set is an institution: an initiated youth changes status
and his relations with his age-mates are imposed on him. Nevertheless he will probably choose, from among the group, one or two
intimate friends with whom he will set up relations which will be

---

[23] In some cases clan solidarity takes precedence over age sets; in some Malinke
villages there are distinct series of age sets each grouping only the men of a single
clan or ward. Lineage rivalry here prevents any possibility of a wider grouping.
Leynaud (E.), *Contribution à l'étude des structures sociales et de la modernisation
rurale dans la haute vallée du Niger* (Paris, 1967) (Ph.D. thesis, roneoed).

[4] Monteil (Ch.), *Les Bambara de Segou et du Kaarta* (Paris, 1924), p. 311.

equally close as those existing between blood brothers. Here there is no need to seal a new contract, by mingling their blood, since the initiation has already made them 'twins'.

Society cannot flourish without these kinds of relationships; this is the moral behind a Dahomean myth which attributes the revelation of the blood pact to the genie, Aziza, king of the forest.[25] A hunter, who came across a doe in the act of giving birth, refrained from killing the mother and the young animal; Aziza, who was secretly observing the scene, imbued the hunter with a feeling of pity for all animals in similar circumstances. (In another version it was Aziza himself, at the point of death from ant bites, who was saved by the hunter.) The genie compensated the man by showing him the secret of farming techniques. On another occasion Aziza allowed the same man to watch people dancing in a clearing to the accompaniment of drums; when he returned home the hunter taught his people dancing and drumming; and it was through these activities, performed on a village green which was extended to represent the whole universe, that they were able to forget for a moment or two their daily cares and woes and perform the 'Game of the World'. By means of a pact mankind was able to learn techniques which enabled them to escape from a hazardous dependence on animals, at the same time discovering life in society.

Is it possible to imagine a former state of society when pacts and age sets were mutually exclusive? In Africa it is very rare to find a society where adolescence is not marked by some kind of ceremony such as a tribal initiation into the first age grade. Nevertheless it is absent both among the Tallensi and the Bete. Equally rare are societies which lack any recollection of blood pacts between individuals, clans, or castes.[26] Having no systematic research to rely on, we shall simply suggest that as a result of equality and a reciprocity of services which both institutions generate among their members, blood pacts and age sets can serve similar ends. In cases where pacts have been contracted between members of a single age set we may suppose that the tie, which had initially bound them, had become lax to such an extent that the persons concerned had forgotten its prime meaning: making them 'twins'.

[25] Hazoumé (P.), op. cit., pp. 11 seq.

[26] Blood pacts appear to have been developed in recent times in some East African societies where the institution of age sets is more highly developed; it was a contract made with strangers and its introduction is explained through economic interest and the need to facilitate journeys and exchanges. Examples in Tegnaeus, op. cit.

We have already said that blood pacts set up relations of equality between partners. Africans have recourse to a locution which is far more emphatic: 'You were two. Henceforth you shall be one.'[27] The same blood now runs in their two bodies. If this is the case how can we explain the presence of pacts in hierarchical societies, pacts between individuals and sometimes groups who belong to very different social strata?

Dahomey provides an extreme example: its kings, in preparing for an invasion, did not disdain from entering into a blood pact with a spy who belonged to an enemy country. He was then sent back to the place of his birth where he at once sought assistance from the local spirits, offering gin and palm oil to the local priest who poured it on the shrine without a hint of suspicion. Victory then depended solely on the bravery of the invaders, since the spirits, having been given offerings which contained ingredients which were abhorrent to them, had already deserted the town.[28]

More enlightening material on this subject concerns the Swazi: there the aim of a pact was not to bring about mutual assistance but involved a rite performed to protect the royal person. When the king was approaching puberty, two young boys were sought out, boys of the same age who were members of two important lineages—Mdluli and Motsa. The parents were not able to refuse the honour and were forced to show as much pleasure as possible in demonstrating their approval of the royal choice. The ceremony took place in private: incisions were made in the right flank of the young Mdluli and the king, their blood was mixed and a 'medicine', made of ground charcoal and herbs, whose names signified 'power' and 'force' and 'loyalty', was rubbed into their wounds. The same performance was then carried out between the young Motsa and the king, this time on their left side. The Mdluli was thenceforth known as the '*insila* of the right' and the Motsa 'the *insila* of the left'. After this the king and his two *tinsila* became mutually identified and everything which happened to one was felt by the other two. The word *insila*, in its primary sense, means bodily secretion: the essential part of any individual. Even if it is washed and scraped off the body it remains intimately associated with the person, to such an extent that anybody who acquires possession of it can harm the person whom it came from. The possession of the king's blood raised the *tinsila* high above all other subjects; they were always in attendance when the king conducted

[27] Westermann (D.), *Die Glidyi-Ewe in Togo* (Berlin, 1935), p. 50.
[28] Hazoumé (P.), op cit., pp. 21–2.

public business. The '*insila* of the right' played an important role in times of war; and the '*insila* of the left' took part in an annual ceremony which renewed the kingship and he also looked after the royal mortuary rites. One of the *tinsila*'s duties was to anoint the king's body with medicines; they also accompanied him to the sacred royal enclosure in his cattle reserve and helped prepare his food. If one of them died before the king his death would not be announced, and his widows were forbidden to bewail his death or go into mourning. It was a tie which was closer and different from any bond the king had with his brothers; his connection with the *tinsila* (sometimes called his twins) protected the sovereign from any evil which might come his way. By keeping in contact with the sovereign the royal blood gives the *tinsila* power to 'sniff out' any danger which may threaten the king's person; without any conscious effort, but at the risk of their lives, they intercept all evil powers directed against him. A similar ceremony is performed when the king marries his Great Wife the 'queen of the right': in this case the mixing of blood protects the king from dangers emanating from the sexual act.[29]

Intimacy and equality are also expressed between Zande partners to a blood covenant through the freedom of their conversational exchanges: they may insult each other publicly without any of the affronts causing umbrage. One of the favourite practical jokes consists of announcing, in a gratuitous fashion, the death of one's partner's kinsman, the father's elder brother for example; this piece of information, if it were true, would mean a serious blow to the strength of the lineage. However, the victim is not allowed to take offence at what would amount to an insult if it had come from anyone else apart from his *bakure*: he must remain unaffected by anything his partner does.

The same exchange of insults characterizes the Malinke *sanàku ya*, 'a kind of alliance uniting and at the same time opposing representatives of certain groups who have different names'.[30] The origins of these alliances are explained either through a blood pact or through a marriage—but a unique instance of marriage only since exogamy is the rule between *sanàku*.

Joking . . . is . . . characterized by a preference for subjects which are normally forbidden (sexuality for example) and it attempts to perpetuate an outrage against the person concerned (by personal insults), his family, his property. Nonetheless it is formally prohibited to hurt each other physically or to have sexual relations with persons even if they would

[29] Kuper (H.), *An African Aristocracy* (London, 1947), pp. 78 seq.
[30] Labouret (H.), *Les Manding et leur langue*, p. 100.

otherwise be licit. In other words joking relationships aim at replacing offences with words which are only seemingly insulting (since they are exchanged 'in the air' so to speak and without having been provoked through any quarrelling).[31]

Joking relationships have an element of ambivalence: prescriptions against being offended by the coarsest of insults make it manifestly impossible for any conflict to arise. Joking is but one aspect of a whole complex of relations which exist between *sanãku*; nevertheless it is basic since it stresses the intimacy existing between the partners; *sanãku* could be translated as a 'duplicate' a 'double' ('You were two, henceforth you act as one'). *Sanãku* share obligations of reciprocal assistance; formerly if one of them discovered that his partner had been condemned to slavery he had to attempt to buy back his freedom; if he were unable to do so he would intercede with his owner in order to secure an amelioration of his conditions. When an old man dies it is his *sanãku* who washes the corpse, dresses it, and prepares it for the tomb; sometimes a *sanãku* even bars the road along which the funeral procession is passing, refusing to let it move on until he has received a small gift from the dead man's kinsfolk: this behaviour recalls that of uterine kin who invade the house of a dead man and create turmoil during the funeral. Not long ago when the 'master of the earth' died in a village in the upper Niger valley his *sanãku* attended the funeral and prepared a 'mock repast', using ashes for flour, water for milk, and stones instead of kola nuts, and the dances performed were of the kind normally performed at a wedding.[32]

Foremost among the *sanãku* are cross-cousins of both sexes. Parallel cousins are called by the same terms as brothers and sisters and elders and younger siblings are distinguished; cross-cousins on the other hand are called *kalame* and they play practical jokes and hurl insults at one another whenever they meet. But the relationship is not always a symmetrical one: a man is the 'slave' of his mother's brother's children, and 'owns' his father's sister's children. Labouret makes the situation clear: 'Originally the term (*kalame*, which has implications of insults and joking) was only used in the paternal line, that is by the "owners"; now it is also used for the maternal line, but in this case it is only done so out of politeness.'[33] The hierarchy which is revealed here is explained by the system of generalized exchange which plays such an important role in so many African

[31] Calame-Griaule (G.), *Ethnologie et langage* (Paris, 1966), p. 381.
[32] Leynaud (E.), *Contribution* . . . vol. ii, p. 73, n. 1.
[33] Labouret, (H.), *Les Manding et leur langue*, pp. 67, 68.

societies and implies a constant superiority of wife-givers (kin through females) over wife-takers (kin through males). Among Islamicized Africans, during the Moslem New Year, 'slave' cross-cousins bring their 'owners' wood for the use of their households and carry out domestic chores, in exchange for clothes. Sometimes the joking behaviour employs themes referring to the symbolic relationship of master and slave, the 'slave' pretending to be master and reproving the latter. P. Smith has observed the functioning of this institution among the Moslem Diakhanke and notes that when they joke each considers the other as a poor copy of himself, yet they admit that 'it is the sister's child who loses value to some extent, compared to the brother's son'.[34]

The Diakhanke welcome marriage between cross-cousins without apparently favouring any choice between 'slave' or 'master': Moslem prohibitions primarily deal with unions between different generations. Among the Malinke, marriages between *kalame* are sometimes permitted, sometimes proscribed: they are nowhere considered obligatory. The Bambara, who have remained faithful to the traditional cults, prefer marriage with the daughter of a maternal uncle, a daughter who is the nephew's by right and for whom he only makes a very minimal marriage payment.[35]

Joking relations between kin are found in an attenuated form between grandparents and grandchildren: the grandfather is said to be married to his granddaughter and the grandmother to her grandson; they quarrel like married couples, enacting mock connubial rows. During their grandparents' funerals grandchildren play a role resembling that of the *sanāku* in so far as they have the right to take anything they wish from the gifts in kind, and even money, which the close affines of the deceased (lineage sons-in-law, that is 'slaves') have brought as their contribution on this solemn occasion. This equality between alternate generations contrasts with the authoritarian relations between proximate generations, those of parents and children. However in this case, as in the relationship between partners to a blood covenant, the words do not reflect African thinking on the subject in so far as the grandson is a kind of duplicate of the elder man; the first of his grandsons often bears the older man's name and is, in a sense, his grandfather's reincarnation. The child's first steps, his

[34] Smith (P.), 'Notes sur l'organisation sociale des Diakhanké. Aspects particuliers à la région de Kédougou', *Bull. et Mémoires de la Société d'anthropologie de Paris*, XI séries, viii (1965), 284.

[35] Dieterlen (G.), 'Les rites symboliques du mariage chez les Bambara', *Zaïre*, viii (1954), 815. This is a patrilineal situation.

games in the family courtyard, are his own, in his mind's eye; both past and present become confused—a photographer might say that they were two prints taken from a single negative.

Freedom in speech is also the rule between younger brothers and sisters of both spouses, called *ni-moro* in Malinke. This is a relationship which contrasts with that of *birana* which imposes distance. A husband's *bira-nke* include a husband and his parents-in-law, and also the elder brothers and sisters of his wife, a wife's *bira-nke*, her husband's parents and his elder siblings. Between *ni-moro*, as with the case of cross-cousins, joking involves the possibility of marriage, since when a man dies it is theoretically his younger brother who takes over his widows; and if the wife should die first, the widower may sometimes receive his wife's younger sister in marriage. A man, meeting his wife's small sister, treats her as a good-for-nothing incapable of looking after a husband; she retorts that he is a lie-abed, and reproaches him for never giving his wife dresses, jewellery or scent.

Secondly, we have the situation of those clans, between members of which marriage is not only undesirable, but is prohibited; they are also *sanãku*. In Mali, as well as in Senegal, nearly all aristocratic clans, of marabouts or free men, maintain *sanãku* relations with at least one other clan: that is all the members of a clan which bear a certain *dyamu*, a proper name or motto, are the *sanãku* of members of the other clan bearing the same name and vice versa. The origin of this relationship is accredited to a blood pact or a unique instance of marriage. Marriage has since been forbidden, they explain, because it always involves the spilling of blood; and *sanãku* should not only avoid hurting each other, but they should provide mutual assistance on all occasions. If blood were to spill—during a get-together at the New Year for example, when young men run through the streets exchanging blows and insults with people they recognize as their *sanãku*, they make amends by sacrificing to the ancestors.

In certain cases the relationship between *sanãku* is generalized throughout a whole community: Dogon farmers and Bozo fishermen, blacksmiths and Fulani:

The ancestor of the Fulani and the ancestor of the blacksmiths came to this country from Mecca together. The blacksmith married and had daughters. The Fulani did not even have a wife. The blacksmith gave him one of his daughters in marriage, on the assurance that his would be the first and only marriage to be performed between the two clans.[36]

[36] Doumbia (P. E. N.), 'Etude du clan des forgerons', *Bull. du Comité d'études historiques et scientifiqes de l'A.O.F.*, xix (1936), 370.

At first it is hard to grasp the point of this exogamy: how can the partners be assured of mutual help if they refuse to exchange women, or without becoming assimilated to real brothers? In the Bete example we saw how both marriage and blood pacts can equally serve to establish peaceful relations. According to P. Smith the fact of their pledging to help each other without making matrimonial alliances means that women are saved for that wider marriage policy whereby clans do in fact seek to establish this kind of alliance. Smith compares this kind of reasoning with that which in the economic domain leads from free competition to a strategy of 'trusts', the very name which, he stresses, alludes to the same kind of confidence which is deemed indispensible between clans which no longer exchange women.[37]

Sanāku relations exist in all West African societies where there are caste groups of leather-, wood-, and iron-workers and griots; it occurs between members of certain aristocratic clans or clan segments and those belonging to certain clans or clan segments of caste groups. The 'slave' *sanāku* in this case is always the artisan, the 'master' is the free man and the relationship is said to have originated in a blood covenant.

It often happens that a free man, not a member of a caste, chooses, of his own free will, to become the *gesere* (Soninke griot) of another man, to whom he wishes to show his indebtedness or submission by throwing in his lot with the latter. In cases such as these it was not uncommon for a ceremony to be arranged whereby the blood of the two contracting partners was solemnly exchanged in order to affirm the reciprocal conditions of the covenant. In all cases of this nature the voluntary *gesere* became a member of the caste along with his descendants.[38]

At ceremonies, 'servants' assume the same role as cross cousin 'slaves' do in relation to their 'masters'. They bring wood and receive clothes in exchange. Even more so than in the earlier case, joking has to do with both the reversal and the affirmation of a hierarchical situation, whereby the man of caste, through his outspokenness, has the laugh on his side. However, the concept of caste translates a complex reality. It is enough to recall the indispensable role of the blacksmith in village life: the services demanded of such men are not purely confined to their role as smiths, for initiation, the making of masks, the guardianship of the sacred copse are all functions which

[37] Smith (P.), op. cit., pp. 293–4.
[38] Monteil (Ch.), *La légende de Ouagadou et l'origine des Soninké* (Mélanges ethnologiques. Mélanges IFAN 23, Dakar, 1953), p. 364, n. 2.
D

fell to the blacksmith in many Sudanese societies. Sometimes he also played a mediatory role, as among the Bobo where the 'blacksmith enjoys particular prestige and special prerogatives: if there is any quarrelling in the village, it is he who intervenes; he knocks two pieces of iron together and persuades the quarrelling men to calm down; and if anyone refuses to listen he is tied up by the blacksmith, who has the right to take anything he wishes from the hut of such trouble-makers.'[39] Members of castes have many different roles to play: as confidantes, messengers, interpreters, ambassadors, and as spokesmen, marriage-brokers, go-betweens in divorce proceedings and other disputes. Since they become involved in all kinds of private and public business, they are able to exercise considerable influence. All aristocratic lineages are keen to be associated with a caste lineage which can fill these indispensable roles; in these cases the myths of origin for the alliance resemble those in the preceding situation: the debtor—that is the inferior partner—is always the ancestor of the caste lineage, if he is not the ancestor of a whole caste as in the case of the Moslem griots, who are all descended from Zuracata.[40]

Two ancestors were traversing a deserted spot; their provisions exhausted, they were becoming visibly weaker and weaker. While one slept his companion cut off a piece of flesh from his own calf, cooked it and gave it to the other man when he woke up, without mentioning where it had come from. In this way his companion's life was saved. When they were about to continue their journey again the latter noticed that his friend was limping and at once understood what had happened. They decided there and then never again to spill each other's blood: their children would not marry, would never share the same food, but would give each other mutual assistance.

Members of castes are known as *nyamakala*, literally 'stalk' of 'manure': *kala* in its original sense means a wisp, or stem, of grass, while *nyama* is a 'pile of grass or leaves which have been swept up— fallen leaves, dead leaves, cut grass, sweepings, piles of rubbish, detritus, dung heaps, scurf'. *Nyamakala* are the 'little people, men of no account, commoners, persons of servile origin, people belonging

[39] Guébhard (P.), 'Notes contributives à l'étude de la religion, des mœurs et des coutumes des Bobo du cercle de Kouny', *Revue d'ethnographie et de sociologie*, ii (1911), 134.

[40] See particularly Sidibé (Mamby), 'Les gens de caste ou nyamakala au Soudan français'. *Notes africaines*, no. 81 (1959), pp. 13–17; and Zemp (H.), 'La légende des griots malinké', *Cahiers d'études africaines*, vi, 24 (1966), 611–42.

to a caste'.[41] By playing on words, a perhaps unconscious pun links the first part of the expression *nyamakala* to *n'yam-ma* (*nyama*): 'life, personality, spirit (of a dead person, of an animal, of a plant, of a mineral etc), a divine spirit, a divinity, a being possessed by a stranger spirit or by a genie'.[42] Griaule is more explicit and defines *n'ya-ma* (*nyama*) as 'instant energy, which is impersonal and unconscious, shared by all animals, plants, and supernatural beings, things of nature; it is an energy which tends to support, in its being, the sustenance required either temporarily (mortal beings) or eternally (immortal beings)'.[43] It is a disincarnate life force and it is universally believed by the Manding that every conscious or unconscious action which causes any kind of moral or material wrong will unleash the *n'ya-ma* of its victim; once freed from its habitual dwelling-place the *n'ya-ma* becomes dangerous, pursuing the offender, attacking him ineluctably when he reaches his lowest physical or psychical ebb. Filth, *nyama*, is naturally very rich in *n'ya-ma*, since it is secreted along with the waste matter and continues to remain part of the individual from whom it emanated. Moslems have only retained this sense of the word and *nyama* is invariably translated by 'filth'; while all those who have remained faithful to the old cults consider the essential source of *n'ya-ma* to reside in men's blood: 'All the *nyama* are in the blood.'[44] It is this which brings about the efficacy of a sacrifice or a blood pact: having absorbed some drops of his partner's blood, each of the parties to the covenant henceforth possess a little of the other's life force. 'A *sanãku* is a kind of twin—inside him there is a little piece of his partner, and vice versa.'[45] Strength and filth—it is easily understood with what mingled feelings of fear and contempt the caste groups are treated. '*Nyamakala* enjoy certain prerogatives denied to aristocrats since they can oblige the latter to perform their will . . . *Nyamakala* are both counsellors and buffoons in relation to their *diatigui*. They entertain by their comical behaviour, their more or less witty, some-times satirical, comments.'[46] How difficult not to compare a *sanãku* caste member—the double who is also 'filth'—with the Swazi *tinsila*—the king's 'waste matter', who are also his twins.

---

[41] Delafosse (M.), *La langue mandingue et ses dialectes* (Paris, 1955), under *nyama*.

[42] Delafosse (M.), op. cit., under *n'ya-ma*.

[43] Griaule (M.), *Masques dogons* (Paris, 1938), p. 160.

[44] Dieterlen (G.), *Essai sur la religion bambara*, p. 90.

[45] Ibid., p. 84. The Kaguru compare the partners in a blood pact to twins (Beidelman, op. cit., p. 331).

[46] Sidibé (Mamby), op. cit., pp. 16–17.

Between *sanāku* of different status direct reciprocity is replaced by a complementarity:

The Dogon blacksmith does not farm. But he does make the agricultural tools: hoes, axes, weeding instruments etc. He is not paid directly for this: after the harvest he makes a tour of the village, carrying his goatskin bag, and it is up to everyone to place some millet in it. In this way the specialist is paid for his work through a system whereby the idea of reciprocal gifts is clearly separated from the idea of exchange; if somebody asks the black-smith to fashion him a tool, he is also honour bound to give him a certain quantity of millet at harvest time.[47]

Farmers and blacksmiths, as well as nobles and griots (the latter sing the warlike exploits of their partners and their partners' ances-tors): each group depends on the other to play a certain role. The myths of origin of this relationship evoke this indissolubility, which is also expressed by insults and exogamy—a strange kind of behaviour it would seem if we were not *au fait* with the original explanation: among the Wolof, during a marriage ceremony, the *dyam*—that is the 'servant'—takes his master's place when the bride is abducted from her home; he puts her on his horse, brings her to the nuptial house, and, lifting her in his arms, places her on the bed; only then does the counterfeit groom make way for the real fiancé.[48] Once again we are reminded of the *tinsila*, the Swazi king's bodyguards.

Myths also stress the asymmetry of the relationship. In studying the Toucouleur, Wane notes that two Dendiraabe will always form a combination of superior and inferior, 'free man' and 'slave'; he adds: 'None the less it is an unstable relationship . . . The *dendiraagal* implies a perpetual emulation, an oscillation—for each individual— between the two poles of superiority and inferiority.'[49]

His role as life-giver being determined for ever, the 'master' must continue to nourish his partner with his blood, a partner who is both his duplicate and his detritus. But if as a creditor he is granted the role of 'master', the debtor none the less continues to increase in strength at the former's expense and he may even end up consuming him: a 'slave' of this type both strengthens and weakens; an arrogant parasite who knows he is indispensable—the Diakhanke say that the *nyamakala* is a person who can demand things and who can go on demanding things. It is during the New Year play that the slaves

[47] Paulme (D.), *Organisation sociale des Dogon* (Paris, 1940), p. 182.
[48] Labouret (H.) *La parenté à plaisanteries*, pp. 248–9.
[49] Wane (Yaya), *Les Toucouleur du Fouta Touro (Sénégal). Stratification sociale et structure familiale* (Dakar, CNRS, IFAN, 1966), roneod.

most strenuously deny this hierarchy whereby the 'master', if he is not careful, runs the risk of exhausting himself to the other's advantage. P. Smith writes that it is as though the Malinke 'recognize the necessity of setting up a hierarchy between affines, differentiating the partner's position, while at the same time refusing, through recourse to joking, to render it rigid or irreversible. This kind of institutional game recognizes the special value attached to each position. It seems to be found at the meeting point of a convergence marked by the act of alliance, and a divergence, marked by the prohibition of marriage—that is on the recognition of complementarity and disjunction.'[50]

Initiated in relations between farmers and blacksmiths, we now have a passage from one type of alliance to another, from the clan system which sees itself as equal to the caste hierarchy: since the 'slave' is his 'master's' duplicate the latter cannot become offended by his insults, insults which, through his mediacy, are diverted to no other person than he who proffered them in the first place.

A passage from one kind of alliance to another is also involved in relations between cross-cousins, with its implications of preferential marriage. By treating parallel cousins as sisters—thus effectively prohibiting marriage—and at the same time encouraging unions between cross-cousins, they are stressing the symbolic character of incest prohibitions, since one type of alliance is only rejected in order to establish another in which exchange is enjoined. Originally, in the Bambara myth, we had two pairs of twins (a male and a female in each case); the men exchanged their sisters, thereby forming new pairs whose single children then practised cross-cousin marriage: a brother may not marry his sister, but the brother's son may marry the sister's daughter.[51]

As a consequence, when the exchange of sisters is supplanted by marriage payments, a distinction is set up between the actors and the objects exchanged—the wife-giver's children (the wife's brother) will be the 'masters' and the sister's children will be their 'slaves' in the same fashion as the descendants of wife-takers, in the myth of origin, are the 'slaves' of the wife-givers' children.

The two types of relations between *sanāku* have therefore been thought out from the same model, but in an inverse sense: both play on the opposition between kinship and alliance, cross-cousins behaving as if they were *not* brothers and sisters in order to be able to marry,

[50] Smith (P.), op. cit. p. 294.

[51] See in particular, Dieterlen (G.), *Les rites symboliques du mariage chez les Bambara*.

while free men and caste groups behave as though they were twins in
order *not* to be able to marry; in the latter case, a fictive identity is
postulated in order to set up exogamic laws: laws which involve caste
endogamy.

In summary, joking and insults always accompany ambiguous
situations:

1. Between cross-cousins, marriage may at first glance seem
impossible, nevertheless it is enjoined: the female cross-cousin is a
sister, but a sister who, through a subterfuge, is permitted as a spouse.
2. Between *ni-moro*—a husband and his wife's younger sisters or a
wife and her husband's younger brothers—marriage is a possibility
in the future, but involves the predecease of the spouse. Joking
implies death.
3. Between clans of equal status where marriage is forbidden,
joking is carried on as a function of their not being permitted to
marry; since members of the other clan contain a small piece of
yourself any union would be incestuous.
In each of these cases, joking is sexual in character. It occurs in a
relationship which is theoretically incompatible: a sister, whom one
may marry; a sister-in-law, prohibited as a sexual partner today, but
who could be your wife on the death of your present spouse; and
finally a woman who should be a permitted partner, but who is
prohibited through a pact contracted by the ancestors. The coarseness
of the verbal exchanges, which causes no affront although it would be
inadmissible from anyone else, stresses the ambiguity of their
positions and at the same time provides an escape from an embarras-
sing situation.
4. The last case concerns the raillery between nobles or free men
and caste groups—masters and 'servants'. Here myth stresses both
their identity and their difference. The 'master' once saved the life
of a man who declared himself to be his 'slave'; but this only happened at the risk of weakening the former's life force. The theme of
the mockery here is not sexual, since they are trying to deny dependence which the mere mentioning of the relationship evokes; neither
one nor the other feels complete without the presence of the other.

The kinds of joking most commonly found associated with the
Zande blood pact are those whereby one of the partners accuses the
other of witchcraft, or informs him of the death of the member of his
lineage; both pieces of information, if they were true, would mean a

diminution of the social status of the person concerned. But since they come from a blood brother, they can only be false; insults do not serve to destroy intimacy, they reinforce it.

We have an inverse situation in the relations between *sanãku* of different statuses, where a slave's mockery does nothing to gainsay his role as a servant; interchanges of the kind fool no one, the slave no more than anyone else; he plays his part without illusions.

In both cases, the form of the message runs counter to reality; falsehood is expressed in order to render truth more manifest. Among the Zande, joking cannot destroy 'equality': between *sanãku*, where one of the partners is an aristocrat and the other a member of an inferior caste, joking stresses distance and at the same time kindles solidarity.

Towards a History of the

Yatenga Mossi

DOMINIQUE ZAHAN[1]

The Mossi region called Yatenga comprises, from an administrative point of view, a vast territory in the form of an irregular hexagon of about 27,300 square kilometres, stretching from the south-west to the north-east in the northern part of the Republic of Upper Volta. It is bounded on the south by the administrative districts of Ouagadougou and Kaya, on the north by Bandiagara, on the west by Tougan, and the east by Dori.

Before the French conquest, the rule of the *Yatenga-Naba*, chief of this territory, was exercised within almost identical boundaries. The inhabitants of the region—around 600,000 to 700,000—were, and still are, grouped into cantons and provinces; each province was administered by an official of the *Yatenga-Naba*'s court, called *ñē-somba*, 'good person', which the French translated as 'minister'.

Yatenga means 'land of *Yadega*', who was the founder of the Mossi dynasty of Ouahigouya, capital of the territory we are dealing with here.[1a]

Culturally, the Mossi of Yatenga belong to a large ethnic group which altogether numbers about three million people; they inhabit mainly five administrative districts, apart from Ouahigouya: Ouagadougou, Koudougou, Tenkodogo, Kaya and Fada n'Gourma.

The people of Yatenga belong to a culture area which is even larger, since it includes that whole group of peoples whom English authors have called the *Mole-Dagbane*; these include, along with the Mossi, the Gourmantche, the Nankana, the Dagari, the Birifor, the Bura, the Koussassi, the Namnam, the Tallensi, the Wala, the

---

[1] *Dominique Zahan* (b. 1915), Dr. es L., Sorbonne. Professor of Ethnology, University of Paris V. Field-work in West Africa since 1948, chiefly among the Mossi of Upper Volta and Bambara of Mali. Main interest: traditional religion and epistemology. The original French text of this paper was published as 'Pour une histoire des Mossi du Yatenga', *L'Homme*, i, 2 (1961), 5–22.

[1a] The word *Yatenga* is, in fact, a contracted form of the words *Yadega* and *tenga* (land, village, region).

Dagomba, the Mamprussi, and the Nanoumba. A great part of this vast block of peoples lives in Ghana.

The map clearly shows the very great extent of the area in the West African geographical region which is inhabited by the *Mole-Dagbane* people, the compactness of which is a noteworthy feature, despite the enclaves of Sissala, Kassena, Boussanse, and Bobo.

Thus defined, the culture group owes its unity primarily to its language whose structure is based on identical systems of vowels and consonant groupings and a common syntax. Homogeneity, however, depends even more on factors of social organization and religion, which are based on what we shall call a bivalence of power, which in fact involves two concepts: the sky and the earth.

Within the whole group only the Mossi, the Mamprussi and the Dagomba have state systems. The others, while clearly sharing a similar social and religious organization, lack any system of centralized authority, ruling over the different groups within the tribe. These remarks, however, are only true to a degree since we are poorly informed about the extent of the so-called 'local rule' in certain groups and, in fact, it would seem that the differences are less of kind than of degree. I am not personally aware of any non-centralized system of political power either in the Upper Volta or in Mali. I would even go so far as to say that centralized rule is a fundamental feature as far as the Africans of these regions are concerned since it forms the pivot of their religious system.[2]

For their congeners the Yatenga Mossi have only contempt. They despise the Mossi of Ouagadougou, Kaya, and Fada n'Gourma,[3] while these groups in turn affect a lack of respect for them.[4]

[2] Authors such as Rattray and Fortes, referring to the *Mole-Dagbane* group, maintain that these ethnic groups are composed of two main communities which may confront each other in a relationship of 'contraposition'. These two communities include one group, which claims to comprise the original inhabitants, and which exercises effective control over land rights, while the others, who call themselves immigrants, form the ruling class.

While admitting the existence of these two groupings, we do not believe that our English authors have grasped the real nature of these religious and social ties. We should also point out that the basic features of the tribes concerned are not peculiar to this group: they form part and parcel of the culture of many other African peoples. The traditions of African states, both north and south of the Equator, almost involve two similar groups: the indigenous inhabitants and the stranger-invader. Almost everywhere this serves to explain state formations among these peoples.

[3] They call them *Gurūsi*, a term also used for a well-known people living in the south-eastern part of the Republic of Upper Volta.

[4] Their scorn is expressed by the word *yadese* (plural of *yadega*).

The history of the Mossi of Yatenga can hardly be separated from the history of the Mossi people in general. However there is a problem here. Those who have done field-work in Africa will know that African concepts of time are difficult to understand and analyse. This becomes somewhat disconcerting when one is trying to determine periods of time and place events in the past through cataloguing and dating them. For Africans in general time is sacred. The history of the world, the traditions of peoples and individuals should not be revealed except at certain times—during initiatory ritual for example, or in order to confirm and validate an important social event, such as the installation of a chief. Apart from cases like these, the course of historical time, going back into the past, soon leads—in the African situation—to an anastomosis with mythical time. It would be more correct to say that Africans possess a sense of the philosophy of history rather than one which involves objective and positive historical data.

For these reasons, and for many others as well, any attempt to write the history of the Mossi must come up against prodigious difficulties: informants will contradict themselves, accounts may differ, periods of time are uncertain, facts and events are presented in a symbolic manner. It was because they had to write 'history' at any price that those who have dealt with the Mossi past have been misled through an acceptance of accounts referring to origins as being literally true.

From an external point of view the history of the Mossi begins broadly with the exploration of the African coast by the Portuguese. We know that this exploration went ahead after the conquest of Ceuta, in 1415, and lasted for almost seventy years. Then came their exploration of the interior of the African continent which continued until the close of the fifteenth century. In fact it was during their last venture that the Portuguese attempted (unsuccessfully however) to come into contact with the Mossi themselves.

Seemingly more precise information about these people is found in the Es Sādi's *Tarikh es Soudan* which mentions four events in relation to the Mossi: the devastation of Timbuktu, an expedition against Walata, another against Benka (all carried out by the Mossi) and Askia El Hadj's expedition against the Mossi.[5]

These facts from the *Tarikh* provide foundation for the different chronological accounts of the Mossi chiefs and, consequently, for the history of the people, Marc, Delafosse, and Tauxier, relying on the

[5] Cf. Es Sādi, *Tarikh es Soudan*, tr. Houdas, pp. 16 and 17, 45 and 46, 112 ff.

dates provided by the Arab historian, have linked them up with the Mossi king-lists given by royal *griots* and placed the beginnings of the Mossi state either in the eleventh century (Delafosse),[6] or in the thirteenth century (Tauxier).[7] Yet the historical value of these passages concerning the Mossi in the *Tarikh* is not great. We do not know which Mossi they are referring to, nor do we know which of the Mossi chiefs undertook the expeditions mentioned.

The history of this people, therefore, does not really begin for us until 1888, when Binger, who seems to have been the first European to set foot on Mossi soil, began his journey. Moreover, the Mossi do not feature in anthropological literature until 1904, when we have Noiret's monography on Yatenga.[8] From this time onwards several works began to appear: those of Vadier (Ouahigouya),[9] Moulins (Ouagadougou),[10] and above all, the studies of Marc which cover the whole of Mossi country,[11] Tauxier,[12] Froger,[13] Father Alexandre,[14] (the last are linguistic works). Up till the present time a bibliography of the Mossi which we have compiled includes about two hundred items.

As for Mossi history, seen 'from the inside' our only sources for the moment are limited to accounts which have been given by Mossi themselves. These accounts are of an extreme complexity and historians will require a great deal of ingenuity if they wish to set them out in any logical order. Moreover, these narratives come from different source materials and must therefore be carefully distinguished one from the other.

As a result of the inquiries which we made into these matters the sources seem to be of three kinds: some are the accounts of royal drummers (*bẽdu wedese*); others are those of the custodians of the earth; while the rest are stories of blacksmith origin. Such distinctions

[6] *Haut-Sénégal-Niger* (Paris: Larose, 1912), I, pp. 306 and 307.

[7] *Le Noir du Yatenga* (Paris: Larose, 1917), p. 672; *Nouvelles Notes sur les Mossi et les Gourounsi* (Paris: Larose, 1924), pp. 16–25.

[8] Unpublished manuscript.

[9] Unpublished manuscript.

[10] Unpublished manuscript.

[11] *Le Pays Mossi* (Paris: Larose, 1909).

[12] *Le Noir du Yatenga* (Paris: Larose, 1917); *Nouvelles Notes sur les Mossi et les Gourounsi* (Paris: Larose 1924).

[13] *Etude sur la langue des Mossi (Boucle du Niger) suivie d'un vocabulaire et de textes* (Paris: E. Leroux, 1910); *Manuel pratique de langue Môré (Mossi du Cercle de Ouagadougou, Colonie de la Haute-Volta, A.O.F.)* (Paris: L. Fournier, 1923).

[14] *Dictionnaire môré-français* (polycopied); *Grammaire môré* (polycopied). These works were published in 1953 under the title: *La Langue Môré*, 2 vols (Dakar, Mémoires de l'IFAN, 1953).

are extremely important, since each of these social categories presents the facts in its own way, thereby throwing light on their role in society.

The first kind of account, which we call '*nakomse* narratives' (that is of royal origin) deal with the chiefship: its origins, establishment in successive localities, the 'conquest' of the country. The chief, in fact, comes from outside; he is partly a stranger. Over the ages he progressively traverses the royal domain until he reaches his present residence where he is finally made to dwell as a 'prisoner', with no right to leave once he has been invested with power.

Tauxier, whom we quote here, has brought together, in a somewhat picturesque fashion, versions provided by different authors.[15]

At one time then, which I shall place approximately around the middle of the thirteenth century, there lived, at Gambakha, a powerful Dagomba king, Nedega by name. He had a daughter who, according to one tradition, was called Yennenga, and according to another, Poko. He loved the girl very much and allowed her to live to all intents and purposes like a man. She led raids organized by the Dagomba all around their kingdom and became a kind of intrepid lord, a veritable Amazon. However her life as a warrior did not entirely occupy her attentions and the young girl ardently desired to marry, a move her father was not really happy about, since he considered her more as a son than a daughter; moreover he would only accept a very powerful chief as his son-in-law, and his like was not to be had.

One day, after a raid, the young girl became lost in a forest, far from her companions. Her horse bolted, and, powerless to control it, she was carried very far, finally reaching a hut where there dwelt a young, handsome and presumably well-made elephant hunter. Hearing the neighing of the horse he came up and helped Yennenga climb down, offering her his hut as a place of rest. It was probably love at first sight, since we know the girl was disposed that way and the young man, for his part, was unmarried. Whatever the case, Riale (since this was the elephant hunter's name) married Yennenga on the spot and the girl, forgetting all about her father, her family, her companions and warriors, henceforth showed no desire to leave her husband.

Who can this elephant hunter be? Tauxier asks himself. His answer follows:

Lieutenant Marc calls him Samba and makes him a Dagomba. Traditions collected in monographs on Ouagadougou, Ouahigouya, Tenkodogo, all call him Riare or Riale. Moulins (*Monographie de Ouagadougou*) seems to

[15] Cf. Tauxier, *Le Noir du Yatenga*, pp. 58 et seq.

want him to be a Boussanse. Vadier (*Monographie de Ouahigouya*, 1909) tells a story which makes him out to be a Malinke: 'A man called Riale [he says], son of the chief of Kaba (Manding) having failed to succeed to his father because his brother had taken command of the chief's lands, went off into the bush by himself to hunt the wild animals and beasts of the Sudan. Going eastwards, further and further into the interior, he built himself a hut near Bittou (near Gambakha). There he stayed alone, without a wife, living off the spoils of his hunting.'

Then follows the story of Nedega and Yennenga. From the union of the Dagomba king's daughter and Riale a son was born; he was called Ouidiraogo, meaning 'stallion'.

After many years Yennenga died. Her tomb became a centre of great veneration. Mossi kings made pilgrimages there up till recent times; on the death of each Ouahigouya- *naba* one of his horses and one of his wives were sent to Gambakha to be sacrificed to the *spirit* of Yennenga.[16]

Riale and Ouidiraogo left Dagomba country and went towards the north. Many Dagomba warriors joined them and they formed a kind of conquering army, precursors of the Mossi conquering invaders.

Ouidiraogo left his father, of whom we hear no more, and he founded the village of Tenkodogo (the present day Tenkodogo) which thus becomes the second place of origin—after Gambakha—for the Mossi people.

From then [says Moulins] his power did not cease growing, through the continual arrival of Dagomba who came in large numbers to offer him their allegiance. On the other hand the neighbouring peoples were very thin on the ground and very divided among themselves. He thus managed to make them accept his rule.[17]

Ouidiraogo had many sons, although only three are mentioned in these accounts: Rawa, Zũgurana, and Diaba. Rawa was the first to conquer present-day Yatenga; he approached the country from the south-east, then, passing by the east, made for the north-west as far as the edge of the Bandiagara cliffs. He was a double person, it was said. He had two residences: one at Sangha, the other at Zadouma, and after his death he was buried, at the same time, in two places. Zũgurana succeeded his father at Tenkodogo, while Diaba established himself at Pama where he founded the Mossi dynasty of this region.

During the lifetime of Ouidiraogo, however, a *Nyonyoga* chief of the Ouagadougou region sent a delegation to Tenkodogo, offering

[16] L. Tauxier, op. cit., p. 60.
[17] Quoted in L. Tauxier, op. cit., p. 60.

Zũgurana one of his daughters in marriage. From the ensuing union was born Oubri, the founder of the Mossi dynasties of Ouagadougou and Ouahigouya, since he conquered the Ouagadougou region and after him, one of his descendants, Yadega, approaching Yatenga from the south, gained control and became the founder of the Ouahigouya dynasty. Like Rawa, Yadega settled down in his new territory, residing now at Lago, now at Gourcy. He also was buried in two different places since he too was a double.

There is an interesting detail in these accounts which tell of the founding of the Yatenga dynasty. Yadega had a twin brother, Kudumie; on the death of their father, Nassibiri, Yadega was busy conquering Yatenga so Kudumie succeeded the dead man. When Yadega heard the news he hurried to La, the royal residence, in order to remove his brother from office. However the council of elders opposed him and Yadega was forced to retreat. As he fled he stole his father's 'royal amulets', aided in this deed by his sister whose role as *napoko* was to watch over them.[18] Kudumie set off in pursuit, but according to the Mossi of Yatenga he was unable to catch his brother; forced to renounce the amulets he only succeeded in bringing back to La some of the droppings from Yadega's horse. Since the Ouagadougou Mossi claim the opposite it is impossible to know which of these two dynasties possess the true 'royal amulets', and which has the paltry copies.

This event marks a separation of the two great Mossi kingdoms into the southern kingdom, whose capital eventually became Ouagadougou and the northern one with its capital at Ouahigouya. As to the hostility between the two twin brothers, it has been given a practical expression in the taboo (still in force today) against either of the two kings ever setting eyes on the other.

In this account and in the *nakomse* accounts in general, we should note the presence in the beginning of the story of the daughter of the Dagomba king—Yennenga or Poko—who is persistently described as a very masculine woman. It is she, in fact, who is the founder of the Mossi people, and the custom of sending a horse and a royal wife in the event of a king's death to be sacrificed on Yennenga's tomb, reveals the importance of this personage as far as the chiefship is concerned. Yennenga symbolizes the perennial nature of the kingdom; she guarantees the transition from one chief to the next. A chief's

---

[18] The *napoko* (literally 'daughter of the chief') is the chief's eldest daughter and on the death of her father she reigns during the interregnum. At that time she dons the dead man's clothes and the insignia of chiefship.

office should never be allowed to fall vacant: a chief may die but the chiefship lives on. The continuity of rule is symbolized in the person of Yennenga; and the institution of the *napoko* has continued this down the ages and until the present day.

This kind of narrative also stresses the importance of the system of alliance which gave birth to the conquering chief, that initial link in the dynasty of the founders of the kingdom. Yennenga marries a Mande hunter. This stranger's character is like that of a god, the divinity, who is the hunter par excellence, he who 'kills' the most important 'game'—man. The fact of his being a stranger emphasizes his extraordinary nature even more: it evokes the unexpected, the unknown, the unusual, all of which, being unfamiliar, attracts attention.

The fruit of the union between Yennenga and Riale, Ouidiraogo, is the grandson of the Dagomba king: he is the person whom the Mossi call by the kinship term *yagēga*. From the point of view of the alliance system, this kinsman plays a considerable role in Mossi society. Every ward has its *yagē kasēga*, that is, its eldest 'grandson', who resides in the village of the oldest *wemba*.[19] This *yagēga* plays a role in his maternal kinsfolk's ward when there are important purificatory rites or funerals, pacts to be made between families or disputes to iron out. As a link between maternal and consanguine kin the *yagēga* is all-powerful with the former. Ouidiraogo himself, when he left his grandfather, took with him a 'present' of four horses and fifty cattle, 'doubtless a good deal' says Tauxier 'considering the times and the situation of the country too far south for the raising of cattle and the keeping of horses.'[20]

The *yagēga* theme crops up again in the *nakomse* narratives when Ouidiraogo makes contact with the 'indigenous peoples' of the future Ouagadougou kingdom. Here it is used to make a different kind of alliance: this is an alliance between the owners of the earth and the conquerors (the *Nyonyose* chief of the Ouagadougou district gives his daughter in marriage to Zũgurana, Ouidiraogo's son). Once again it is the *yagēga* of the chief of the owners of the earth who becomes chief and supplants the authority of his maternal grandparents.

In those parts of the accounts concerned with establishing a new authority over the so-called conquered regions everything takes place,

[19] The term *wemba* pl. *wemdemba* refers to daughters and married sisters. They always occupy a different ward from their paternal kin since the Mossi practise exogamous marriage.

[20] Op. cit., p. 60.

in fact, as if the immigrant chiefs infiltrated into the sphere of the custodians of the earth through a claim to kinship. In fact the people whom we have grown accustomed to calling the Mossi and who possess the chiefship at present are not so much enemies of the *Nyonyose*, the indigenous inhabitants, as their close kinsmen. Between these two human groupings we have the same social relationship, *mutatis mutandis*, as that which exists between a *yagēga* and his grandparents, particularly between a grandfather and his grandson, through a daughter.

We shall not proceed any further in an analysis of the ideas behind the *nakomse* accounts since, from the birth of Oubri onwards, they no longer deal with relations between Mossi chiefs and the custodians of the earth, but with the kingdom's internal organization.

The second category of narratives, those we might term of *nyonyose* origin, derive from the milieu of the custodians of the earth called Nyonyosé or Foulsé. (They also call themselves Kourouma or Kouroumba, plural form of Kouroumde, rendered in Fulani as Kouroumankobe.)

These tales do not portray warlike events and show no passion for conquest. They are imbued with a remarkable pacifism. Their main aim is to present the expansion of the custodians of the earth as a function of their two major occupations: firstly fishing, then agriculture. Here lineages also play an important role since the watercourses and the earth are the 'property' of groups each of whose members descend from the same ancestor.[21]

The Kouroumba of Yatenga maintain that they originated in a region situated between Say and Niamey, on the other side of the Niger. From there, they appear to have spread to an area north of Yatenga, settling at Loroum or Pobe. Then, moving southwards, they settled at Gambo, Bougouré, and Ronga. At first they were fishermen but took up farming with the discovery of cereals.

Parallel to this group of custodians of the earth, other families were also settling at Womsom, Gourcy, and Koundouba adopting the same way of life in southern Yatenga.

We have included all these place names since they may help in an understanding of the Nyonyosé. In fact their names (excepting Loroum and Ronga) correspond to the months involved in the beginning of the agricultural cycle in Yatenga and they mark the *bega,* an itinerant ceremony which is spread over five months of the year.

These accounts, in fact, only reveal one aspect of the origins of the custodians of the earth. In the same way as the Nakomsé they tend to present a picture of groups of 'strangers' arriving to settle pacifically, according to them, in a region already populated by Dogon. Here we find once again the concept of 'stranger' being used to establish as far as the occupation of the land is concerned, a pre-eminence over others, as a result of the value accorded the unforeseen event of a man coming from the outside. In fact the Nyonyosé are also justifying their own chiefship which existed alongside that of the Dogon before finally supplanting it.

The similarity between the way the Nakomsé set up their rule and authority and that of the Nyonyosé—through a so-called invasion—is remarkable, but we should not be surprised overmuch at this. Among both groups, chiefship—and by this we mean a centralized chiefship —is very strong. Even today the supreme head of all the Nyonyosé, installed at Loroum, is the counterpart of the supreme chief of the Mossi of Yatenga, who resides at Ouahigouya. The former rules over the earth, while the latter controls the internal and external affairs of the kingdom.

The other aspect of the origin of the custodians of the earth is to be found in other Nyonyosé tales, tales which tend to portray them in the exercise of their functions. These can be reduced to two principles: the working of the soil, properly speaking, and the 'exploitation' of rain. According to these accounts, all Nyonyosé of Yatenga, either came out of the ground or descended from the sky. As far as we could make out, those who claim to have come out of the ground are in fact guardians of agricultural techniques, controlling those processes which make grain grow—endowing it with a soul, removing it at the right time and returning it at the period of sowing. In their turn the 'rain makers', the masters of clouds and winds, possessors of techniques involving a mastery over the atmosphere, snakes, and fire, declare their place of origin to be the sky. Among the owners of the earth, therefore, there seems to be a major cleavage determined by their functional roles, and this cleavage divides the Nyonyosé into two clearly differentiated social categories.

We suspect that similar divisions are present among other peoples. We have found the same idea among the Samogo. Meyer Fortes—the author of an intensive work on a people related to the Mossi—notes the same thing for the Tallensi. However as far as he is concerned, the birth of the ancestor of the *Tendaan Genat* (chief of the earth), out of the bowels of the earth, is but an affirmation of the dogma that they were the first occupants of the land.[22]

Narratives coming from the blacksmiths deal with the migration of the whole of the blacksmith population of Yatenga and clearly seek to explain the dispersal of these families and caste groups among the Mossi peoples. In fact Yatenga blacksmiths are only rarely found in compact groups. They usually consist of small endogamous families forming wards—*zaka*—within Mossi communities. In a general way, excepting the villages of Kalsaka, Guite, and Seguenega, they consider themselves to derive from the same stock as the Nyonyosé who came from the Say region. They consider themselves, therefore, as 'owners' of the earth.

According to their accounts, in the beginning, when the Nyonyosé began to people the country, blacksmiths all lived in the village of Tougou, north-east of present-day Ouahigouya. It was here that they were found by a Mossi chief called Ouemtanango (a son of Oubri and a grandson of Zŭgurana) who forced them to join his warrior bands and then dispersed them throughout the country. The relations between this Nakomboga chief and the blacksmiths merit some consideration.

The portrait we get of Ouemtanango shows him to be a cruel chief (cruelty is, moreover, one of the characteristic features of all the chiefs and all *yagẽga*). In one village, during one of his raids, he wanted to force a woman to kill her child; in another village where he resided for a while (Guite), he had a deep tunnel dug, joining his quarters to his private well, so that no one should see his wives when they went to fetch water. His cruelty was such that he once had the feet cut off one of these women because, being very tall, she was unable to pass along this passage without hitting her head on the top.

He was very severe with the blacksmiths, it is said. Obliged to follow him on all his expeditions, he once forced them to cut through a 'mountain' which was in his way (at Sabouni people still show you this 'mountain' through which the blacksmiths dug their famous trench). He also forced them to dig out the aforementioned passage from his house to the well. In order to make them easily recognizable he made them all wear a piece of charcoal around their necks. And when he talked to them they were not allowed to call him *naba*, like

[22] See M. Fortes, *The Dynamics of Clanship among the Tallensi* (London, 1945), pp. 23 and 24.

other Mossi, but *jorro*. Finally—and this is the episode that led to the dispersal of the blacksmiths—he once asked them to go and find some toads which he needed for a sacrifice. They set off to get these animals in the rocky hills but, returning empty-handed from their expedition, they provoked the wrath of Ouemtanango who decided to put them all to death. Before the chief could carry out his design the blacksmiths took fright and fled in all directions. From that time onwards, it is said, these caste groups could be found all over the country. In an allegorical fashion these tales describe the relations between blacksmiths and chiefs. We want to bring out clearly the patterning of these tales, which, along with those concerning the Nakomsé and the 'owners' of the earth, are indicative of a basic social structure.

The blacksmith, in Mossi society in Yatenga, is a person associated both with the custodians of the earth and the chiefs. He forms a link between these two poles of social life. A *saya* (the Mossi word for blacksmith) is Nyonyoga by origin. He comes from the same region and is of the same stock. Particular tales also bring him down from the sky on a wire thread. His occupation links him closer to those 'owners' of the earth who are 'rain makers', because the blacksmith is the uncontested lord of the water, in spite of the fact that he works with iron and fire. However, the same *saya* is also closely associated with the chief, whom he protects. It is he who 'clears' a path for the king at his installation, symbolically opening the road of his kingdom.[23] Sometimes the blacksmith is even regarded as a peer of the king; both may, if need be, share the same mat.

It is of some interest to show why the blacksmith tales we have mentioned should bring in one of the most cruel chiefs known to Yatenga tradition: his rival was the famous *Naba Kago* of the eighteenth century (according to the historians) who amused himself, it is said, by feeding human corpses to the vultures. Yet cruelty is not only a royal prerogative, since it may also be attributed to the blacksmiths. Was it not the smith who inflicted man's first wound by the painful operation of circumcision? Is it not the smith who fashions arms to destroy and kill: knives, arrows, spears, and guns? Did he not invent agricultural tools which initially inflict 'wounds' on the earth?

The blacksmith is often portrayed as a civilizing hero, who was the first to provide mankind with perfected farming techniques (even

[23] We are here referring to a rite which takes place during the royal investiture ritual; it consists in the king passing through a new door which has been specially opened for this purpose in the wall surrounding the blacksmith quarters.

Ouemtanango, himself, also had a human side since it is said that he
saved his brother Kimso, when he became lost when riding an ostrich
he had mounted instead of a horse). On the whole, however, the
negative qualities of the smith—his role as destroyer and annihilator
—are forgotten. Yet it is enough to hear the kind of songs sung by
newly circumcised boys along with their reaction to the skill of the
man who has been cutting into their flesh, to be aware of the fact that
the blacksmith is both life and death, just like the cruel king whom the
Mossi themselves call a 'blackguard'.

From the foregoing accounts of the origins of the inhabitants of
Yatenga we may derive some useful information for the understanding
of the social and religious foundations of the Mossi kingdom of
Yatenga which are also relevant no doubt to other peoples culturally
related to them.

Since the early studies of this Voltaic people, the Mossi kingdoms
have always been described as consisting of one relatively small
segment, which corresponds to the ruling group with a king at its
head, and several subject peoples. In the kingdom of Yatenga these
subject peoples comprised the Nyonyosé, Dogon, Fulani, Samogo,
Yarsé, and the blacksmiths.

The ruling classes in these societies were considered to be the
descendants of a small number of invaders, who came from the south
and brought about the submission of the peace-loving populations
there, particularly the Nyonyosé; these people lived in their ancestral
lands as the original occupants, the custodians of the earth. This is a
phrase which has come to be synonymous with 'indigenous people'
and in this way it has become usual to contrast the two different
groups as if we were dealing with two different races.

This contrast between 'invaders' and 'indigenous peoples', as far
as the social organization of these people is concerned, has not
impressed French writers overmuch. Among English anthropologists,
on the other hand, the idea took firm root. From the time of Rattray's
writings on the peoples of the northern territories of the Gold Coast
it began to be presented as a theory. This eminent English anthropologist concluded that the political institutions of the invaders had
been superimposed on those of the first inhabitants, thereby producing a mixed form of power, 'a kind of dual mandate'. The secular
power of the incumbents of the chiefship, descendants of foreign
invaders, was contrasted with the power of the 'custodians of the
earth' who 'continued to assert their original title as guardians and
trustees of the land of their people'. The 'custodians of the earth'

continued to exercise those functions which they had held prior to the invasion by the political chiefs, but they were nominally placed under the authority of the latter. Conquerors and conquered most commonly live in a perfect symbiosis; but on certain ritual occasions their antagonism over land matters came to the surface.[24]

Meyer Fortes came to similar conclusions in studying the Tallensi. The *namoo* represent 'an immigrant stock': they control the chiefship and exercise their authority over the whole population as far as policies are concerned. The *tendaana* represent the indigenous section of this people. They possess the chiefship of the earth and are vested with religious and mystical prerogatives as far as the indigenous clans are concerned.

For all these peoples, origins and migrations are related in a fashion which is analogous to the account described above in the *Nakomse* tales. For example, the traditions of the Dagomba drummers attribute the origin of the Mossi, Dagomba, Mamprussi, and Nanoumba kingdoms to the direct descendants of a certain Toha-Jie, the 'red hunter', of Mande origin, husband of the daughter of a Gurma chief.[25] These traditions also give the son of this same Toha-Jie and a woman who was the daughter of a 'custodian of the earth' as the ancestor of the Tallensi and the Nabdam (ibid.). These legends are in every way comparable to the ones which makes Ouidiraogo, son of Riale and Yennenga, the initial link in the Mossi dynasties. Everywhere we have this theme of a maternal grandson occurring in all the accounts referring to the monarchy.[26] The importance of the *yagēga* is therefore basic to our understanding of the origin and the meaning of the chiefship. The *yagēga* symbolizes the continuity of the line of the maternal kin, a line which has been interrupted by the birth of his mother. He is, in a way, seen as his mother's own brother. The fact that he is placed at the head of a royal lineage has a symbolic rather than a historical value. He symbolizes the fact that, despite the greatest risk a lineage may run (the birth of all females and no males), its continuance will be for ever assured. The *yagēga* is a symbol of the resurrection and the permanence of life. It is because of this that he

[24] R. S. Rattray, *The Tribes of the Ashanti Hinterland*, vol. I (Oxford, 1932), pp. xii ff.

[25] *Enquiry into the Constitution and Organisation of the Dagbon kingdom* (Accra), p. 42.

[26] On this subject it should be pointed out that from a sociological point of view this 'relative' is most often considered in reflection to his maternal uncle and in this case is called the uterine nephew. In fact his social role among the Mossi, as well as among the Bambara, is also applicable to the relationship between a grandson and a maternal grandfather.

plays a role in funeral rites. Associated with chiefship, he marks its indestructibility, its eternal nature, in a manner of speaking. On the other hand, however, the *yagēga*, because he is considered to be his mother's brother, has well-established rights in the home of his maternal grandfather. In fact he is the latter's legitimate heir. Normally he may demand anything he fancies from his maternal kin.

For all these reasons the *yagēga* is a perfect choice as head of a royal line. Through his agency the king becomes the *yagēga* of his subjects, of those people he is supposed to have conquered. And in this way the rights of the *Nakomse* to appropriate the wealth of their subjects is also explained. They cannot be accused of abusive behaviour or theft. It is a right obtained through this kind of relationship set up between maternal kin and consanguineal kin, by placing a daughter's son at the focal point of these two lines. The historians of the Mossi have failed to grasp this essential feature of their legends of origin and have arbitrarily opposed the group of 'conquerors' to the group of 'original inhabitants'.

Of course the 'invaders' and the 'indigenous people' do possess their own institutions which mean that the groups tend to confront each other as real antagonists. However, this state of affairs derives less from a genuine sense of opposition than from a ritual which is found in their common religion, a religion shared by both 'social cleavages'. They both claim to be part of an overall political and religious organization which functions as a single whole. The secular aspect of political chiefship has a no less religious significance than the chiefship of the 'children of the earth' (*Tēgābisi*); it is only one aspect of the totality of religious beliefs of the whole society. And while, on certain occasions (ritual segregation, the exchange of insults with *Tēgābisi* at burials, etc.), the 'chiefs' appear as enemies of those who call themselves the 'original inhabitants', this is not to stress a real historical fact but rather because their 'inimity' also plays its part in their religious dogmas. Social unity, a dominant feature of Mossi society, and so well brought out by Meyer Fortes for the Tallensi, is assured by these commonly held beliefs, in which the *Nakomse* adopt the character of the sun and the sky while the *Tēgābisi* assume characteristics associated with the nourishing earth. Together they consider themselves to form the unity of the world.

There are many signs that the chief and his descendants belong to the same category as the sun. At his installation ceremony the chief, who has just been invested with power, will begin a tour of his terrain after the sun's disc has touched the horizon. His journey, on horseback, carrying the heavy shrines of the chiefship on his shoulders—symbols of the burdens of the kingdom and the world—is interpreted as the 'progress' of the sun. The coming of day and light, and the accession to power of a chief, illustrate a single concept in Mossi thought. On his death, on the other hand, an inverse phenomenon is evoked. A special official of the palace, where the chief has just died, has the task of bringing out the fire and extinguishing it in front of the west door of the palace. Everyone then becomes aware that, like the embers which are ceasing to glow, and the setting sun, the chief has passed away.

As for the *Tēgābisi* their chthonian character is so obvious to anyone familiar with Mossi 'customs' that there is no need to dwell on them here. In general they all share a common taboo as regards the horse (they may not eat it and some may not even ride it), the *Nakomboga* mount par excellence, since it is a solar symbol. They all perform rites which only have to do with the earth, water, and grain. However, there is a degree of specialization found among them, apart from those already mentioned; some perform rites dealing with the earth, properly speaking, while others are only concerned with the wind and rain. Activities associated with hills and mountains (the mining of certain ritual stones and certain coloured earths, for example) are the prerogatives of the 'owners of the earth' from Gambo. Hollows and caves are controlled by the Nyonyosé of Ronga. Finally all rites concerning the earth's surface and agricultural work proper comes under the aegis of the *Tēgābisi* of Bougoure.

These facts allow us to make two important conclusions:

1. In Mossi society we have two categories of persons, or two major segments if we are to use a current sociological expression: the *Wēdrāse* and the *Tēgābisi*. The former comprise those normally called the Mossi, the latter are the Nyonyosé or Foulsé. These two social groups should not, it would appear, in the present state of Mossi studies, be opposed to each other as separate ethnic groups. We have, rather, two functional categories in one and the same society. Each of these segments has its own ruling class: the *nakomse* among the *wēdrāse* and the *tēgā soba namba* among the *tēgābisi*. Schematically this social structure can be represented by two pyramids joined at their bases, with the top, in each case, representing the chiefship of each social segment. At the same time these pyramids

also represent the sky, on one hand, and the earth, on the other (see figure). Associated with the sky, the *nakomse* are in possession of the chiefship with regard to the celestial principle; they are responsible for the smooth running of the kingdom, both in internal and external affairs, in the same way as the sun, which—according to them—was given by the Creator the role of assuring the perfect functioning of the world. Associated with earth, the *tẽgãbisi* are responsible for chiefship in its terrestrial aspects. They look after agricultural pursuits and everything which connects man with the earth.

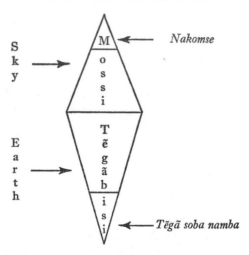

The relationship between the Mossi (or *wẽdrãse*) and the Foulsé (or *tẽgãbisi*) or, if one prefers it, the *nakomse* and the *tẽgã soba namba* is one which involves two cosmic elements essential to human life: the sun and the earth. They are not antagonistic but complementary. The complementary nature of the two social segments is reflected, basically, in the accounts of the origins of the *nakomse* and *tẽgãbisi*.

The former, in their movement of 'conquest', go from south to north like the sun in its course between the two solstices. In the same way their own particular festival, the *filiga*, takes place at the time of the winter solstice when the days are beginning to grow longer and when the sun is about to move from the south to the north. This festival coincides, moreover, with the beginning of the kingdom's new year. As for the *tẽgãbisi*, once they had emerged from the earth, they moved from east to west and from north to south, like rain clouds, and their own festival, the *bega*, assumes certain qualities of the wind as it brings water all over the land. This festival is the one which leads the soul of the grain, in a grandiose ceremony, from Womsom to Gamba, Bougouré, Gourcy, and Koudouba, one after the other.

2. The usual distinction between 'an administrative and political chiefship' and a 'mystical and spiritual chiefship' is too broad and certainly an inept concept if applied to Mossi society. A chief also enjoys religious and mystical prerogatives with regard to his subjects; a *tēgābiga*, for his part, has a political and administrative authority over the *tēgābisi* of the community under his jurisdiction. The inexactitude would be even more flagrant if we were to talk of the 'secular' power of the chiefs as opposed to the 'spiritual' power of the owners of the earth. Both these persons are chiefs; both possess regalia which suit their respective roles. Both wear the red cap of authority; but while the *nakomboga* has the right to a horse, since it represents the celestial aspect of his power, the *tēgābiga* has to be content with the axe (*litila*) which is used to open the earth and also to 'split' open the clouds, harbingers of water. The opposition here, therefore, is not between 'secular' and 'spiritual' but between 'sky' and 'earth', and it is, moreover, understood that each of these two elements is as sacred as the other.

The blacksmiths are found between these two social segments, an ambivalent element in Mossi society. In relation to each human grouping the blacksmith serves to provide a link between two segments. It was on purpose, therefore, that Ouemtanango, according to legend, dispersed these artisans throughout the kingdom. The presence of the blacksmith recalls the presence of the chief—of the fire and sun. Yet he is also a being of the earth, like those among whom he lives. He even comes first among the 'children of the earth' since without him there would be no food.

It would be interesting to study the social role of the blacksmith along these lines. It would become clear that, far from belonging to a caste whereby endogamy condemns him to exist, turned in on himself, in a manner of speaking, the blacksmith is the perfect mediatory. He ensures social exchanges between the two poles: the 'children of the sky' and the 'children of the earth'. The blacksmiths provide a neutral milieu, which is clearly brought out by the institution of the *buguba*, in which both the *nakomse* and *tēgābisi* are involved.

These three groups thus constitute a frame for Mossi social structure. Associated with this framework we have some customs involving *nakomse* chiefship and others involving the chiefship of the custodians of the earth. These three social segments provide

Moaga society with its unity. The Mossi prefer to present this unity in the simple and naïve form of a legend, which conveys the consciousness of profound social and religious truths.

There was once, says the legend, a man who had three sons. As he lay dying he called them to him and said: 'My children I am about to leave you, but before I go I want to give each of you your inheritance. Here are three sacks: each of you will find his share in one of them. Now choose.' Thereupon the eldest of the brothers ran up and picked the heaviest bag. In it he found all the tools of the forge; he became the ancestor of the blacksmiths. The second eldest then rushed to take up the bulkier of the two remaining sacks. In it he found a saddle and harness and a red cap; he became the ancestor of the kings. The youngest son eventually opened the bag left by his brothers; it was less bulky and lighter and in it he found an adze; he became the ancestor of the chiefs of the earth and the rain.

The father in this *solumde* (legend or fable), according to a commentator on this tale, is *wēde* (divinity) and all of those who live in the land of the *yadega* are descendants of his three children.

*

All the foregoing would warrant a good deal of scepticism as regards the historicity of accounts of Mossi origins. It is an indubitable fact that the Mossi in general, and the Yatenga Mossi in particular have not always lived in the same place; it is equally obvious that important movements of peoples have taken place in the Volta basin, just as in other parts of Black Africa. But how are we able to distinguish the indigenous peoples of Yatenga from later immigrant groups? Historically, and considering the present state of knowledge, such distinctions would seem impossible to make. The population, from a cultural and religious point of view, has in fact a high degree of homogeneity. Mossi culture is neither an improvised nor an artificial one; it is rather an aggregate of elements superimposed one on the other; it has all the features of an old-established situation, the unity of which has profoundly marked the society.

However, although we may give up the search for any historical elements in these tales of origin, we still have to explain the relationship which exists between Mossi society and the town of Gambagha, in modern Ghana. It will be recalled that during the royal funeral rite a wife and a horse belonging to the dead Mossi king used to be sent to Gambagha, where they were sacrificed on the tomb of Yennenga, the woman whom tradition credits with being the ancestress of both kingdoms. Do these close ties with the village of Gambagha prove that this was the original home, the point of departure, of the Mossi invaders? We do not think so.

In the first place, who is this Yennenga? According to traditions she is the daughter of a Dagomba king who lived at Gambagha. In fact it is more likely that this town was never located in Dagomba country, but that it was in Mamprussi country. Even if it were to be maintained that the Dagomba had occupied this region in ancient times, and founded Gambagha, it would be expected that they would still claim religious rights in the town today, even though it is in fact occupied by Mamprussi at the present time. This is a common feature of African cultures. In Yatenga, emissaries from the Dogon cliffs regularly, each year, visit spots which were formerly sites of Dogon cults, and perform sacrifices there.

However, it does not seem that the Dagomba have ever claimed similar rights in Gambagha. Their traditions do not even mention this village as one of their ancestral homes. Yennenga, therefore, was probably never the daughter of a Dagomba king living at Gambagha. Was she, then, the daughter of a Mamprussi king? We can find no proof of this. It would seem, therefore, a reasonable hypothesis (and much of the information collected in Mossi land supports this) that, given the legendary character of this woman, we are concerned less with a historic figure than with a personification of power (*nam*). As her son, Ouidiraogo, the Dagomba king's grandson, symbolizes the continuity of the kingdom and Yennenga is the symbol of power. In fact, in Mossi society, the king goes through a ceremony of marriage with his own kingdom during his investiture. He is considered to be the 'bride' marrying a 'husband'—that is his kingdom. The kingdom is represented by the queen-mother. And as the kingdom is the king's power, the queen-mother is the symbol of this power.

Moreover, the sending of a horse and a wife of the dead Mossi king to Gambagha may be explained from a different point of view than the historical one usually adopted. Gambagha, for the Mossi, is symbolically the home of the 'maternal kin' of the royal family. Since the king is the wife of his kingdom, on his death part of his personality is sent off to his 'kinsfolk', in exactly the same way as is regularly done at a woman's funeral. The sending of tribute therefore has no connection with historical facts concerning the origins of Mossi migrations from Gambagha to the north; it simply attests the fact that power (*nam*) was given once upon a time to an ancestor of the king of Ouagadougou by the authority of Gambagha. In this way the chiefship does not belong to the *nakomse* of Ouagadougou and Ouahigouya because of their genealogies which are traced back to the king of Gambagha; they obtained it because of a transfer of power. At a certain point in time, the chiefship of this town invested certain *nakomse* from the north with political power, which they afterwards transmitted to their successors. Therefore, it was not actual people, bearing the chiefship, who emigrated from Gambagha, but the chiefship itself in so far as it is a principle which confers on a dynasty authority over the others.

We should add that Gambagha does not maintain social relations solely with the *nakomse* whom they invested with this power, but also with the *tēgãbisi*. Each year, in fact, the latter receive the soul of millet from Gambagha. This soul is then diffused throughout the whole of Yatenga, thanks to a lengthy ritual which takes place over a period of several months. Yet nobody has ever claimed a Gambagha origin for the *tēgãbisi*.

The opinions we are giving here in no way detract from the reality of movements of people which may have occurred within the Mossi kingdoms. Our only aim is to shed a clearer light on the so-called 'Mossi migrations'. In each kingdom population movement certainly took place. Towns have disappeared and others have sprung up over the centuries. The capitals of the kingdoms have changed sites because of the chance whims of kings, according to political considera- tion and also, no doubt, for more profound reasons. There is no need, in fact, to consider these variations solely as the outcome of civil war, even if the historians of the Mossi people seem to give this impression. Above all we must be careful not to attribute a bellicose character to the establishment of Mossi chiefship over the other people who lived in the territory. *Nakomse* rule has spread, primarily from the interior, in exactly the same way as a culture or a religion diffuses.

Our present knowledge of the functioning of Mossi society is only a drop in the ocean; before the reign of Naba-Boul, king of Yatenga from 1894 to 1899, we have no data at all. Historians have taken oral traditions too literally; perceiving only a historicist meaning they have completely falsified the real aspect of *nakomse-tēgãbisi* society. At the present time it is proving difficult to go back into the historical past. Whenever one tries to get information on the traditions of chiefship among the Mossi many informants simply send the ethnographer back to the works of Tauxier and Dim Delobsom! These pioneers certainly performed a useful task; but they viewed the evolution and functioning of these societies through a prism of occidental logic.

This kind of historicism has lost sight of such things as the real relations which bind the Mossi kingdom of the south (Ouagadougou) with the kingdom of the north (Ouahigouya). Now people simply point out the 'historical' enmity of the two kings, an enmity which was transferred to the two kingdoms and attributed to the stealing of the Ouagadougou royal 'amulets' by Naba-Yadega's sister on behalf of her brother, the founder of the Yatenga kingdom. In fact this so-called enmity is merely a ritual activity between two twins, analogous to the *tẽgâbisi* and *nakomse* relationship. The two kingdoms are twins, one in the south, the other in the north. Their organization as a whole corresponds to a spatial organization based on the two major cardinal directions. Here again one represents the sky and the other the earth, and the distance which they keep between them reflects the same distance maintained between the sky and the earth in order to have a perfect cosmic functioning.

We know with what facility African societies even today derive religious and cultural values from one another. Has not Naba-Kango been accredited with the introduction to the Mossi court of a number of practices involving protocol which have been copied from the Bambara court? Spiritual values circulate among all these societies the more easily as in this part of Africa where the people's attitude to problems of the self and their relations with the cosmos seem to be much the same.

We may possibly never have the chance of determining the beginnings of Mossi history in any scientific fashion. The only sources which we have for this purpose are those which the people themselves are able to place at our disposal. For the Mossi, a sense of history does not consist in the mere valorization of events as a function of time, nor in their repercussions on social progress; it comes rather from religious and mystical ideas which control the behaviour of men in society.

2

Traditional Social Structure
and Economic Change

GEORGES BALANDIER[1]

In studies dealing with any aspect of the economic development of
a 'backward' country it has become almost the rule to make some
reference to traditional social structures. Nevertheless, by calling on
the sociologist in this way, an equivocal step has been taken; it con-
ceals a transfer of responsibility behind a recognition of the difficulties inherent in the diversity and relative inertia of social systems;
it allows us to ignore for a while the boundaries of classical economics
at a time when this discipline is attempting to make its field of application a more universal one. In this way the political challenge of so-
called under-developed countries in their claims for equality is
paralleled by a scientific challenge.

The proof of this is of such importance that it requires a revival of
initiative. We should at once ask ourselves what are the intellectual
tools of the sociologist and the anthropologist who refuse to despise
those 'subverted' societies? Our balance sheet is a poor one: scant
material results of studies aimed at examining the forces behind
social change and the form it takes, a few concepts and some frag-
mentary theoretical constructs; the latter are very vulnerable, the
former are lacking in diversity.

Nevertheless, these assets, despite their imperfections, should
not be neglected. We have here the initial elements of a dynamic

[1] *Georges Balandier* (b. 1920), Dr. es L., Sorbonne. Professor of Sociology at
Panthéon Sorbonne University (Paris I) since 1969, and formerly of African
Anthropology at the Sorbonne; Director of Studies, Ecole Pratique des Hautes
Etudes, Section VI, Social Sciences; Director of the African Research Centre,
Panthéon-Sorbonne University; Editor, *Cahiers internationaux de sociologie*. Field-
work in Senegal, Guinea, Gabon, Congo (Bra.) His doctoral thesis (*Sociologie
actuelle de l'Afrique noire*, 1956) was the first French work directly concerned with
the effects of colonisation on African societies; with major interests in general theory
and studies of modern social change he has strongly supported inter-disciplinary
research teams in African studies. The original French text of this paper was
published as 'Structures sociales traditionnelles et changement économiques',
Cahiers d'Etudes Africaines, I (1960), 1–14.

E

approach which can take into account those changes affecting traditional societies today. The incidence of the 'modern economy' is often studied in terms of rudimentary capitalism which first began under the impetus of the coastal trade and later developed through mining and other specialized industries. This theme occupies a central position in most recent published works. Monica Hunter, describing the contact situation in South Africa where colonialization was a 'blow which was primarily economic in nature', remarks: 'A society with a poorly developed economy, one which stresses group solidarity rather than individual strength, finds itself up against a highly developed society which is industrialized and has an economy based on individualism.'[1a] Max Gluckman, also dealing with South African examples (the Zulu), points out that modern social systems, which have come about as the result of a development over a period of a hundred years or so, have acquired a relative stability which is explained 'by the social cohesion imposed by new economic relationships'.[2] These two quotations have the advantage of portraying in a clear fashion the dual incidence of external economic forces which affect traditional societies: those destructive effects which lead to a breaking down of old structures, and positive effects which result in new structures and new modes of social integration.

The contribution would indeed be mediocre if a demonstration and affirmation of the role played by economic factors as a factor in social change were all we had to go on. However, before studying some examples in greater detail we should make some introductory remarks of more general signficance. Studies, which aim at examining and explaining social changes which bring about the modification of traditional societies, not only shed light on the development of these societies but also on their earlier structure and organization. During the 'trial' period which these societies undergo it is the relatively vulnerable social institutions which are revealed, that is those relatively fragile equilibria and social models which are so valorized that they continue to exist in spite of their inability to cope with the new situation; the relative importance attached to these different constituent elements can then be grasped with greater clarity and with less arbitrariness. In my analysis of the colonial situation I have been led to show how those crises undergone by colonial societies reveal issues which provide us with an insight into both phenomena of contact and domination, and into the earlier structures of the societies

---

[1a] Monica Hunter, *Reaction to Conquest* (London, 1936).
[2] Studies by M. Gluckman in *Bantu Studies* (1940), and *African Studies* (1942).

concerned: 'They provide an access to basic ensembles and interrelations.'[3] This is a point of view also followed by English anthropologists of the Manchester School. Gluckman has shown, on the basis of his experience in South and Central Africa, that modern developments are related to structural weaknesses in the traditional societies. More recently V. W. Turner, in the published results of his researches among the Ndembu of Zambia, defines his method as 'diachronic micro-sociology', and he devotes his energies to making a minute and fruitful study of modern 'social dramas' which are revelatory of the contradictions and conflicts implicit in traditional social systems.[4]

A dynamic approach would appear indispensable on other counts. It provides an insight into the heterogeneous nature of all societies which contain features derived from different times—a consequence of the historical process—and which co-exist in a more or less contradictory, more or less effective manner. H. Lefebvre, tracing the 'perspectives of rural sociology' has clearly brought out the 'dual complexity' of peasant society; a duality involving a 'horizontal complexity' found in those structures which have the 'same historical date' and which 'reveal basic differences extending to an antagonism'; and a 'vertical complexity' which involves the 'co-existence of formations of different ages and dates'. These two levels of complexity 'interrelate, overlap and react on each other'; they create 'an interweaving of factual data which only the best methodology can untangle'.[5] J.-P. Sartre has recently discussed this analysis and expressed his agreement with the methods involved—methods which, according to him, are valid 'in all fields of anthropology'.[6] By recognizing this multiple complexity, dynamic studies of traditional societies 'in transition' will be able to correct the simplified picture of those social structures which have too often been considered from the viewpoint of their 'purity' or their 'primitivity'.

On the other hand, the study of social structures in a context of swift and multiple change, reveals—through a kind of enlargement effect—the 'approximative' nature of their role in the total society. It reveals contradictions existing between the different principles of structure and organization, as well as the gaps which are found between an 'official' aspect of society and actual social practice. In fact

---

[3] G. Balandier, *Sociologie actuelle de l'Afrique Noire* (Paris, 1955), pp. 35–36.
[4] V. W. Turner. *Schism and Continuity in an African Society* (Manchester, 1957).
[5] H. Lefebvre, 'Perspectives de la Sociologie Rurale', *Cahiers Internationaux de Sociologie*, xiv (Paris, 1953).
[6] J.-P. Sartre, 'Questions de méthode', *Les Temps Modernes*, 139 (Paris, 1957).

124 Georges Balandier

it is through this kind of conjuncture that we can catch a glimpse of incompatibilities and discordances, conflicting interests, and the kinds of strategies to which both groups and individuals have recourse. In this way we are safeguarded against any inclination to over-emphasize the static aspects of society and the (implicit) affirmation of the quasi-perfection of traditional societies envisaged as systems.

In an article dealing with anthropological methods F. Boas remarked: 'It is not sufficient to know how things are; we must also know how they came to be as they are.'[7] This approach is incomplete, however, it should also include those dialectical movements which take into account processes making things stay 'the way they are', at least temporarily, and unveiling forces which impose new kinds of structuring.

Finally, researches devoted to under-developed countries which are being disturbed by the introduction of modern productive techniques and modern forms of economies are concerned with a 'moment' in their development which might be said to differentiate, in an essential way, various types of global societies. In the one case (the systems we call traditional), individuals find themselves in direct relationships; they have a concept of relations in which the products of human activities do not intervene decisively. They are part of a network of social relations which are organized on a small scale, and the pattern repeats itself from the smallest unit up to the most comprehensive one. In the other case (our so-called modern systems) the product of collective activity determines those relational networks which now obey new models: tensions arise because of the mode of production and the distribution of goods; differentiation replaces repetition; social relationships are expressed on a different scale (a widening of the field of action) and change their nature (multiple links now mean that individuals no longer communicate in any exclusively direct way). These are the aspects I have stressed in my researches in Equatorial Africa[8] and which G. and M. Wilson also touched on in their essay on social change.[9]

This introduction seemed to me necessary if we were to understand how contemporary sociology, preoccupied with social dynamics, provides anthropology, in its study of traditional societies on the move, with improved techniques. Above all, however, we must

[7] F. Boas, 'The Method of Ethnology', *American Anthropologist*, vol. 22 (1920).
[8] G. Balandier, *Sociologie actuelle de l'Afrique Noire*, 'Conclusion' (Paris, 1955).
[9] G. and M. Wilson, *The Analysis of Social Change* (Cambridge, 1945).

demonstrate its usefulness in solving problems posed for economic
theory by the consideration of structures, modes of behaviour, and
processes which have been outside its field of study until recently.

II

The confrontation between traditional social structures and a
modern economy (or, rather, for a long period a special kind of
capitalism) has consequences which are revealed at very different
levels of generality and complexity. The most common observations
deal with the rapid decline of those economies we call subsistence
economies: they are expressed in global schemas similar to those
presented by G. and M. Wilson and based on researches carried out
in Central Africa. A necessarily simplified representation of this
total view can be presented in the following diagram:

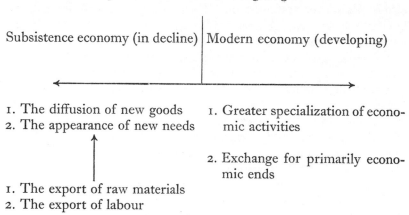

Subsistence economy (in decline) | Modern economy (developing)

1. The diffusion of new goods
2. The appearance of new needs

1. The export of raw materials
2. The export of labour

1. Greater specialization of economic activities

2. Exchange for primarily economic ends

---

1. Regional discrepancies in development and population changes
2. A widening of the field of social and economic relations
3. New social differentiation, accompanied by affirmation of the
   'inequality' and the upsetting of the former systems of pre-
   eminence.

Here, of course, we are only dealing with a referential framework
which reveals the most obvious processes of development. But, as
such, it is not without its use and means, moreover, that we are not
induced to neglect the differential incidences of a modern economy
(as evidenced in the very field of observation) nor the heterogeneous

character of the economies and societies that are studied by experts today.

Within the more exclusively sociological framework of such an approach we may grasp another series of consequences. Among these is the example described by Monica Hunter for the Pondo of South Africa; at the level of kinship structure—a decline in the extended family (*umzi*) and a decline in the effective nature of kinship and affinal networks; at the level of the system of social status and types of authority—new economic relations tend to determine, in an exclusive fashion, the respective roles of groups and individuals and to generalize competition for power; at the level of institutions which ensure co-operation and security—economic insecurity, depending on market fluctuations, and, more broadly, social instability (resulting from multiple and concomitant transformations) lead to a search for kinds of protection which are more or less illusory and also result in protest movements. These are the kinds of elements, all having a sufficiently general character, which fit within the boundaries of the schema we have just set up.

However, even in its more complex form this schema can only serve as a rough guide; it can hardly take into account the diversity of actual cases and situations. Complementary contributions can be found scattered through the pages of studies which not only offer factual data but also provide the first results of attempts to set up theories. Here it is to be noted that certain 'models' are still determining social relations without playing any part in the new economic and political situation: structures are transformed at a faster rate than systems or institutions which 'officially' organize their interrelationships. This gap becomes even more serious if the forces of change come from the outside and also if modern institutions are imposed to the detriment of the old order. This is why the so-called dependent or colonial situation delays the moment of total restructuring and effective reorganization. Because of such delaying actions, it will be understood how the passage from one socio-economic system to another is achieved without (as in the natural order) any brutal or global change; we can also see, with greater clarity, the heterogeneous and approximative character of economies and societies considered as systems. The periods in which this character is brought out to maximum effect—as in Africa south of the Sahara today—include those which offer the greatest possibility of manoeuvrability in dealings between individuals and groups. Confusions inherent in transitional stages have a cumulative aspect. The works of

Gluckman and Turner to which we referred show that the situation engendered by colonization has exaggerated the structural weakness of the colonized societies, upset their equilibrium, and released antagonisms which had remained, until then, suppressed. This is one of the manifestations of the phenomenon we have just mentioned.

The complexity of the interplay of antagonisms, taking advantage of multiple strategies, should not hide more general contradictions. Those societies which are being studied in Africa today rely on two principles of structure and organization which are contradictory: on the one hand we have wide relationships of kinship—'blood ties' and affinity, plus a mythical justification for the correctness of social relationships; on the other we have differentiation and competition resulting from their participation in the market economy, 'economic nationalism' and self-interest which is becoming more and more imperative both for individuals and groups. These changes mean that the African is now involved in a social universe which is more heterogeneous and more unstable; and it is also more *abstract* than that world which, until recently, was regulated by tradition.

It is by reference to this kind of contextual situation that we should consider the problem of 'economic individualism', a new situation which has been tackled by certain Africanist anthropologists. Lucy Mair, considering the Ganda of East Africa, stated that it was hardly a satisfactory answer to contrast (traditional) 'collectivism' and (modern) 'individualism'; this would involve an adherence to a distinction which is too stark and unjustifiable.[10] Nevertheless while the formula has only a conditional utility it does express one of the tendencies of social change. Within the limits of Ganda traditional society, factors of economic activity could be analysed under two aspects: (*a*) the low volume and lack of diversity of the goods produced, the small amount of durable goods (domestic slaves, herds of cattle, land), the low level of needs: (*b*) on the other hand relative wealth depended on the possession of power (automatically in the hands of a restricted aristocratic class) and was balanced by the functions inherent in the possession of power as well as obligations to be generous: generosity being the condition of lasting prestige. Modern conditions are radically different: (*a*) goods are now numerous and diversified; they are desired because they are convenient and because of a 'valorization' which endows their owners with a prestige formerly only derived from generous actions; (*b*) internal competition

[10] L. Mair, *The Growth of Economic Individualism in African Society* (1934); text taken from *Studies in Applied Anthropology* (London, 1957), pp. 23 ff.

for goods has begun and is becoming general, to such an extent that the economic interest of individuals has come to override customary obligations, to the detriment of former solidarities; economic initiative primarily directed to economic ends and wealth no longer involves a compensatory social responsibility. The expansion of cotton cultivation has accelerated this movement and superimposed on the old-style peasantry a class of small landowners, and one of great landlords, some of them absentees in control of multiple enterprises.[11] The basic difficulties of analysis, plus the impossibility of utilizing exclusively concepts of economic individualism and social class in interpreting the new situations, derive from the fact that the two systems (or, rather, some of their features) co-exist in a closely intermeshed fashion at the moment of description.

An additional factor emerges. The effect of modern economics on traditional social structures cannot be considered solely from an internal point of view; the effect of the domination exercised by external centres of economic power, the relationship set up between neighbouring societies, both play a decisive role. The Ganda situation provides a useful example. It shows the effects of a colonial economy: on the system of land tenure (with the development of land rent); on the orientation and levels of economic development; on the social structure and inter-tribal or inter-racial relations, etc. But it also reveals to what extent the type of relationship which existed between less developed neighbouring peoples has been perpetuated. Inequality exists and works to the advantage of the Ganda; it means that they are provided with wage-labourers who were not available on the spot and as a result, according to Lucy Mair, they 'consider themselves as an employer class, as in earlier times they confined themselves to specialised crafts and government'.[12] It appears, therefore, that the relationship between societies of unequal development —even when the differential disparity is reduced—soon results in a situation which is more favourable to the group which is in a better position.

III

Our remarks up to now have remained general. They do not take fully into account the complexity of inter-relationships, the very

[11] B. Mukwaya, *Land Tenure in Buganda* (Kampala, 1953). References are found in the Marxist analysis of R. Mukherjee, *The Problem of Uganda, a Study in Acculturation* (Berlin, 1956).

[12] L. Mair, *An African People in the Twentieth Century* (London, 1934).

marked heterogeneity of socio-economic systems observed in a period of transition and of the ambiguity of developments which are being studied long before they have worked themselves out. For this reason we shall consider a single case and look at one or two enlightening aspects. The people concerned are the Bakongo, a people who live on both sides of the Congo River, in the neighbourhood of Brazzaville and Leopoldville [Kinshasa] and extend south into Angola where the old capital of the tribe was situated. It is a society with matrilineal lineages, a certain degree of centralization of power, a unitary historical tradition and a long record (from the sixteenth to seventeenth centuries) of relatively close social interrelations.[13]

The major system of relations, which is to be found right at the core of Kongo society and culture, is that which involves clan land, lineages, and the ancestors; they constitute a system of relationship intense in nature and highly esteemed, which is articulated into a wider pattern through alliances deriving from matrimonial exchanges. It is through reference to this system that economic relations and various other social interactions are organized and become involved with each other. A very schematic diagram brings this out clearly:

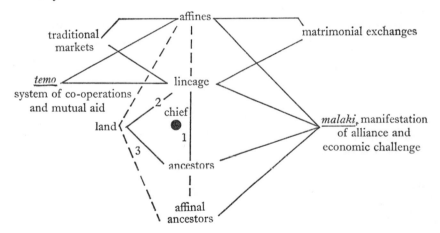

This kind of arrangement suggests the difficulties experienced when we try to grasp the phenomena involved in a complete fashion, and one which is fully significant in the terms of any one discipline; in this case there is no way of dividing up the problems scientifically.

[13] See relevant chapters on the Bakongo in my *Sociologie actuelle de l'Afrique Noire.*

Nevertheless certain present-day problems are revealed quite clearly in this way.

For example, we can begin to understand the gravity of the issues at stake in the conflict between 'maternal' and 'paternal' rights, a conflict which has resulted from colonization and recent developments. These are those central relations, numbered 1, 2, and 3, which would be cut off if the conflict were settled in favour of the 'paternal' side; the traditional system would then be injured at its very roots. We can also see, more clearly, how chiefs and important men such as lineage heads have 'modern' economic motives when they defend the traditional order; they use the attachment of villagers to the traditional order to their own advantage. The control of extensive land, the authority exercised over the men of the lineage who live on these lands, as well as over their former 'slaves' who still dwell there, the income received from strangers (people outside the clan) who have only rights to residence and usufruct: all these are elements which, owing to the new economic conditions, suffice to transform former notables into 'landowning aristocrats'.

However, let us first of all look at a single example of an aspect which clearly brings out this linkage between social and economic factors: let us consider those changes which affect the capitalization of wealth and the use to which savings are put. Traditional procedures of accumulation were all directed at the *eventual* control of more women, slaves, or dependents, and by so doing to gain *prestige* and *authority*, through the extension of spheres of influence. This kind of wealth brought but few material advantages to important men; satiety was quickly achieved, and between slave and lineage head differences in standard of living were not striking. In fact lineage heads were deemed to be caretakers of wealth of a collective nature, wealth which had been acquired by communal efforts. It was used for specific purposes: making 'sacred investments' which assured the health and fertility of the group (periodic ceremonies in honour of the ancestors, expensive tombs, etc.); in policies involving the group's alliances and prestige; in ensuring material security to all through the existence of a kind of rudimentary 'social security' which was the responsibility of those who were both rich and dependable. The influence of these men derived from the sucess they achieved in meeting these different obligations.

Profound changes have taken place over the past fifty years or so. It is becoming less and less easy to conform to traditional methods of capitalization. The disappearance of domestic slavery and female emancipation movements have limited the opportunities available for capitalizing in 'wives'. The first cause, associated with the opportunities for economic emancipation open to every individual, also reduces the number of dependents likely to attach themselves to some important man; the frequent fissions which occur within the lineages provide evidence of this. Finally, it becomes difficult to accumulate new areas of land: the system still involves restrictions on the alienation of land and land disputes consequently multiply. Nevertheless the new expressions of accumulated wealth and the uses to which it is put became evident only slowly for reasons connected with the level of development of Bakongo economy and a general social inertia. Part of an individual's savings are used in the construction of permanent buildings (which often have little more than a 'display' function), the acquisition of furniture and manufactured objects which constitute the 'treasure' of an important man; another part forms the monetary reserves of the lineage and is used to pay expenses collectively incurred or mutual help obligations. The most modern of the uses to which savings are put is the organization of 'economic units' which more or less coincide with the extended family and which integrate multiple activities sometimes assuming a half-urban, half-rural character. This system associates together both individual capitalization and collective capitalization: the stress is still on the latter and all durable goods remain the property of the lineage segment concerned.

The existence of types of behaviour associated with two basically different economies is brought out very clearly in the two kinds of strategy between which an individual with capital savings must make a choice. He may seek genuine 'economic investments' and go after personal profit and advantages: this 'entrepreneurial' mentality cuts him off from the social milieu into which he was born; for this reason there are not many examples and those that do occur are to be found primarily in urban centres and their neighbourhood. On the other hand he may opt for 'sociological investments', taking advantage of the new economic situation to achieve—or reinforce—a pre-eminence of the traditional type; here the number of his 'clients' and the extent of his generosity will be proof of his success; his profits will be expressed in terms of prestige and authority. This is the choice which is most frequently made: economic strategy is still only a means to an end determined by the older social and cultural system.[14]

[14] Incidental remarks of the same nature are made by Turner, op. cit., concerning the Ndembu.

An institution like the one known as *malaki* reveals the ambiguous nature of the situation. It has initially the character of an annual (dry season) celebration which served to exalt the unity of the lineage, honour the ancestors, and reinforce affinal ties.[15] On these occasions many goods which had been accumulated during the course of the year were consumed collectively in a real atmosphere of pleasure and display. The savings of the lineage heads were a means of 'renewing' kinship and affinal relationships. The *malaki*, owing to its periodicity and the amount of wealth involved, was one of the most important driving forces and regulating features of Bakongo economy—an economy which contributed very little to an individual's profit or even to that of a 'class'; it was primarily aimed at reinforcing the lineage and its affinal connections.

The institution also served to regulate the succession of an important man, the transfer of his goods and his statutory offices. The new lineage head was publicly proclaimed in the presence of other lineage members, affines and friends from outside the lineage group. The *malaki* clearly was associated with some of the procedures which assured the distribution of power. It will easily be understood that it has come to be manipulated by those who have acquired wealth and wish to use their riches to obtain prestige and authority.

Finally, in its traditional role, the *malaki* provided a kind of 'backdrop' to economic relations. All kinds of goods and partners were more or less directly involved in a system of multiple and ambivalent manifestations: co-operation and affinity did not exclude prestige rivalry and challenge. We might express these different aspects by a rather ugly neologism—*econodrama*. This 'game' gives people the opportunity of widening their network of alliances and co-operation, by circulating their wealth and not only their women. It is an example of a moment in economic development (the kind of moment which is difficult to date) when the surplus of produced goods presents men with a new problem: these goods are interposed in the system of personal relations and deform it. This aspect becomes more obvious as the total wealth of the Bakongo country increases.

If we look at the institution in its modern form we find that it has partly assumed the aspect of a speculative gamble. In fact it involves a monetary contribution (*fundu*) which gives rise to a veritable system of accounting. The contribution, from year to year, is doubled in a cycle of gifts and counter-gifts between groups involved in the *malaki*. The sums involved therefore increase with considerable

---

[15] Cf. *Sociologie actuelle de l'Afrique Noire*, pp. 347–52.

rapidity and the partner who falls into difficulties—that is, a man who is only able to reply with a gift which is equal to the last sum received—is the loser as far as economics and prestige are concerned. This system permits individuals with economic power to convert it into power of a traditional kind: this is how former domestic slaves have been able to acquire their 'freedom' (the status of being a free man through purchase), wealth, and then authority—one after the other.

Here we can see that the uses to which savings are put are still mainly determined by old values and social models. The *malaki* is found at the centre of a complex field of relations (social, economic, political, and cultural) which involves men, their material goods, and their values. The diagram below will help to make this clear:

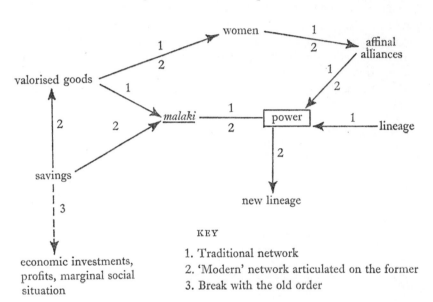

KEY

1. Traditional network
2. 'Modern' network articulated on the former
3. Break with the old order

STRATEGY OF THE USE OF WEALTH

These remarks do not pretend to form a complete inventory of the problems which modern economy imposes upon Bakongo society, but they do provide an illustration of these. They show the complexity of inter-relations and those contradictions which are born or reinforced during the course of a process of economic development and modernization. They suggest the power of inertia contained in some models of social relations and behaviour (the genuine frame-work of the traditional system) and also the plasticity of institutions which are formally maintained, but whose functions and constituent parts undergo change. The *malaki* is an example of this type of institution; the *temo*, which we have only mentioned in passing in this essay, has a greater use as a model; initially it played a pacifying role by substituting exchange and cooperation for conflict; then it inspired the new organization of mutual aid groups, firstly, for work parties, and secondly, for savings groups; finally, it has today begun to direct native initiative towards the creation of co-operatives.

We should emphasize again the extent to which the facts mentioned here bring out clearly—because recent developments have accentuated it—the heterogeneous character of social systems and the economies which support them. They also show how certain processes of change have a revelatory role *vis-à-vis* those structures and organizations which occupy a central position in the traditional disposition of society. Thus a dynamic approach and a structural analysis may become allies; synchronic researches and historical studies may be found side by side in a process modelled on the very processes of societies and economies.[16]

[16] Part of this study was presented at Brussels during the founding session of the 'Association of French-speaking Sociologists'. These are the first results of a study which has been made possible thanks to financial support from the Ford Foundation.

The Study of Marriage
and Urban Research

PAUL MERCIER[1]

In organizing all field research two kinds of approach are basically involved and these are closely connected. Firstly the framework and the general conditions of the inquiry should be settled. It might be said that this kind of organization is carried out on three levels, which are, schematically: (*a*) the fixing of the boundaries of the field of inquiry, or in other words, defining (which cannot amount to perfect precision) the subject under study;[1a] (*b*) the determining of a common orientation to bind together the multiple aspects of the inquiry—this is the level involving research methods in the strict sense of the term; (*c*) the choice, adaptation, and if the case arises, the constructing of the means and instruments of research—this is the level of research techniques. These are three indissociable aspects subordinate to each other, in the order we have presented them of one combined approach. If this is incomplete a precise estimate of the value of the research will be rendered difficult, if not impossible.[2]

Nevertheless, within a given framework—however well defined it may be—no inquiry can ever be made which will be exhaustive. We should therefore also try to determine what we may call the 'economics' of the inquiry; this will correspond—in the stages of

[1] *Paul Mercier* (b. 1922), Dr. es L., Sorbonne. Professor of Anthropology, René Descartes University, Sorbonne (Paris V) since 1970. A fellow-student and close colleague of G. Balandier. Extensive periods of field research in Senegal and Dahomey. Main interests in social change, urbanization, and modernization, also in general problems of theory and method in the Social Sciences. The original French text of this paper was published as 'Etude du mariage et enquête urbaine', *Cahiers d'Etudes Africaines*, I, 1 (1960), 28–43.

[1a] We never meet with a closed ensemble and one is therefore never able to achieve an exhaustive characterization of a social reality in its totality.

[2] Some authors should be reproached for having neglected a description of their techniques in favour of an account of their methods when presenting their research orientation: or vice versa, which is more frequently the case; V. G. Pons, N. Xydias, and P. Clément, 'Effets sociaux de l'urbanisation à Stanleyville' in: *Aspects sociaux de l'industrialisation et de l'urbanisation en Afrique au Sud du Sahara* (UNESCO, Paris, 1956), pp. 253–542.

organization and realization—to the progressive delimitation of a minimal research programme.[3] We shall only mention two aspects of the efforts required here. One involves the necessity of rendering studies bearing on the same subject, but carried out in different places,[4] more amenable to comparison.[5] A second concerns the determination of the more favourable approaches to a given social reality. By this we mean those phenomena or institutions which are relatively easily defined and the study of which enables one to deal with the largest possible number of aspects of that social reality, a study which constitutes the fullest possible series of landmarks of the processes of social change, etc. It is to this last problem that I wish to direct the brief remarks which follow, remarks dealing with researches carried out in an urban environment.[6]

Touching this field of research a general problem arises: what are the requirements to be met by this kind of study if it is to contribute to determining the rhythm and the direction of social change as manifested in cities and at the same time to the comparison of concrete urban situations? At this stage, if we wish to be precise, we must begin with the concept of urbanization. A multitude of definitions have been proposed.[7] Discussion is still continuing and it is not our concern here to open the subject afresh. In so far as our prime intention is to recall certain more general methodological problems which arise at this level, it will suffice if we mention some of the more essential aspects which concern the process of urbanization: the more schematic types of definition suffice to express these in a quite satisfactory manner.

Settling in a city, even for a temporary period, involves a person in an immediate, and to a certain extent, total incorporation in a new situation; this situation is characterized by—economic relationships and motivations for action which are radically different from those prevailing in rural areas; by different methods of social grouping and hierarchies; by different links to space, etc. In its most general form, the concept of urbanization denotes the development of modes of

[3] This is carried out—according to its own particular perspective—on two of the levels mentioned above: that of techniques, and that of method.
[4] And in more or less contrasted global contexts.
[5] Such an identity can never be more than an approximation.
[6] This cannot be entirely divorced from a preceding problem which will be approached secondarily.
[7] This diversity appears, either implicitly or explicitly, in the series of texts in the collection: *Aspects sociaux de l'industrialisation et l'urbanisation en Afrique au Sud du Sahara* (UNESCO, Paris, 1956).

behaviour, norms, structures, and social relations corresponding (which does not necessarily mean adapted to) the new global situation. They may be defined by themselves, or they may also be defined in contradistinction to types of behaviour, norms, structures, which characterize the 'traditional' environment which the town-dwellers have left (for, in the majority of cases to be studied today, townsmen of the first generation predominate). Traditional institutions are far from having lost all effectiveness in towns; the problems relative to an urban population should therefore be posed in terms of ambivalence. It is only in order to simplify things that they can be expressed in terms of divergences or time-lag; divergences between new social forms and the situations to which they are supposed to correspond; divergences between the traditional social institutions as they appear and operate in cities and as they did in the milieu which gave them their fullest meaning; and finally divergences at certain privileged, institutional levels, between new social forms and corresponding traditional ones.

A basic problem of method involves therefore devising tools of research and systematically applying them; in view of a comparative study, for example, they will permit an estimate of the stages of development and the amplitude of the divergences. Two types of approach may be pursued in order to achieve this. The first consists of discovering simple criteria, limited in number, which will enable us, through their combination, to define indices oriented towards the comparison of urban situations—usually in the form of indices of stabilization; in any case it requires the setting up for a given town of a schema which will indicate the general outline of its own special situation (taking into account, in particular, any internal differentiation in the population comprising it).[8] However, when it is a question of evaluating the degree of modification in behaviour imposed by the urban milieu, the extent of the urban involvement of different categories of townspeople, the degree of stabilization and adaptation to urban life, indices established from numerical data and susceptible of a simple expression[9] run the risk of proving themselves unequal to the task. We soon reach limits beyond which the criteria adopted

[8] Too often the indices proposed tacitly aim at a general application, when they are really only valid for a certain type of town, at a certain stage of its development. A preliminary study should include the setting up of a typology, if only a rudimentary one, of urban centres.

[9] Cf., for example: J. C. Mitchell, 'Urbanisation, détribalisation et stabilisation en Afrique méridionale: comment les définir et les mesurer', in *Aspects sociaux de l'industrialisation* . . . (UNESCO, Paris, 1956), pp. 741–61.

become too general in nature to be fully significant. It is always possible to work out more complex indices. But this can also lead to a dead end: their handling becomes more and more difficult and even their construction poses delicate methodological problems, particularly as regards the adequacy and the homogeneity of the criteria employed. For this reason a second mode of approach seems to offer greater possibilities. Since it is not limited to quantitative forms of expression it allows the implementation of research methods which are much more flexible. This method consists in the systematic examination of phenomena or key-institutions which will allow through their multiple adjustments, the evaluation of urban situations in their widest possible aspects. They are favourable jumping-off points for approaching the social reality in the sense indicated above. Marriage—which has already been shown by certain of the simple stabilization indices to be a basic element—is an example of such a key-institution; its instrumental utilization in this field may reveal itself of great value.

In order that tools of this kind can be put to a valid use they should correspond to two main imperatives. In the first place they should be registered in a dual perspective. At this point we should stress and amplify some of the remarks made previously: it is essential to define each urban situation as a function of the relative importance given to processes of disorganization and reorganization, both of which take place simultaneously and are interwoven in a complex fashion. This has been clearly recognized by now in the more important studies which have been published in recent years.[10] We can in fact distinguish two major phases in the progress of research devoted to African towns. At first there was the strong impression made by the rapid pace and extent of social and cultural changes taking place in towns and above all by those manifestations of rupture with the traditional environment which were involved in the move to an urban environment. Moreover, in the first phase of these studies there was an emphasis on the social and cultural 'cost' of urbanization—to use an expression employed later by various students and in the wider context of development. Aspects of disorganization and disintegration of value systems associated with them were stressed. Thus, in the beginning, a concept such as that of detribalization emphasized less the divergences between traditional and modern institutions, than the inadaptability of the older institutions, and above all the

---

[10] See, for example, the work of G. Balandier in the French sphere and the British research group at the Rhodes–Livingstone Institute.

cultural void in which the new townsmen found themselves. However, a new phase of research began in the fifties in which students have been concerned to stress the existence of a dual process of socio-cultural change, which I touched on above. They have found it necessary to point out that the destruction of traditional structures was not always so radical as one had at first imagined; and that they presented, in a more or less schematic way and in forms which were of varying effectiveness numerous possibilities of refuge, defence, and semi-adaptation for the urbanised masses.[11] Through this approach, a richer and more comprehensive one, the intensive study of key-institutions will assume its true value as an instrument of inquiry. It will suffice merely to mention briefly here our second imperative. Our tools should enable us to locate the greatest possible number of levels of social reality (morphology, group structures, inter-group relations, forms of hierarchization, values, etc.). This requires us to limit our studies to a small number of basic institutions.

II

Marriage has already been mentioned as one of the key-institutions on which there should be concentration. The ensuing remarks are merely intended to emphasize the importance which an intensive research devoted to urban marriage might reveal. A summary presentation of the results of one inquiry will give us the opportunity of suggesting how far such studies may contribute to a general attempt to interpret and compare urban situations.

In researches devoted to traditional social structures and organization it is hardly necessary to mention the fact that the study of marriage forms and the significance of matrimonial alliances are one of the basic preoccupations of social anthropology in Africa. In the process of field-work it is an essential guide-line in the analysis of group structures, the definition of inter-relations, the delimitation of global societies, etc. An exhaustive description of concrete matrimonial networks provides an approach to most of the aspects of the social organization of a given society. This is a question of basic method. However, in recent years a certain number of important works have shown that the study of contemporary social change can also be

[11] See, for example, K. A. Busia, *Report on a Social Survey of Sekondi-Takoradi* (London, 1950).

approached fruitfully through the perspective of matrimonial data.[12] In societies whose organization depends on a few relatively simple themes—this is the case, for example, for most societies which lack state-type political organization—it is one of the surest indices, and of the widest significance, to be kept in mind in any evaluation of present disequilibrium or orientations involving change. Within such a framework, researches dealing with marriage are primarily devoted to the following problems: analysis of modifications arising in relationships and tensions between the sexes; the study of new types of competition for women and their monopolization; analysis of changes in the economic significance of marriage; examination of any rupture in group equilibrium as a function of changes modifying the rhythms and circuits of matrimonial circulation. Some of these approaches may be of the utmost value in studying the phenomenon of urbanization.

However, since we are not able to discuss them as a whole here, we shall restrict ourselves to emphasizing the range of the use of tools provided by data relative to marriage in the interpretation and comparison of urban situations. The fields of inquiry which may provide meaningful points of reference are numerous and we shall mention only some of them:

(*a*) *Relations between town and country*. These may be clarified by a study of the matrimonial situation of temporary town-dwellers; of polygynous households split between town and country; of the frequency with, and the conditions in which permanent townsmen choose a wife from their own region; of the role played by country relatives in the marriage of permanent inhabitants of the towns.

(*b*) *The cohesion and vitality of extended kinship groups:* particularly lineages; they can be precisely evaluated by studying the degree of individualization in the choice of a wife; the circumstances of family participation in marriage expenses; the constitution and distribution of marriage payments; the levels and spheres of parental authority etc.

(*c*) *The new forms of social stratification:* variations in celibacy rates, polygyny rates, and the importance given to the personal choice of spouse, are some of the basic and revealing facts playing a part in the differentiation of behaviour found in strata of urban populations which constitute—at least in some cases—embryonic social classes.

---

[12] The importance of this approach has been emphasized in some remarks made by I. Schapera in *Married Life in an African Tribe* (London, 1939).

(d) *The complexity and ambiguity of economic motivations:* here we are essentially dealing with the role played by a concern for balancing the amounts of bridewealth payments in relation to attempts to improve one's living standards, changing one's way of life, etc.

(e) *The opening of social groups* which in the traditional situation were more or less completely closed; that is those castes and ethnic groups in which a more or less strict rule of endogamy was one of the main characteristics.

These pointers for research were among the most important which were covered in a series of inquiries carried out between 1953 and 1955 in the major Senegalese cities.[13] The brief indications included under each heading are sufficient to indicate how far a systematic study of marriage would lead to a total coverage—and how far, in each case, favourable approaches could be made to basic processes of social change taking place in an urban environment.

III

In our field researches certain orientations in the study of marriage were given particular emphasis since they provided more numerous and more efficient data. The more basic of these themes are the following: the difficulty of finding an appropriate spouse in a city (because of the sex ratio, the economic situation, etc.); the circumstances and place of choosing a spouse (from a wider perspective than the one mentioned above, since the problem of town–country relations is only one aspect of this problem); the function and degree of participation of kin groups and their representatives in the project; the conclusion and sanctioning of the marriage; the character of conjugal life and the demands made on each spouse by his or her partner; the changes in the institution of bridewealth; the changes in the structure of the restricted family, monogamous or polygynous; changes affecting endogamy, exogamy, and prohibitions involved in traditional marriage. Some of the data collected during our inquiries concerning the two last-mentioned orientations for study will be presented summarily here.[14]

1. All of the cities studied in Senegal (and almost all modern African towns) are characterized by the ethnic diversity of their

[13] These inquiries were organized by the *Section de Sociologie de l'Institut Français d'Afrique Noire* in Dakar, Thiès, and Saint-Louis in Senegal.

[14] One of these specifically introduces a theme of research mentioned above; while the other approaches several of them at one and the same time.

populations, a diversity which is more or less pronounced according to each case.[15] The mingling of tribal groups in an urban centre, whether they are settled in separate quarters or not, vary considerably; certain groups remain very closed, others are prone to mixing with outsiders. The cultural inter-penetration of elements of different origins living in a town environment proceeds more or less swiftly— depending on numerical ratios, the divergences between the different cultures, cleavages of a religious nature, etc. City life wipes out traditional enmities (and at the same time generates new kinds of differentiation and internal oppositions). The processes of cultural unification, of gradual reduction of intertribal conflicts should be studied from several points of view (for example: the composition of new kinds of associations, labour relations, character of leadership, etc.). The examination of just one aspect—the frequency of intertribal marriages—enables us to present indices which are both precise and of general significance, and which can be expressed in a relatively simple manner.

Some of the data collected at Dakar and Thiès[16] can be presented here to indicate this method. In Dakar (the most ethnically mixed of the two) 29 per cent of monogamous males were married to women from a different tribe; in Thiès the figure was 23 per cent (data for polygynists were collected from such a small sample that they are of little significance). Tribal endogamy does not exist in theory, but it can become a tradition which is respected more in those ethnic groups which have, for various reasons, become more particularist. It may also apply to more recent arrivals in the town, or those who are the least Westernized. The global facts should therefore be analysed further; once more we meet the problem caused by using necessarily simplified indices and the advantage of employing a more flexible approach. In this case we find very clear differences particularly between the different socio-professional statuses and the various ethnic groups as the figures shown in the tables on the following page indicate.

These two sets of data obtained from inquiries made from a sample population in the two towns should not be considered without reference to each other. On the whole, it is true, variations in rates of intertribal marriage according to socio-professional status reflect the

[15] It is at its maximum in Dakar, for example, which is a large port, an industrial centre, and the administrative capital of AOF.
[16] The numerical data derive from the results of systematic inquiries carried out on sample populations taken from both towns.

Intertribal marriages
according to socio-professional status (monogamists)

	Dakar %	Thiès %
Farmers, fishermen, etc.	13	15
Labourers—unskilled	16	32
Labourers—skilled	29	28
Junior clerks, administrative employees	35	24
Senior employees	36	44
Professional classes	41	33
Traders	16	16

Intertribal marriages
according to tribal groups (monogamists)

	%	%
Lebou	45	
Wolof	14	7
Serer	26	7
Toucouleur	31	40
Bambara	52	61
Moors	26	15

degree of Westernization and the extent of stabilization as well as the resultant weakening of tribal ties. We can observe several noteworthy exceptions, however: thus, at Thiès, the category of unskilled labourers provides an example: this is a class of persons which is there on the whole more stable and longer established in the town than is the Dakar group. However, we must also refer to the ethnic composition of this category—since it varies from town to town—in order to interpret these exceptions. Divergences are much more marked on this level as our second chart shows. They express a large diversity of situations and the explanatory facts here are multiple: an accentuated particularism, distance from the home regions, differences in demographic composition, etc., between ethnic groups in the town.

Data of a quantitative kind, collected along the lines previously indicated, obviously do not allow for the setting up of a simple schema. It might have been completed through the use of very diverse materials dealing with this subject: specific aspects involved in the eventual consent of heads of kinship groups to a marriage; the place and circumstances of the choice of spouse; the particular tensions associated with this type of marriage and its own causes of instability. Thus the analysis of the facts of the break with traditional endogamy has proved, from this point of view, particularly effective. Moreover, it touches on a more general aspect of the development of urban marriage which involves the whole set of traditional rules, concerned in the choice of a spouse, which are undergoing important modifications. In considering the problem of the 'opening up' of groups we should note that all these rules do not disappear at the same rate; some of them are particularly resistant. An example are those obstacles put in the way of marriages between members of different and theoretically endogamous castes. Unions between different castes are certainly recognized by customary courts today, provided they were knowingly contracted. However, while some ignore traditional prohibitions, and this practically happens only among the most Westernized elements of the population, the majority of cases meet with the irreconcilable opposition of the respective families: those who are able to accept the break with their kinsfolk which such a marriage probably entails are few and far between.

2. The various lines of inquiry suggested earlier constantly cut across one another. This can be seen by an examination of just one of them. Let us take as an example the study of data relative to polygyny. The first question generally put when inquiring into this institution is the following: does urban life lead to a diminution of polygyny rates and the relative proportion of polygynists? As far as Senegalese cities are concerned a glance at the total figures would seem to provide a negative answer. However, the essential problem is brought out when we discover that divergences within a single town are considerable: divergences between ethnic groups, between categories defined by socio-professional statuses, and of course between religions. In Dakar a preliminary inquiry showed a proportion of 28 per cent polygynists among married Moslem men (polygyny was exceptional among Catholics and in any case information was less easily acquired).[17] At Thiès a study of a sample population taken from the census showed a higher proportion of polygynists—30 per cent. In the two cities it would therefore seem that the proportions are either equal to or even higher than those known in certain

[17] The Dakar census of 1955 gives, for all married men, a percentage of 18 per cent for polygynists. Christians represent little more than 10 per cent of the population and this, in any case, gives a lower figure than the one we obtained from our first inquiry. The divergences between Dakar and Thiès should perhaps be somewhat widened.

rural areas of Senegal—particularly among the Wolof. Only the examination of contrasts between different elements of the urban population brings to light meaningful data.

It should not be necessary to stress the basic opposition, on this level, between Moslems and Christians, unless it be to point out that it is reflected in certain contrasts found between ethnic groups, contrasts which by themselves are not very significant: certain tribes are partially, some almost entirely, Christian. Thus, according to the data of the Dakar census the Mandyak (from the Casamance) are 97 per cent Catholics and 95 per cent monogamous. Among the Serer, the proportion of polygynists is clearly low because more than one-fifth of the members of the tribe residing in Dakar are Catholics, etc. Avowed polygyny among Catholics is never absolutely absent but it is nevertheless very rare. Among Moslems we have noticed that polygyny has a varying frequency according to membership of brotherhoods, to which almost all belong.[18] In Dakar the proportion of polygynists among the Tidjanis is equal to the mean figure, lower than this figure for the Kadiriya (among whom a special tribal group, that of the Moors, predominates); it becomes higher among the Mourides and Layen (the fact that the Lebou, who are not an immigrant group in Dakar, represent the majority of this group, suggests that factors other than religion are involved here). The situation appeared little different in Thiès where the polygynists were 35 per cent among the Tidjani, but only 22 per cent among the Kadiriya and 42 per cent among the Mourides (this is the only brotherhood in which there were polygynists with more than four wives). The polygyny rates for the three groups were respectively: 1·44, 1·27, and 1·67.[19]

The incidence of polygyny varies of course with the age of the married men. Thus in Dakar the polygyny rate, which is 1·21 for the whole of the population is only 1·03 for the 20–24 age group; it only rises above the average after 40: 1·74 for the 40–44 age group, 1·42 for the 60–64 group, 1·45 for the over-seventies. For a group of 178 men each with two wives who were studied through the use of questionnaires more than two-thirds were over forty. Inquiries carried out in Thiès gave much the same results. The data do not imply that there are any regular variations in marriage behaviour, nor in ideas

[18] It is, moreover, not differences in doctrine or religious discipline which count but the play of various factors which are not religious in nature.

[19] The figures for Thiès were primarily compiled by L. Masse; cf. 'Contribution à l'étude de la ville de Thiès', *Bulletin de l'IFAN*, B, xviii (1956), 1–2.

about conjugal relations, etc., according to generations; moreover, a precise comparison with earlier periods is not, unfortunately, possible. At all events it seems clear that polygyny is associated with relative material success which in the majority of cases only comes with age; it also remains an uncontested source of prestige for the greater part of the urban population. Monogamy, more frequent among younger men, may be the result of choice (a choice which of course is not irrevocable) but this seems still to be a minority position.

Clear differences are to be discerned between ethnic groups, although they are not in all cases particularly significant. It is only rarely that we can clearly distinguish the presence of a tradition which belongs to this or that group. As we mentioned above adherence to different religious faiths plays a role, particularly at this level. On the other hand, however, the various ethnic groups are not associated with the different socio-professional status groups in the same proportions. In Dakar the Lebou and the Wolof show a high percentage of polygynists,[20] 26 per cent and 20 per cent respectively while the average is 18.[21] These are groups which do not suffer from lack of females; women are in fact a majority. On the other hand, they live very near their home areas and relations with these are constant. Finally, they have a relatively high representation in those socio-professional categories which possess more favourable material opportunities. A series of other ethnic groups are characterized by percentages of polygynists which are closer to the average; but the same interpretation cannot be offered for each situation. The Serer case (11 per cent) has already been mentioned. The Toucouleur, the Fulani, the Bambara all range from 13 to 15 per cent (noticeably lower than data for these people in their home areas). The fact that they are much more highly represented among unskilled labourers, domestic servants, etc., whose standard of living is low, plus the fact that their establishment in the town is of more recent origin and that they show a deficit in female population, account for these figures. Some of the ethnic groups, finally, have a specially low polygyny rate: all the groups which come from the Casamance (5 per cent) where the religious factor must be taken into consideration, and the Moors (3 per cent). The latter have a female deficit; they are primarily temporary inhabitants of the town; and intertribal marriages

---

[20] These two groups, together, form more than one-half of the Dakar population.

[21] In this paragraph we have used the most recent figures, those of the 1955 census.

play a limited role. Moreover, in their home region there is a marked tendency towards monogamy.[22]

In Thiès the Wolof position still contrasts very clearly with that of the other ethnic group: out of 100 married men, 39 are polygynous, a figure which is higher than the average. All the others in fact are below the average: 22 for the Toucouleur, 9 for the Moors, for example. Data relative to polygyny rates vary in the same way. It is 1·42 for the population as a whole. Only the Wolof have a higher rate: 1·55. It is 1·25 for the Toucouleur and 1·1 for the Moors. For all the other ethnic groups it is 1·26. Moreover, it is rare to come across a polygynist with four or more wives, even among the Wolof.

Nevertheless more marked contrasts appear if we compare the data relative to the principal socio-professional status groups which we have distinguished. They do not, however, have the same significance on each level. Here we should note the distinction already alluded to between monogamists who have not—for various reasons—been able to achieve a desired polygyny and monogamists through choice. It is, of course, only possible to point to tendencies. We may consider basically four important groups of socio-professional statuses. The Dakar example provides clear indications here. Farmers and fishermen (together) and traders have a polygyny rate markedly higher than the average: 30 and 40 per cent respectively.[23] These are people who have stuck more closely to traditional ways of life and values. In a second group—that of skilled and unskilled labourers and foremen—we can discern a regular progression in the proportion of polygynists which ranges from 15 to 28 per cent, then up to 55 per cent.[24] In this case polygyny seems to be clearly a function of stable employment and income level. As for unskilled labourers who figure among the two lowest categories as far as polygyny is concerned the case is particularly significant: we have an actual monogamous situation although, as mentioned earlier, it is not necessarily the desired one. In a third category composed of white-collar workers and administrative employees it appears that *de facto* monogamy and monogamy 'by choice' both occur together. In fact we can discern a progression in the proportion of polygynists from lower grade

[22] We should point out that the masculinity rates and proportion of polygynists do not always have a direct relationship. The masculinity rate (or from a different point of view the sex-ratio) is only one of the factors involved here.
[23] Here we are dealing with data acquired through the use of questionnaire; the average established, as we mentioned, was 28 per cent.
[24] In the last case the small absolute size of the sample makes this a somewhat doubtful figure.

white-collar workers and administrative employees to those in superior positions (the professional classes); 24 and 31 per cent respectively. Thus once again the importance of income levels intervenes. However, on the other hand, when incomes are the same, the proportion of polygynists is clearly lower than it is among skilled labourers and foremen. A changing situation is clearly visible here. Finally the members of the professional classes—considered broadly [25]—constitute a fourth series which reveals the lowest proportion of polygynists: 11 per cent roughly. It is this category which disposes of the highest incomes on the whole: the development of a tendency towards monogamy is very marked here. Nevertheless it is not as great as the net figure would indicate: we should also note that the percentage of Christians is slightly higher for this category than for the population as a whole.

At all events, even if the religious factor is not taken into consideration, the degree of acceptance of certain values and Western ways of life influence in the most marked way the choice of monogamy. The importance of this can be determined, as an initial approximation, by examining different standards of education. The following are some brief indications. Among men who have never attended school the proportion of polygyny is 30 per cent; it is even a little higher for men who began primary school and left off. These two categories taken together show a polygyny rate which is higher than the Dakar average. A second group, with a percentage slightly below the average includes both those who have finished primary schooling and those who attended upper primary schools and technical professional schools. The figures range from 22 to 27 per cent. Finally a third group, made up of those who have experienced the greatest Western influence, includes men who have had a secondary education—even if incomplete—those who have attended the large federal schools of AOF, and those who have gone on to university level; the proportion of polygynists is respectively 10, 14, and 0 per cent. This obviously provides only a skeletal schema and the few figures should be completed by the addition of qualitative data. The general trend, however, will be the same.

Inquiries made at Thiès on the whole give the same kind of results. In this town we tried to compare socio-professional categories within a single ethnic group which constituted about two-thirds of the population—the Wolof. We might take as an example the data which refer to polygyny rates. Among farmers and traders it is 1·85 and 1·55

[25] Here we have included, particularly, all members of the teaching profession.

respectively—that is above and equal to the mean figure (1·55). We find the same regular progression as in Dakar—from unskilled labourers (1·12) to skilled labourers (1·50) and foremen (2·00) on the one hand, and from lower grade clerks and administrative personnel to the higher grades (1·50 and 1·61) on the other. Nevertheless the gap between these two series is much less.[26]

In the same town we tried to discover whether there were any significant differences between townsmen of the first or second generation. As far as the problem considered here is concerned a comparison of men born in Thiès and men born outside the town gave the following results. The former had a proportion of polygynists of 26 per cent and a polygyny rate of 1·33; while the second showed figures of 32 per cent and 1·46 respectively. If we take into account the fact that the first group has a higher percentage of men with higher incomes and that about one-tenth of the second group includes persons born in other Senegalese urban centres, the divergence will be seen to be even more marked. Inquiries made along these lines show that the distinction is a significant one. In a way we have here two stages in the complex development of an urban milieu. During the first stage rural traditions favouring polygyny still exert a great influence and this influence is maintained until a certain income level is reached. Thus the proportion of polygynists may even exceed that found in the home areas of the townsmen—this is the result of a differentiation of living standards. In the second stage, what might be called an urban tradition favourable to monogamy develops, which is linked to a preoccupation with improving one's standard of living, the accepting of new ideas concerning relations between married partners, the education of children, etc. These two stages overlap and this is a factor in the complexity of the urban situation on this level. Research, dealing with attitudes and opinions concerning monogamy, has shown that it was already highly valorized in those socio-professional categories where an option in its favour had only partially been realized.

These few examples, presented in their most schematic form, allow us to suggest the degree of diversity of the insights made possible by the systematic study of marriage and the multiplicity of approaches which can be utilized in this sphere involving the analysis of social change occurring in urban milieux. Considering only the second of the subjects treated here we can see that it affords an

[26] The category of professional classes was numerically too poorly represented to provide any valid comparisons.

introduction, in particular to the following questions: motivations of economic activity; ideas and values attached to material success; the persistence of traditional forms of prestige; a differentiation in the population with the appearance, already, of a series of categories characterized by relatively contrasting modes of behaviour; and an elaboration of new systems of values and a cultural heterogeneity in urban society, etc. It illustrates the importance which the most complete inventory of matrimonial questions has in posing—for a given town—a precise diagnosis of the situation and in undertaking comparisons between cities of a similar type at different stages in their development.

Regional Studies. Thoughts on the

Monographic Formula in Human Geography

GILLES SAUTTER[1]

As with anthropologists, geographers cannot deepen their studies unless they restrict their field of operation which leads to studies of a monographic type. This term involves three ideas: a 'field' of study which is localized and circumscribed; a limited spatial area or a restricted number of people (according to whether the geographical or anthropological aspect is uppermost); and finally, within this framework, a study which is exhaustive or one which at least aims at a complete coverage of some of the perspectives pertaining to the student's discipline. We also have to deal with the problem of scale. Once the framework is widened a monographic type study is no longer feasible; but within these limits the same methods can be adapted to units of very unequal size. From the local residential group of a few dozen individuals, who are primarily concerned with subsistence and kinship organization, to the nation, or polyethnic, state where the emphasis shifts to political institutions, the anthropologist has a wide area of choice. Similarly the geographer has to choose his topic from a series ranging from village to country. Within this hierarchy the region in fact has pride of place. Many signs attest this fact, particularly the role played by so-called 'regional' geography in French university courses and the very use of the term in course catalogues. 'Regional' is then used in its broadest sense. Nevertheless common usage accepts that each distinct part of the world—here dubbed 'region'—should in turn be divided up and dealt with as being composed of regions, properly speaking. If proof is required

[1] *Gilles Sautter* (b. 1920), Dr. es L., Sorbonne. Professor of African Geography, Panthéon-Sorbonne University (Paris I). Director of Studies, Ecole Pratique des Hautes Etudes, Section VI, Social Studies. A geographer with anthropological and sociological interests, has pioneered inter-disciplinary work as co-founder, with P. Pélissier, of the field-work teams for the *Atlas des terroirs africains*. Main interests: problems of land-use and agricultural development, human ecology. The original French text of this paper was published as 'L'étude régionale. Réflexions sur la formule monographique en géographie humaine', *L'Homme*, v, 1 (1961), 77–89.

we need only leaf through the massive volumes of the *Géographie Universelle* which was published between the two world wars. In France, at least, monographic studies, carried out essentially on a regional basis, are considered an ideal means of applying geographical methods and are an inexhaustible reservoir on which so-called general geography can draw for primary material and points needed for comparisons. There are two approaches, the combination of which constitutes geography as a modern science: one is the study of phenomena in their inter-relationships and the other in their individual extension. The former is far and away the more specific, but it demands a limited and precise framework and within such a framework we inevitably find studies of the monographic type. Here we are dealing with the region again. But why precisely the region—that is, speaking generally, a portion of the dimensional spectrum which ranges from a couple of dozen to several hundred kilometres of linear distance? Firstly because of its size. Let us consider a district which includes a single rural community. This is a framework within which we can examine an intimate structure, the relations between man and his environment which are the basic articulation of all the rest which constitutes human geography. But the area is too limited to discern whether the coincidence of human and natural facts shows any significance (in the sense understood by statisticians). Observations made on this level, whatever their interests, never permit any kind of generalization. On the other hand a territory would appear to be too large. The relationship between men and their environment becomes confused by the multiplicity and complexity of the connecting relays between them. Moreover, those political and other structures which appear on this level are largely independent of natural conditions. A geographer is therefore more likely to ascend the scale, using his knowledge of a region to consider units of a superior kind, rather than moving down, like the economist, from the territory to the region.

Another factor comes in here. It is only in a region that we find a free confrontation—if I may express myself thus—between physical and human facts, considered on an equal footing. The district and the territory, by definition, favour human as opposed to natural facts. The environment on these two levels is viewed only through a special frame of reference and this, in itself, already represents a construct which is specifically human, architecturally and dimensionally lacking any necessary relation to the physical environment.

Everything therefore points to the region. But what exactly is implied by this term in human geography? First of all it is a part of the landscape: that is a particular combination of concrete facts, on the scale of visual observation, including houses, roads, fields of a certain shape and size, farming of this and that type. These 'geographical facts' materialize the efforts of a human group to make use of a natural situation and to settle down in an environment. Reciprocally the countryside registers the reaction of the environment to human intervention and its possible decay. Certain landscapes have been humanized only recently, but most of them betray, if one knows how to read them, periods of more or less ancient occupation. The present and the past, the distant and near past, are found juxtaposed and combined on one level. We are reminded of those composite buildings where stones and centuries intermingle. The successive inhabitants of a region or a single group passing through successive stages of development are imprinted by a characteristic sediment. Men usually inherit an environment profoundly modified by their predecessors. Apart from nature they must cope with an inheritance of improvements, constructions, planted trees. Since they have become incorporated into the landscape, changed from effects into facts, these features introduce into geographical evolution the powerful factor of inertia. Among sedentary farmers, features such as inhabited sites, networks of country roads or the contours of fields manifest a special resistance to time. In many European landscapes, agriculture still suffers from the restricting influence of a local organization of space which dates back to the early middle ages, even the neolithic. In England during the enclosure movement the old system of open fields was not broken without a real technical, economic, and social revolution. However, we shall ignore for a moment all this material heritage with its accompanying limitations. Even if we consider only the 'way of life' of a population, the way it regards its relationship to nature and space, we are confronted by the past time and time again. Once they have been installed in a new milieu, a transplanted group stubbornly continues—often indefinitely—to use the same techniques which they had adapted to suit their former habitat. With good reason, the geographer makes a reasoned study of the landscape and tries to grasp, through concrete manifestations, those relations—involving confrontation or adjustment—between men and their environment. However, if these are to be fully convincing they should be framed in a diachronic perspective. The logic of his interpretation is only valid if it is based on a knowledge of the history of the group and the archaeology of the landscape.

F

The concept of a regional landscape needs both precision and nuance. It is probably not worth while stressing here the distinction which is made between an immediate bird's-eye view of the situation —taken from a vantage point or seen from an aerial photograph, and the landscape itself, a term which we are tempted to write with a capital L, in so far as it is something which gradually becomes elaborated in the mind of the geographer. A slow decanting process leads—through a successive number of recorded images—to a kind of visual synthesis which places the most characteristic features in their normal positional relationships. Anyway, it is almost possible to find a favourable spot from which a view conforming effectively to this representation can be had. However, the regions which can be covered by one landscape-type are very rare. Let us leave aside variations in detail which can be reduced to facies. From one place to the next, within a region, clear contrasts are the rule rather than the exception. They can be seen to repeat themselves, more or less regularly and with a variable frequency, as one proceeds over the regional space in all directions. Thus the Parisian region in its several parts combines two rural landscapes which are in great contrast: that of wide valleys left to family farm exploitation and frequently given over to market gardening and the plateaux which have been converted to large-scale farming. These kinds of juxtapositions—vegetal and agrarian—like morphological *catenas* do not profoundly disturb the unity of a landscape. By broadening one's view, by seeking a higher vantage place, one can easily fit them into the framework of the typical landscape. Neither do small hamlets and large villages, scattered throughout the countryside, break the unity of a specific combination of facts.

Things change, once the scale is increased and the repetitions are replaced by a collection of sub-regional landscapes, each unique in its own way. Thus geographers have recognized as individual units each of the innumerable individual 'pays' of rural France and in setting up a nomenclature they have brought back the old names. What happens to our 'regional landscape' then? At best the special combinations which have taken its place have a family look about them, enough common features to lend themselves to a grouping. There remains a degree of arbitrariness in an approach which prefers to stress resemblances: with so many differences in landscapes, guessing at a geographical order implies some complacency towards the regional concept. A step further, and with all the good will in the world, we cannot bring together the oasis and the desert around it, the high mountain and its piedmont, the town and its surrounding rural districts. In each of these cases a regional synthesis is derived from the very contrasts which these violently opposed landscapes reveal. Here the link docs not consist of a passive resemblance between features more or less strongly imprinted by the human and natural environment; it is of a functional nature actively based on living relationships. In this way we are beginning to draw a new portrait of the region, no longer as a landscape but as a structure, in which towns, communications, networks, the politico-administrative organization all play an essential role. Between the landscape region and the structure region there is no sharp break. These two factors of regional unity may quite well be found in combination, in any proportion, or be mutually exclusive; they may coincide on a geographical level or be discordant. It is clear that, given time, with the elaboration of political structure and the intensification of production and exchange, functional elements will gain in importance. Yet things are never straightforward and in countries of ancient civilization or those found at the peak of economic development, the unity of the landscape remains true for most regions and remains a valid criterion. We might even ask ourselves, when this unity is destroyed or upset with the passage from a subsistence to a market economy, whether this unity does not tend to become apparent again once trade assumes larger dimensions and goes beyond the limit of the regional framework, whole regions beginning to specialize in narrowly determined productive functions.

The concept of regional geography, endowed by the nature of things with a certain ambiguity, originated in Europe, primarily in France where, from the beginning of the twentieth century, several grand theses, prototypes of many others, founded and applied the first rigorous methods of regional analysis. France, it is true, provided an ideal field for these kinds of studies. Historical regions, natural regions, economic regions can all be distinguished with particular neatness. Descended either from fiefs and appanages or from royal intendencies, many of her ancient provinces have retained their personality; a centralizing economic link, radiating from regional capitals along modern systems of communication, has often taken over former political and administrative ties. As far as land is concerned history has—this time under the guise of geology—again determined the natural regional divisions of the French soil. A climatic influence, related to latitude and distance from the sea, completes the individuation of each sedimentary basin, each fold of mountains and

Gilles Sautter

old massifs, recognizable at first glance on a map. This picture is probably less clear cut when we come to the economic side; the countries are not really strong until after the industrial revolution; nevertheless exploitation of the northern coal basin and the ascendancy of Paris in relation to neighbouring districts—to mention but two examples—have had time to bring about an original differentiation. We have three principles of regional segregation therefore, but certainly not three independent principles: the land has to a large extent provided the framework for historical and economic development and they in turn have reacted constantly on each other. Even when we come across cases of real discordance, one or other of these factors normally proves to be clearly the matrix of regional formation. Despite their physical unity the Vosges hills can only with difficulty be considered as a geographical region; modern economy and history have meant that the Alsatian and Lorraine slopes have always been strongly opposed. Neither historical ties nor social relationships would allow us to include the Pyrenees in an Aquitanian ensemble leaving out their eastern end.

Given these pre-established harmonies, we should not be surprised that the French geographers have come to consider regional systems as a kind of necessity, inscribed in the very nature of things; or that they have shown a tendency to postulate their existence everywhere their curiosity has taken them. Moreover, these implicit views have often been confirmed. In the ancient countries of the Far East many authors, as expert as P. Gourou and Ch. Robequain, have succeeded in isolating very clear examples of regional personalities. From works on India, the Mexican and Andean plateaux, as well as a large part of the Mediterranean and Near East, we obtain a similar impression of well-ordered diversity. However, the model which had been constructed in Europe could not always be transposed without mishap. In Black Africa in particular, regional entities can hardly, if at all, be distinguished within an undifferentiated and amorphous landscape, in a state of flux and rapid change. In order to detect them we shall need a good deal of ingenuity, perhaps imagination, and certainly intuition; and even more if we are to delineate their limits. What is the reason for these difficulties? It is partly due to the natural environment, made up of great climatic and morphological ensembles: the huge *cuestas* of Sudanic Africa, the enormous alluvial basins of Chad, Congo, and Niger, the extensive peneplains of East Africa, the equatorial forests beneath which even the relief loses any individuality; these are all features which are hardly commensurable in regional terms, not to mention the climate whose zonal uniformity makes any division an artificial one, except in some favourable cases. Only rarely, then, have men and their activities been able to insert themselves into a prepared framework on a scale with their historical hold.

What is more, even history fails us. Or at least it has not so far crystallized, as in Europe, into well-marked regions. Here the mobility of the population, rarely anchored to the soil like a genuine peasantry, seems to be the operative factor. This should in turn be referred back to a primary cause: men usually attach themselves to a piece of land only in so far as by parcelling and transforming it to suit their needs they shape it away from its original condition. In this respect Africa can, at the most, provide only negative evidence. In short, techniques appear to be responsible: temporary farming on cleared land, nomadic pastoralism, human or animal transport, buildings made of perishable materials. Along with this we have throughout the greater part of the continent the absence of any urban civilization which, as the Maya and, to some extent, the Yoruba examples show need not require advanced material techniques. One fact in particular shows how powerless the land was to preserve a record of history: in the major state structures of traditional Africa the province, the unit immediately subordinate to the central power, normally had in fact only a limited degree of material reality. It involved little more than a network of inter-personal obligations with a corresponding territory, vague in extent, with shifting boundaries and often broken up in different parts of the country. At best it corresponds to a tribal or sub-tribal group whose limits formed the province's boundaries, but without any real geographical necessity or ties. Here we return to history which, in Africa as in other parts of the world, emerges under a tribal rather than regional guise. French geographers, accustomed to the consistent reality of their old provinces and familiar with historical concepts and methods, are at a loss when confronted with this hitherto unfamiliar situation—the gap between historical processes and contemporary developments.

This feeling of being out of one's element recalls in a way the equally awkward situation of the anthropologist when he sets out to study modern societies. Here perspectives are reversed: the anthropologist moving forward along the corridors of time sees the special forms and structures he has learnt to study deteriorate and melt away into a wider organization. The geographer who travels overseas goes back in history: he now finds in their nascent state, hardly emerging from a matrix of confused traits, both natural and human, those regional structures he took so much for granted.

This comparison is not merely a formal one. It draws attention to the essential kinship between the tribe and the region as subjects of study. Everything seems to point to the fact that the region—as a level of organization—replaces the tribe at a certain stage in human evolution. We are not, however, confronted with a mutation, nor with a natural descent process but rather with a transference of substance, since one—the region—may become apparent long before the other—the tribe—disappears. At this stage it is not rare to find a geographical correspondence between the two, a complete overlapping, in fact. In Africa this meeting-point becomes obvious when geographers talk of 'Mossi country', 'Bateke plateau', 'Nuba hills'. They do not, however, imply that such a superimposition involves an assimilation. Together with the name of a tribe, recognized as a powerful factor of regional originality, they still use a technical term, as evidence of the role played by the milieu, to isolate, beneath the vestment of the humanized landscape, a portion of the terrestrial surface, identified by its position and endowed thereby with a reality of its own. Without in any way changing their unique character, a number of peoples have succeeded in changing their habitat, even performing great perambulations from one physical environment to another. By fair definition, however, a region is for ever untransportable. Not all of them are bound under the yoke of a rigid natural framework. We see some of them expanding, changing shape, contracting over time. However, these fluctuations only involve the periphery of a fixed and permanent core: they can be reduced to balanced movements between neighbouring regions. After a migration many a human group has lost its territorial cohesion and we have frequent examples of people being scattered among other peoples in limited areas. Here we have a definite discordance between tribe and region.

We have put our finger here on the fact which makes these two orders of facts irreducible. Ethnic groups are formed in time, regions are spatial entities; one depends on historical continuity, the other on contiguity. For a diversity of persons to contribute effectively to regional diversification three conditions have to be fulfilled: the tribes must be of sufficient population density, they must be territorially cohesive, and thirdly, they have to be permanently attached to the soil.

If we push our analysis further we shall find that the ethnic unit of the geographer is not always the same as that of the anthropologist. The latter demands criteria which include, essentially, differentiating factors such as those of social organization, religion, and a whole collection of traits many of which exercise, at the very most, only an indirect influence on the landscape. For the geographer the important part of the cultural complex is that which immediately conditions the humanized landscape, a landscape which is cultivated and inhabited. But while the facts of habitat are closely controlled by the social structure and religious expression, food habits, and techniques of exploiting the environment belong to a sphere which is somewhat less dependent, to a kind of exterior world which is much more exposed to outside influence and contamination. Thus it often happens that the distinctions between 'ways of life' or 'modes of exploitation' cut more or less across purely ethnic limits, without at the same time being moulded by natural limits.

As far as the region and tribe are concerned, the discordances which we have mentioned do not prevent the existence of a common dimension. There is a natural relationship between them and for this reason it is not always easy to distinguish what the tribe owes to the geographical environment and what the landscape has derived from tribal culture. In these circumstances it would be surprising if the geographer and the anthropologist, who are both concerned with the same kind of inquiry, were not confronted by similar difficulties. This is, in fact, the case. From various points of view it certainly seems as if the geographer has the best of it. He starts off with a concrete landscape, with definite clear-cut facts, which sharpen his curiosity, provide a guideline for study and encourage immediate hypotheses. In this respect he is covering the same concrete field as the ethnographer. He does not run the risk of seeing the reality he wishes to interpret faithfully being modified by his physical presence in the field. Looking at a farm or a house does not have the same terrifying capacity to upset a balance or provoke a human reaction on the part of human beings to a situation they were previously unconscious of, as does a maladroit question on the part of the anthropologist. The geographer is immersed in concrete facts and for this reason he can come to grips with reassuring certainties; he does not have to take on those responsibilities of the observer who becomes involved with the subjects of his observation. However, every coin has its reverse side and here this reverse side involves a certain disproportion between the field of observation and the field of study, between the few details which the eye can encompass and the region as a whole. This makes the geographer heavily dependent on cartographical and photographic material, leaving him somewhat ill-equipped when these materials are lacking as is frequently the case in Africa.

In spite of the differences in the constraints imposed on each discipline the basic problem of the monographical approach is practically the same for the geographer and the anthropologist. They both accumulate facts and observations for the sole purpose of presenting a synthesis. Herein lies the difficulty. How are we to be sure that the proposed construct will remain faithful to the model (assuming for the moment, of course, that the latter has any reality)? Everybody knows that a tribe is never reducible to a catalogue—even a perfectly conscientious one—of material objects and behavioural sequences classified under headings. Every society has an internal order, whereby a conglomeration of diffuse features is adjusted into a coherent whole, as well as a system of representations and a scale of values which sustain it. The anthropologist is expected to clarify these. Beneath the apparent functioning of social relations we expect him to uncover the hidden springs of which even the people concerned are far from being conscious. The most profound researches are not sufficient, however. It is only by reflection that we can be sure of getting to the bottom of things. The same applies to a geographer trying to define and represent his region. In this field as well, investigations should not be limited to a mere inventory of concrete facts and material activities. The mere collecting of observations, however objective may be their inventory and classification, excludes the possibility of discerning the organic reality of a region, of communicating to a reader a true feeling of its real life and its unity. The facts which immediately spring to notice are never more than indices, the concrete emergence of a play of subtle activities and relations between human beings and the milieu they live in, a play in which, moreover, the past continually interferes with the present. On the other hand the broad lines which define regional structures become entangled among themselves and with others again, producing a complex network which has to be disentangled in order to discover the organizing force behind them. The range of possible judgements which the geographer can use in his interpretation of a region puts his *savoir-faire* and talents to the test. The immediately graspable facts are only hints. For this reason a monographic study is doubly revealing both of the region and of a method—or an art. The geographer, in carrying out this exercise, runs the same risk as the anthropologist, that of giving the reader, in his presentation of the region, only a mere reflection of the many schemata he is armed with, or at best an image which is deformed by his personal thought processes or those imposed on him by the fashions of science or the period.

The most venial sin as far as regional and anthropological researches are concerned involves the exaggeration—or, on the contrary, the minimizing—of the influence or importance of this or that factor. This is how the picture of a region can become gravely deformed and unbalanced. On another level, it soon becomes apparent that it is extremely difficult to appreciate strictly the degree of reality, the relative clarity of the region, considered as a whole. If he concentrates overmuch on the landscape and the human beings concerned, the scholar may, because of a kind of auto-suggestion, overestimate the geographical 'necessity' of the overall framework in which—before he had a real knowledge of it—he has chosen to work. Regions will then crop up out of the blue with over-defined features which do not carry conviction (or perhaps carry too much, according to another point of view). Cannot the mere fact that the existence of a region has been posited already give it a kind of reality? Anthropologists have experienced this reaction. It is much less obvious in human geography, where the opinion of the persons concerned can only with difficulty prevail over the established facts. Even when he succeeds in avoiding these pitfalls, the geographer who undertakes a regional monographic study of the classical type almost inevitably comes up against another stumbling block: that of boundaries. It is in fact exceptional for a geographer to be able to delineate unequivocally his region by a bold outline on the map. The problem is exactly the same as it is for tribes: the passage from one region to another involves a gradual shading off and all boundaries will necessarily be arbitrary ones; or the boundaries which are drawn up through a consideration of each criterion separately never coincide and, whatever the choice, one element in the regional complex is usually emphasized. When structures are so discordant and overlapping they do not offer any safer approach than the landscape. While it is possible, in theory, to divide regions according to lines drawn where there is a greater weakening of geographical communications, in practice we should always have too many outlines, each of which would be equally satisfactory by itself and as a result equally unsatisfactory. This explains the geographer's predilection for islands where everything stops abruptly at the coast. Everywhere else the problem involves the same difficulties: we have two regions (or three); between them there is a subregion of the size of a French 'pays', endowed with mixed characteristics the attachment of which wavers between one side or the other.

Since, some fifty years ago, the regional monograph achieved a form which one could believe to be definitive, profound changes have altered the ideas we have of a region and the orientations of our researches in this field. The origins of this development are threefold. First of all it is unquestionably true that geography has been caught up in a general current which has affected all the social sciences. In all fields the old 'classifying' mentality has given way to a growing interest in relationships and structures. Of course human geography is too young a discipline ever to have taken the presentation and ordering of facts as an object of study in itself. From the beginning it declared itself to be a discipline concerned with relationships and liaisons. Nevertheless, as far as the actual behaviour of research workers is concerned, this new interest has gained ground over a certain initial complacency as regards description and categorizing. In its recent development, in European countries, geographical reality has played its part in questioning the traditional models of the monograph. In France itself the growing dynamism of the past few years has led to an overall crumbling of the old regional structures inherited from the Ancien Régime and the industrial revolution. New groupings developed, new units were formed, and the older ones have undergone a kind of moulting process, changing in appearance and articulation. Regions are less and less considered as belonging to a pre-established geographical order. Their evolution can no longer be confined within limits regarded as stable when considered within the purview of a single man's life. The very framework is being brought into question. While the large regional unit remains an essential cell it is progressively losing its functional autonomy, becoming instead a specialized element within national or pluri-national ensembles. The master-concept of poles of development, geographically understood, as well as the complementary concept of 'backward regions' derive their significance from their interdependence. The factor of 'geographical position', due to the place and role which it assigns to the region in a wider whole, weighs more and more heavily; it adds its own determinism to those of history and the natural environment. Confronted with important changes such as these it becomes obvious that the usefulness of the monograph will diminish more and more in its original form. To all this we should add the special experience—

which converges in so far as results are concerned—of expatriate geographers in America, Africa, and Asia. Their search for regions in the European sense of the term has often proved a vain one. Should we, therefore, because of the lack of a suitable framework, discard such a satisfying formula as the monographic study? As far as geographers are concerned this would be an unjustifiable abdication. And students have escaped from a seeming impasse by various routes. Some of them have concentrated on well-circumscribed physical environments for field work, environments which are susceptible of influencing human life; nevertheless we are aware that such natural units are the exception rather than the rule. Others have opted for tribal studies, as a field which presents a confrontation between man and his environment. The approach of these geographers seems to resemble that of the anthropologist. We are thinking in particular of monographs such as those on Indian communities in Central and South America, where the physical environment is given detailed treatment, since it plays such an influential role in all human activities. However, in choosing an approach similar to that of the anthropologist the geographer has jumped out of the frying pan into the fire. The delimitation of human groups is as overladen with problems as that of regions and the doubts begin to pile up when—having defined the tribe—they have to plot it on the ground. There seems to be only one way out—a reforming of the traditional formula of regional studies. Today many geographers are busy making their contribution to this wider-ranging endeavour.

What have been the results of the efforts simultaneously undertaken in very different geographical fields to renovate the discipline? We certainly have more flexible concepts of monographic inquiries and exposition. We shall restrict ourselves to mentioning only some of the new tendencies which are discernible concerning both research and the presentation of its findings. In a general way less attention is being paid to a region's limits than to its contents; in other words more importance is given to the complex of facts and relationships which constitutes a region than to the framework which has so often been imposed by history or milieu. Instead of determining the regional field by criteria which are more or less anterior and exterior to its own reality (if only since a rigidly conceived boundary means that a region is formed only in contrast to its neighbour) we now consider its extent solely after uncovering its distinct geographical pattern and as a function of this distinctiveness.

Regional monographs have long been a kind of 'genre', obeying strict rules, even if these remained unexpressed. The geographer was confronted with a double imperative; he had to make an exhaustive study of all aspects of 'his' region and then distort the results of his research to suit a rigid type of presentation. Even today certain works have the character of inventories, lists of facts set out under different headings. The constituent elements of the natural environment, the historical phases of the peopling of the area, the cultivated landscape, the facts of the rural habitat, the town or towns, communications, and exchange—these are the kinds of rubrics and the general order followed. And along with this succession of chapters we have a review of the 'pays' which constitute the larger regional unit. This schema, of course, is not a rigid one: the chapter headings are subject to variations and transposition. Nevertheless we always find this insistence on a logical ordering, on the structuring of the whole work into a framework of geographical causality. One begins with the 'conditions', the 'factors', the 'natural data', 'historical antecedents', and then proceeds towards the resultant landscape and the region which has been elaborated. Many authors were able to rise above this formal sequence of headings and, by means of a series of sectional views, have succeeded in presenting a closely reasoned study. Reading through some of the older theses of the French geographical school one is impressed by the extent of their explanatory rigour. Nevertheless the risks of such a formula are very real; at each stage in this precisely elaborated itinerary one is tempted to dwell a while longer, to begin to study facts for their own sake, not as part of a global study. In its extreme form a region may become merely a pretext for a series of studies, artificially attached to a conventional framework.

A reaction against the formalism of this approach began to show itself a few years ago. Firstly research was made more selective. Now we are trying to understand the regional picture through its most typical manifestations, leaving aside data which were not specific to the problem. Some carry this further and consider the region they are studying from an exclusive point of view, one which brings out its distinctive character. All research becomes concentrated on a selected aspect: population density (whether it be abnormally low or high); special methods of rural exploitation; an unusual aspect of the agrarian landscape, such as wooded farmlands ('bocage'); or perhaps the urban network, if it plays a determining role. Other data are only introduced in relation to this emphasized aspect. As well as polarizing their researches, this grouping facts around certain major themes —or even a single theme—also provides material which is better adapted to the geographer's preference for interpreting facts. Instead of beginning with natural factors and the human past before arriving at the concept of the region, its contours and contents, the monograph writers now follow an analytical approach. From those features which contribute most to the general geographical unity of the area, they move backwards along a chain of causality to the factors, antecedents, and environmental influences which are responsible for them. As an element in the contemporary context, a historical sequence or a physical situation, an explanatory fact is presented only when it is needed for the argument and not as a matter of course, along with facts of a similar kind or of the same period. This new way of presenting research results is more flexible than the older methods; it also brings out the real conditions of research in the field and in the library (with the vicissitudes and hazards of the inquiry). The reader, in a sense, plays his part in the research. The region is presented as it appeared to the writer, in the form of a problem to be solved, or as a group of interconnected problems. This is not an artificial means of enlightenment, if one recalls how the 'choices' made by a population as expressed in the landscape and the context of a region, almost always reveal a degree of independence rather than any simple determinism. These are the lines along which geographical monographs are now seeking to provide the answers.

We have already mentioned the fact that European regions have changed in nature in recent times. They have lost their fixed character as they begin to participate to a greater extent in structures of a superior order. Confronted with this kind of mutation in his field of studies the geographer has reacted by according a greater interest to the structures, as supports and the instruments of regional dynamism. *A fortiori* we find the same situation in the tropical zones and the colder areas where the differentiation of space is taking place under our very eyes, starting from structures often created from scratch. The way space is organized round a town, as a function of the town's existence; the economic development of a zone affected by a transport route; the insertion of the countryside into a hierarchical urban network; these are some of the themes which keep cropping up with a significant insistence. Other studies deal with geographical fronts. This choice involves a similar approach for those who try to grasp a problem as part of a gradual growth. A frontier is not an ordinary boundary, it is that of a region in the process of expansion, of a peopling, or a method of exploiting the environment, or an organization of space all of which push back nature's wilderness or make headway over a territory hitherto less effectively organized and used. It does not possess the hybrid character of the usual inter-regional no-man's-land. On the contrary, the identity of the stronger region, the prevailing one, bursts out here in traits which are particularly clear. Therefore, in these circumstances it is legitimate to try to understand a region through the study of its periphery. This method is absolutely essential in those pioneer fringes—and South America offers several examples—where men and their activities are highly concentrated and, moving ahead, leave behind them an exhausted countryside, emptied of most of its inhabitants. In fact one wonders whether it would not be truer to say that in these extreme cases regional reality has become merged in the frontier phenomenon. We might then find ourselves faced with a unique example—which contradicts all our rules—of a region on the move. Geographical logic tends rather to consider this category of frontiers as the evidence of a failure. The study of these 'hollow shells' is, in the long run, one of still-born regions.

Let us conclude. As far as the region is concerned the geographer in 1960 is a prey to a certain anxiety. Like the anthropologist faced with the possible disappearance of the subjects of his researches he dare not place too much reliance on it for fear of seeing it slip through his fingers. Sometimes, as in tropical Africa, he has the feeling that he has arrived too soon; used to studying spatial articulations he finds here only unformed, embryonic regions. Elsewhere, on the other hand, and this is happening in the older countries of Europe, he can no longer recognize the familiar subjects of his researches. The region has lost its permanence, its relative geographical autonomy. Its contours are growing blurred. It tends to be conceived as a kind of geometrical locus satisfying a collection of conditions which were previously determined. Formerly the result of a free confrontation between nature and human initiative, it has now become the final end of a conscious and anticipatory process. At one extreme the monograph has come to the point of preceding the region, in the files of the planners. Seduced by this new picture the economist discovers a reality he did not know before, simultaneously changing its nature in the eyes of the geographer. Reduced to a field of forces, expressed in equations, the region is becoming further and further removed from a concrete concept, divorced from the landscape.

Must we give up then, and admit that we are out of fashion? Certainly not. We have just explained why. Renewed in both form and spirit, regional monographs intend to come to grips with the living reality. Moreover geographical knowledge is indispensable for modern attempts at a voluntary remodelling of space. Only geography—the analysis of landscape—can point out, beneath a seemingly random appearance, those precise adaptations, delicate equilibria which must not be tinkered with without careful precautions. It can draw attention to the resistance of the natural environment and the inertia of men, prisoners of their techniques or their social organization, as well as provide information on boundaries and delays which any action must respect. Behind statistical abstractions geography can reveal the teeming reality, stress the variety of local facies, and inspire a subtle preparation of programmes.

However, is this spatial geography still a regional geography? Is the region not another of those concepts like those used by physicians and naturalists? At one stage they are justified by their organizing logic, but once they have brought about the series of discoveries for which they had provided the original impetus, they are finally recognized for what they have always been—figments of the imagination. Accepting this simile would be going too far. No matter what demolition is undertaken, the region will always provide an imperishable basis, that is, a framework for geographical research, midway between a rural district and the nation-state. As we saw in the beginning, it is its dimension which makes the region a suitable framework for our researches. However, this dimension is far more than a simple commodity. Paraphrasing Cl. Lévi-Strauss, it is possible to define it as the largest area in which men and geographical facts are in direct and easy communications. This is what makes for the unity and the strength of traditional regions. And to this favoured dimension, there corresponds—both for the modern politician and the technocrat—a kind of threshold; once you have crossed it space becomes so vast, so complex that it must needs be divided and organized in order to remain in control of the situation. If we admit these facts, the resurgence of regional notions at the present time does not smack of a new fashion; it is a manifestation among responsible people of an awareness of a fundamental dimension of action. This is a development which bodes well for the geographer, who can see opening before him a large field of application, eminently suited to his most legitimate preoccupations.

Problems of Modern Political Terminology

in African Languages

PIERRE ALEXANDRE[1]

It is a striking fact that almost all political and administrative activities in modern African states are expressed basically in French or English.[1a] Independence has not altered this situation; there has even been a certain regression in the use of some Negro-African languages which had at one time been used as a kind of code, a code which had not been very accessible to the colonial authorities and therefore served as a fairly obvious instrument for subversive activities and propaganda. Even on the level of the struggle for national emancipation, moreover, the doctrinal and ideological formulation of demands and programmes used mainly (and in West Africa, exclusively), the language of the colonizers. In the history of Negro-African nationalism linguistic claims have played nothing like the role they did in the rise of European nationalism.

In states which were formerly under French rule we are tempted to interpret the local language situation as a sequel to those colonial policies which dealt with public education, in so far as the exclusive use of French in schools and in the administration, in some way, hindered, if not paralysed, their adaptation towards the expression of those new situations which sprang from colonization and its aftermath. In doing so we are perhaps neglecting the sometimes considerable

[1] *Pierre Alexandre* (b. 1922) LL.M., Ph.D. (Paris), Dipl. in Social Anthropology (London). Professor of Bantu Languages, Sorbonne Nouvelle (Paris III) since 1960. Head of African research section, National Foundation for Political Sciences; editor, *Cahiers d'Etudes Africaines*. Trained first at the Colonial Service Cadet School (ENFOM), did post-graduate work both at LSE and SOAS (London) as well as at the Ecole Pratique des Hautes Etudes (Paris). Field studies mainly in Cameroon. A general practitioner rather than a specialist, his outlook has developed from both the Griaule tradition and the later Balandier trend in African studies. The original French text of this paper was published as 'Sur les possibilités expressives des langues africaines en matière de terminologie politique', *L'Afrique et l'Asie*, 56 (1961), 13–28

[1a] Also in Portuguese by Africans of these countries: however, the few Angolan leaders I have met prefer to express themselves in French or English in order to get their ideas across to an international public.

linguistic achievements of religious missions which were active in French territories. Furthermore there was an almost equally noteworthy predominance given to English in the former British colonies, although here Negro-African languages were widely used administratively and in schools.

These statements obviously run the risk of breathing life into that old *canard*, which some people still bring up now and again, of the 'basically concrete nature of African languages' and their supposed 'inaptitude to express abstract values'. These twin assertions, so dogmatically and frequently repeated, derive from a total ignorance— or too superficial a knowledge—of the languages in question, from either a certain incapacity of the persons concerned to conceive of any other system of abstraction apart from their own, or from an erroneous conception of the nature of language. We might even suggest that these three factors are often found together.

In fact Negro-African languages seem to have quite the same possibilities for abstraction as Indo-European or Semitic languages, involving mechanisms to facilitate the passage from the concrete to the abstract which are both flexible and numerous; and we find that these forms correspond to those in many other languages, from special stylistic processes (metaphors) to morphological processes (special affixation, etc). It does not follow that they need necessarily share the same catalogue of ideas as one or other of the European languages, nor that any two Negro-African languages will possess lexical lists which are automatically and exactly superimposable. Abstract words, or so-called abstract words, form part of the lexical system of each language, in the same way as words which we call concrete, and the whole system itself is organically linked to the physical and socio-cultural context for which it serves, of course, to provide meaning and expression.

Here we are dealing with factual evidence; yet we tend to forget the obviousness of these facts, perhaps as a result of wrongly interpreting the Saussurian principle of the arbitrary nature of linguistic signs. What is 'arbitrary' in fact, is that for a signified object, 'horse' we have the signifiers [hɔːs] on one side of the Channel and [šval] on the other. On the other hand it is not at all an arbitrary fact that there is nothing to correspond to either of them in Eskimo or Bulu, since the animal 'horse' is absent both from the Bulu and the Eskimo context. What is so obviously true as to be a truism for 'horse' is all the more so for 'proportional representation', 'nation' or 'self-determination', for example. The distinction concrete/abstract is only an absolute one in elementary books on grammar. Linguistically it may offer a certain taxonomic or heuristic interest on the morphological level; all the same any rules which we set up almost always suffer from innumerable exceptions. On the semantic level things are much more complex, less well-defined, and labels such as 'concrete' and 'abstract' are sometimes little more than dangerous oversimplifications.

Let us take a look at the social and political vocabulary of an African society, which we shall hypothetically assume to be in a state of stability and functioning euphoria. The social structure will involve a certain number of relationships and each of these relationships will have one or more subjects and one or more objects. For each perceived relationship or one represented in the consciousness of society's members, there will be a corresponding term—probably an abstract one—and in the same way that each subject or object is involved in the relationship there will also be a corresponding term for them, probably 'concrete'. The whole will constitute a terminology which has been determined socially rather than linguistically. Let us take an arbitrary example: given two societies which share a similar social context, it does not matter if one of them has a term for 'chief' which derives from a root meaning 'chiefship', while in the other an inverse process derives 'chiefship' from the root for 'chief': the two terms, linguistically different, are not any the less equivalent socially, the difference in morphological structure not preventing a semantic similitude. It would be quite possible to translate the meaning exactly from one language to the other. Conversely the translation of this kind of terminology would be impossible if we have two societies which are linguistically proximate but socially very different.

The situation postulated above is obviously a non-existent one in present-day Africa. Whatever our notions about the extent of social stability in pre-colonial Africa—and they are almost always exaggerated—it is clear that it is now nothing more than a memory or a myth. Colonialization resulted in the setting up of arbitrary and artificial boundaries which now enclose societies of the most heterogeneous nature and also imposed on these societies a non-African socio-political system of foreign domination. And today they have been succeeded by independent régimes also founded on ideological, economic, and political systems of European origin. Along with their language, the colonizers introduced educational systems which were more or less inspired by their own. However, and this is the important point, the diffusion of the imported languages was not co-extensive with the spread of administrative and political systems of the same origin. No matter how direct the character of the administration or its impact on the country, no matter what the level of schooling or the educational methods, European activities everywhere resulted in the division of the people into two new groups of unequal importance: on the one hand there are people who speak one or more local languages; on the other there are those who speak English or French as well (or more rarely both). The second group, demographically, is in the minority yet is sociologically dominant.

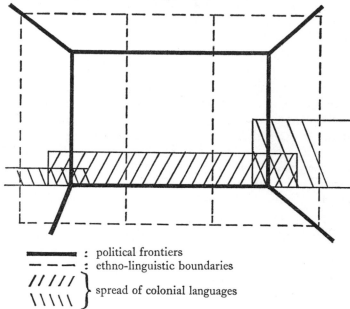

━━━━━ : political frontiers
─ ─ ─ : ethno-linguistic boundaries
/////
\\\\\ } spread of colonial languages

The ethno-linguistic situation in a modern African state.

In general the members of the first group, besides speaking their mother tongue, have a more or less extensive knowledge of several other African languages, particularly in ex-British and ex-Belgian territories where primary schooling was given in more or less arbitrarily chosen local languages. This often led to the growth of a written literature, sometimes a press, which was composed purely in the vernacular.

As for the members of the second group, there are those who speak one or more European languages as well as their African mother tongue (and sometimes several other African languages).[2] During the

[2] It should be noted that many educated Africans, especially those in British and French universities, speak their own mother tongues badly, particularly if they left Africa early to pursue further studies.

colonial period this knowledge gave them access to socially privileged key positions and with the end of colonialization they found themselves in a position to take over administrative and political techniques from the European rulers with whom they had been the first to associate. It is very important to note that, especially as far as political techniques were concerned, the transfer was made so swiftly that the necessary conceptual tools *had not had time to become Africanized*.

Afro-European bilingualism assured its possessors of a real technical monopoly, but it did not happen without posing serious problems of development for the new states. The difficulties were less serious under the colonial régimes, which were essentially of an administrative and institutional nature: they were limited in extent and most often had been superimposed, not without deleterious effects, on traditional structures without replacing them. Coming into contact with a number of relatively restricted social roles, new relationships and institutions, which had no African precedent, the colonized peoples soon gave them names, often Africanizing the European terms: the European administrator became the *disi* in Kiswahili in Kenya, the *kumadã* in Bambara (Mali), the *ngóvina*, in Bulu (Cameroon). Among the Bulu, taxes—unknown traditionally—became *toya* (from the English 'tax'), agricultural officers were *fasikale*, from Monsieur Marius Pascalet who introduced cocoa, and the recruitment of forced labour was known as *njok*, from the name of a village situated in a particularly murderous region along the Yaounde–Douala railway line. These innovations, in fact, provided no more difficulty, than those which consisted of naming such purely material novelties as rum (*bilám*) or the motor-car (*metóa*). In each of these cases the phenomena involved were very widespread; and they all had direct repercussions on the life of most of the villagers and they were neither equivalent nor even parallel to elements already socially integrated. Furthermore, acclimatization took place over a fairly long period.

The situation was very different in the post-colonial period. The number of new institutions increased very rapidly during a very brief period of time, and on top of this the spirit in which the innovations were made was of a very different nature to that which accompanied the introduction of colonial institutions.[3] Unlike the colonial rulers (particularly the British), the new national rulers usually tried to unify the system of political relations at almost every level, by

[3] I am ignoring for the moment the problem of religious proselytization, although it is a subject which has much in common with that presented by political ideology.

substituting a new system for the old one, as far as possible with the consent and the active support of the masses, to whom they had to explain what it was desired that they should desire. These new systems, even if they are couched in the new language of Negritude and Africanism, are conceived in European terms, and if they are to be communicated to the masses in order to convince them, shake them out of their apathy, or merely avoid their opposition, these terms must be translated *or adapted* (not the same thing), as quickly as possible, and the terminology is both abundant and complex. All this must be done in a way which is as homogeneous as possible, in spite of the linguistic and socio-cultural heterogeneity of the peoples concerned. On the translation or adaptation depends not only the internal political future of the new states but also, very largely, their relations with their neighbours and other countries (especially the former colonial rulers) in so far as a reciprocal understanding of each other's political concepts may help or hinder their relations.

Here we might be tempted to think that such efforts can perhaps be dispensed with, since the present political élites both form their ideas and express themselves predominantly in English and French; the problem might be resolved by a massive education scheme in the European language, a scheme which would put an end to the socio-linguistic dichotomy mentioned above, and in so doing reinforce the struggle for national unity. However, this ignores both the immediacy of the problem and the practical difficulties involved: even in those countries where the education level is relatively high, the huge majority of adults—the voters—speak African languages only and it would not be feasible to teach them a European language in a sufficiently short period. It also ignores the importance of cultural and linguistic factors in African nationalism and runs the risk, not without some apparent justification, of accusations of cultural imperialism.

Having therefore recognized the necessity for the African politician to Africanize his terminology, he has now only the choice between two extreme solutions: either simply to adapt French and English terms, allowing them to conform to the phonemic structure of the language concerned, or to look for terms or periphrases which will best translate the European terms in the local languages.

The first solution, as we saw above, existed in those *ad hoc* situations where colonial administrative terminology was translated by the use of such terms as '*commandant—kumadã*', 'D.C.—*disi*', etc. Most likely this method will be used readily for many terms for roles

and institutions which lack any precedent or equivalent—such as
'deputy', 'minister', 'president'. It is rather like the way certain
technical or scientific terms are diffused through our Indo-European
languages, either from the language of the inventors (*sputnik*) or put
together from common Greco-Latin roots (automobile, telephone).
This process succeeds particularly well in regions where the languages
of the colonialists were sufficiently diffused and where political
acculturation was early and most intensive. The semantic content of
these borrowed words may vary a lot. Here we come up against the
concrete/abstract opposition. It would perhaps be better to view as a
distinction between simple, tangible (or verifiable) non-ambiguous
signifiés,[4] and complex, non-tangible ones, the latter corresponding to
relationships rather than to the objects and subjects of these relationships. Let us take 'deputy' and 'communism' as concrete examples:
introduced either as they are, or phonetically modified, into a Negro-
African language, the first word will quickly take on a much more
precise meaning ('that nice fellow X' or 'that bastard Y') than the
second ('the devil and his train', 'happiness in this world'). According
to the effect which the African politician wishes to make on the
masses, he may either be led, particularly with words of the second
type, to make borrowings from European languages or otherwise use
vernacular expressions which are adequate for this purpose.

This second method is not without difficulties. I mentioned above
that the vocabulary of a language forms a system peculiar to that
language because it is conditioned by the total ecological context of
the speakers. As a result it is highly likely that the vocabularies of two
languages with different ecologies will not be exactly superimposable;
or in other terms, that no literal, word-for-word translation will be
possible, from one language to the next. If the semantic field of the
two given words are not absolutely identical, they will partially
overlap, the semantic field of *one* word in language A overlapping in
this way or being intersected by the semantic fields of *n* words in
language B. Translation from A into B—which would really be more
of an adaptation—will consist therefore of choosing one of the *n*
words in B language which have fields cutting across that of the A
word we are translating. This word may have a connotation, a
feeling, which is different from that of the 'translated' word. At one
extreme the differences may be such that an honest translator will
prefer to keep the word we are trying to translate—'in A in the text'.

[4] In de Saussure's terminology, i.e. the non-linguistic elements of the total context which are expressed by significants, i.e. the linguistic signs.

However, politicians are not necessarily honest translators. Moreover, two words which are exactly superimposable as far as the *signifié* is concerned, may be radically opposed to each other as regards their expressive implications: remember the anecdote of the grateful Hindu who said to a Paris policeman, '*Brigadier*, you are a real cow.'

The African politician who wants to 'translate' a certain European notion, is, in certain cases, able to use a word which corresponds to a relationship or role which has lost its former function as a result of the social disintegration caused by the colonial impact. He gives it a kind of new currency. On the other hand he may have recourse to a word which still has a highly charged semantic content, either, for example, because he wishes to transfer to a new relationship or role the high or low prestige with which the word is endowed, or else he wishes to change the semantic load of the word because of the high or low prestige of the relationship or role.

In fact, in many, if not the majority of cases, the choice of an African word to 'translate' an English or French term is more an accidental than a conscious one, something which is 'better than nothing'. The semantic inertia of the chosen word still tends to colour or inflect in a certain sense one or more aspects of local political life. If we consider the lack of ethno-linguistic homogeneity in most Negro-African states, we see that there is a certain peril which affects party cohesion and also, as a result, national unity. The first solution, which we mentioned above—involving the borrowing of European words which have been Africanized, phonetically—is not enough to avoid this peril since the structural elements of the phrase, particularly the predicatives, vary sufficiently from language to language for the 'translation' from the same text into two idioms, which are geographically (but not linguistically) neighbours, to produce quite different emotional resonance. Non-specialists are not always aware of the fact that the forms used to translate our verb 'to be' are semantically very different from one language to the next—they may indicate essence, identity, physical presence, presence in a place, presence at a certain time, existence, staying, the fact of not being absent, or a relationship. The same applies to the verb 'to have'. Finally we again have the difficulty of translating verbal tense conjugations (past, present, future . . .) in a language with aspective conjugation (action unfinished, finished, repeated action, action beginning, etc.).

These difficulties crop up more or less often according to the language concerned, but always very quickly. The surprising thing is,

perhaps, that there have not been more of them and that a mere
fifty to a hundred years of contact should have produced, in many
cases, phenomena of linguistic interference which are sufficient in a
number of cases to solve these difficulties. Whatever the case they
allow us to observe and understand a phenomenon which is found in
all—or almost all—contemporary Negro-African political parties,
and which is moreover unaffected by differences in organization:
doctrines, ideological principles, and often general programmes are
formulated, and, if need be, discussed in French and English at the
higher levels; propaganda—of various kinds—in the vernacular
languages, which are aimed at the masses, are merely simplified and
schematicized, reduced to the 'larger issues'.[5] It might be commented,
it is true, that analogous facts can be found in European political
parties; there is, however, one basic difference and that is that in
Europe the difference between political expression at the top and
bottom echelons of the party is quantitative, in the main, while in
Africa it is qualitative and marked by a total modification of conceptual
and expressive tools: there is in fact a discontinuity, even if it is
unintended. The same considerations explain the fact, even in a one-
party state, that the lower sections of the party, even including those
in urban centres, remain highly tribalist.[6]

Negro-African languages *in their present state*, are incapable of
expressing political doctrines conceived in European terms. African
political leaders who are attempting to formulate an ideology for a
practical programme, adapted to the context of the twentieth century,
are therefore obliged for the time being to use tools which are not
accessible to the masses they govern, while at the same time being
irrevocably committed to keeping in polyglot contact with masses
whom they must keep informed and whose opinions they must mould.
We might therefore expect—and here there is no need to imply a
conscious machiavellianism on the leaders' part—to find a pronounced
difference between the party's doctrines as they are formulated and
agreed upon at the summit and the way they are 'translated' (adapted)
for diffusion to the masses—and as a result the way they are 'applied'
among the people. After all, these things are probably less shocking
in Africa than they may seem to us, living in a liberal democracy of

[5] W. H. Whiteley: 'Political Concepts and Connotations: observations on the use
of some political terms in Swahili', *St Anthony's Papers 10 (African Affairs 1)*,
(Chatto and Windus: London, 1961), pp. 7–21.
[6] Cf. I. Wallerstein, 'Ethnicity and National Integration in West Africa', and
A. R. Zolberg, 'Effets de la structure d'un parti politique sur l'intégration nationale',
Cahiers d'Etudes Africaines, vol. i, no. 3, pp. 129–39 and 140–9.

the European type, as long as we take into consideration the initiations and rites de passage traditions of many African peoples.

The fact remains that, as long as this situation lasts, that is as long as all the people of a given state do not share a knowledge of the language used by its leaders, or until the local languages have sufficiently evolved under the influence of the new situation to be able to express imported or adapted notions, the whole political situation will remain affected. It would be useless, in any case, to try to compare the situation of a contemporary polyethnic African state with that of a multilingual European state such as Switzerland or Belgium as certain optimists are wont to do: they ignore the fact that Flemish, French, German, and Italian all possess, at this stage, expressive and conceptual potentials which are similar, due allowance being made for their special ecological contexts,[7] which are themselves all involved in twentieth-century industrialization, a context which the Negro-African state has hardly begun to enter.

APPENDICES

I *The adaptation of certain current political terms into Bulu (Southern Cameroon Bantu)*

Some of the following examples are taken from my own notes, but most have been found in texts (the journal *Mefoé*, propaganda, or counter-propaganda pamphlets published by the American Presbyterian Mission, later the Presbyterian Church of the Cameroon).

'Party' is translated sometimes by [9]*ngam*, sometimes by [3]*nsámbá*. *ngam* is a nominal derived from the verbal root *kam*, meaning 'to keep for yourself' > 'prohibit' > 'forbid' > 'protect' > 'take sides over' > 'favour' (note here the parallel between the French '*défendre-interdire*' / *défendre-protéger*). *ngam* originally had the sense of being 'a party to a trial' (remembering that all traditional trials were between groups not individuals) or 'a team playing against another in a game'; from the beginning the connotation is therefore basically dual or bipartite.

nsámbá once meant 'a group of people brought together temporarily for an expedition of limited duration, with a precise end in view: a group journey, a warrior raid, a collective hunt, portering goods to the coast, etc.'. These temporary and voluntary associations group

---

[7] But only as far as this context is concerned; a perusal of anthropological monographs, reveals immediately the inaptitude of European languages for expressing relationships, functions or roles which evolved in an African socio-cultural context.

together members from several villages or clans: when they meet or
break up there is a sacrificial rite and a communal meal. The connotation of opposition and the dual nuance of *ngam* are absent; on the
other hand we have the idea of temporariness and the idea of having
a single precise end in view.

The word *nsámbá* is also used to translate both 'society, association,
group of people' and 'social class'. This latter notion is also translated
by [5]*aválǝ bot* ('kind, category of people').

The following schema results:

$$
\begin{array}{ll}
\text{'party'} \\
\text{'class'}
\end{array}
\left\{
\begin{array}{l}
ngam\text{—idea of dual opposition} \\
\left\{
\begin{array}{l}
ns\acute{a}mb\acute{a}\text{—idea of temporary association} \\
\text{with a single objective} \\
av\acute{a}l\partial\ bot\text{—neutral notion of} \\
\text{category}
\end{array}
\right.
\end{array}
\right.
$$

whereby *nsámbá* is in some way neutralized by the cutting across of the
fields of 'class' and 'party' (as long as the confusion does not result in
the identification of 'class' with party).

The term 'member' (of a party or a class) is rendered by the
following terms:

[1]*mot*—'person, *homo*', followed by the name of the party or its head
[1]*mɔ́n*—'child, son of' followed by the name of the party (a construction
    identical with that for tribal membership: *mɔ́ná Bulu*: a Bulu)

these two words being considered as equivalent to our suffix '-ist';

[7]*ejula*—'comrade, companion'
[9]*mvón*—'initiate, member of an initiatory ritual association'
[5]*awɔsó*—'men belonging to the same initiation class'
[7]*enam*—'member (leg or arm)', 'sleeve of a garment'

and finally

[1a]*ébǝ*, *mbɔ́*, *ébǝlǝ* which correspond roughly to our prefix 'co-'.

The affective connotations of these words differ noticeably. The
most neutral of them is probably *ejula*; *mvón* is exclusive in nature,
being opposed to *ebis* ('non-initiate, profane'), and it clearly implies a
kind of rejection of those who do not belong to the party; *awɔsó*
traditionally implied a very close tie, a kind of pseudo-kinship; it is
only used vocatively, almost metaphorically; *enam* is borrowed from
the translated New Testament, the metaphor 'member' of an
association is therefore an importation and is primarily applied to a

member-communicant of a church (whom the pagans call *mvón*, 'initiate'): it has retained a certain flavour of its Christian origin. Some translate 'citizen' by *enamá si*, 'member of the land, of the country'.

Phrases with *mot* and *mɔn* denote a kind of basic tie, such as those between members of a tribe or kin group; *mot* Lumumba is therefore stronger than 'a Lumumbist'; it is more like 'one of Lumumba's men'. In the same way *mɔna komunis* marks off a man as a communist very definitely, just like 'white man' or 'French man' or any other characteristic which is only acquired through birth or adoption into a family.

Note finally the choice made for ideas of political 'competition' and 'opponent'; their overtones may well have influenced the general coloration of political life in Southern Cameroon—unless it was the other way round.

For 'competition' there has been some hesitation between

mɔsiŋ—'open-handed wrestling', a traditional national sport on which
    depends the prestige of village communities
[8]*bitá*—'war'
[6]*mɔlúman*—'quarrel, brawl, affray'
[9]*ziŋ*—'permanent enmity, hostility'.

The last two are the ones mostly used and hence we have 'opponent' translated by: [3]*nsiŋ*—'enemy' (strong sense) rather than by:[1] *nsiŋ* or [9]*siɲi* which means 'a person against whom one fights or with whom one plays a game'.

II *A test of dual translating in Mbɛnɛ (Bantu of the Southern Cameroon)*

In order to study the correctness of the translation of a political manifesto from French into Mbɛnɛ, this text, chosen at random from a collection published by *Présence Africaine*, was given for translation to a Basaa student (*mbɛnɛ* is the name of the Basaa's language), educated to pre-university level and accustomed to talking politics in his mother tongue. The Mbɛnɛ translation was then given to another Basaa who retranslated it into French without seeing the original text.

English translation of the original French text (taken from Sékou Touré, *The Guinea Experiment and African Unity*, Présence Africaine, Paris, 1959, pp. 282–283):

Communiqué from the Political Bureau of the PDG:

'The Political Bureau of the Democratic Party of Guinea, the P.D.G., after a study in depth of the political situation in Africa, following on the referendum, and after analysing the conclusions of a meeting of the Bureau of the Committee of Coordination of the R.D.A. (Rassemblement Démocratique Africain), held in Paris, on the 7, 8, 9 October 1958.

'Considers that the decision of the Bureau of the Committee of Coordination to bring about the separate adherence to the Community, territory by territory, sanctifies a definitive balkanization of the Federations and gravely compromises African unity, which all the sections of the R.D.A. had given as their basic reasons for approving the projected constitution.

'The P.D.G. is astounded by the clear declarations of the President of the R.D.A., in defining the Community, not as a means of emancipating the African people on the road to sovereignty and independence, but as a structure which will integrate in a permanent fashion the African states as separate units within the French Community.

'The P.D.G. affirms the manifest incompatibility of its conception of the character, dignity, and genuine aspirations of Africa and their membership of the R.D.A., the president of which now extols, in an unambiguous fashion, the keeping of Africa in a position of subordination, sacrifices African personality, and renounces to make use of the clearsightedness of Secretary General Sekou Touré whose political awareness has enabled Guinée to make a decisive choice and to turn the African masses' aspirations to independence into a living reality.

Upon the platform of national independence and full sovereignty for Guinée, the PDG makes the solemn declaration that it no longer considers itself a section of RDA, and that it is henceforth the natural ally of any section of RDA, PRA or any other democratic organisation which will openly take its place in the actual fight for African unity, a fight unseparable from the fight for national independence, in view of a common final aim which historically remains the formation of the United States of Black Africa

Counter-translation (from Mbɛnɛ)
Communiqué of the *Political Bureau* of PDG

Having considered the *political* situation in Africa after *the referendum* as well as the decisions of the meeting of the *bureau* of the *committee* of *coordination* of the R.D.A. which met in Paris on the 7, 8, 9 October 1958;

the *Political Bureau* of the Autonomous Party of Guinea, thinks that the resolution of the *bureau* of the *committee* of *coordination* by which each country should separately join the *community* is a cause of serious division between the parties, and is also opposed to the unity in Africa of the *sections* of the R.D.A. which have agreed to establish common links;

the declarations of the *President* of the R.D.A., which say that the *Community* is not a means of sending Africans on the road to *self-government* (in English in the text) and independence, but aims at confining, separately, the African peoples in the *French Community*, surprise the *P.D.G.*;

the *P.D.G.* declares that its conception of the character, honour, and true problems of Africa does not accord with its presence within the R.D.A., whose *President* has clearly affirmed that Africa should remain a dominated land, thereby betraying its nature, and since he has also rejected the experience of the *Secretary general*, Sékou Touré, whose political skill has allowed *Guinea* to choose a good method of showing the true face of African unity, corresponding thereby to the aspirations of Africans for liberty;

in the interest of the country's independence and the genuine sovereignty of *Guinea*, the P.D.G. firmly states that it has ceased to be a *section* of the R.D.A., and declares that from now on it is linked in a brotherly fashion with each section of the R.D.A., the P.R.A. (Parti du Regroupement Africain) or any party whatsoever which declares its supoprt of the fight for African unity, which is inseparable from the fight for national independence, in order to achieve the great desire for union of the Negro-African peoples.'

We should note the proportion and nature of terms kept in French in the Mbɛnɛ text (italics); basically they are technical terms referring to the central organs of the party; on the other hand the idea of 'party' and the general objectives of the party are translated (keeping in mind the fact that the Cameroon party of which this translator was a militant supporter has the same organization, the same origin, and the same policies as the P.D.G.). The initials of the parties are kept as they are, but they should really be considered as African proper names (Pededze, Erdea, etc.), rather than the initials of foreign words.

A comparison of the counter-translation from Mbɛnɛ and the original French text reveals a degree of condensation and concentration which does not however do any great injustice to the stylistic qualities of the original. The essentials remain and the general sense is faithfully preserved; although certain images could not be translated, the connotation of certain periphrases has been changed and the affective feeling of the whole is no longer the same—it is rather more peremptory in translation, in spite of the loss of the classic Marxist adjectives such as 'effective', 'historical', etc.

Among other points of detail, note that:

the neutral expression 'integrate in a permanent fashion in the community' becomes in Mbɛnɛ 'imprisonment' within the community; a highly unfavourable connotation, but it paraphrases quite correctly, if more brutally, the spirit of the text; the alternative in fact would have been to use an expression meaning 'adoption', which has a clearly favourable connotation and is therefore opposed to the general tone;

'any other democratic organization' becomes 'the domination groups whatever they be', with which we might find fault;

the term *Afrika*, borrowed both from German and English is quite as difficult to pronounce in Mbɛnɛ as *Afrique* would be; the choice of the German form is to be compared with the spelling *Kamerun* for 'Cameroon' which is always used by Cameroon extreme nationalists.

Translation into Mbɛnɛ (Standard Protestant orthography) with juxta-linear counter-translation.

'Communiqué / Bureau Politique / bi / P.D.G.'
'Communiqué / of / the Political Bureau / of / the D.G.P.'

Ki / i ntibil bengé / libag[8] / li Politique / i kété / Afrika / i mbus /
As / it has well looked at / state / of Politics / in / Africa / after /

Referendum / , ki / i ntoñol / makidig / ma lidoda /
the Referendum /, as / it has examined / the decision / of the meeting /

li Bureau / i Comité / i Coordination i R.D.A. /
of the Bureau / of the Committee / of Coordination of the R.D.A. /

li / li bitagbe / i Paris / dilo / 7, 8, ni 9 / di soñ / jôm /
which / happened / at Paris / day / 7, 8, and 9 / of the month / ten /

i moi 1958. /
of the year 1958. /

Bureau Politique / i / nlôñ[9] / u / ane[10] / loñ[11] /
The Political Bureau / of / the party / of / ruling / (of the) country /

Guinée / i nhoñal / le / liteag / li / Bureau i
(of) Guinea / thinks / that / the resolution / of the / Bureau of the

Comité / i Coordination / i nté[12] / le / hiki /
Committee / of Coordination / (which) has decided / that / each /

loñ / yo mede / yon / i nlama / job / i Community /
country / itself / that / should / enter / into the Community /

li nlona / soso / mbogla / i minlôñ /
it (the resolution) brings / big / separation / of the parties /

[8] Nominal form of v. *ba* 'to be', literally 'being' or 'way of being'.
[9] Literally 'group, meeting' cf. Bulu *nsámbá*.
[10] 'Ruling, command', here used in the sense of self-government.
[11] *loñ* (Bulu *ayoñ*) refers more to a 'people' or literally to a 'tribe', rather than to a 'country'; here the best equivalent would no doubt be 'nation' (cf. its pre-revolutionary nuance in French).
[12] From the verb *té*, literally to 'raise up'.

li johag / ki / adna / i Afrika / i bisection[13] /
(and) it fights / also / the union / in Africa / of the sections /

bi R.D.A. / gwo / biso / na / bi bi neebe / i té / matiñ,
of the R.D.A. / those / all / who / have agreed / to establish / knots.

Mapdog[14] / ma President / i R.D.A. / ma / ma nkol / le /
The words / of the President / of the R.D.A. / which / say / that /

Communauté / i tabé / njel[15] / i niiga / bon ba Africa[16] /
the Community / is not / a way / of teaching / the Africans /

i pes[17] / i ane / be mede / ni / i kunde[18] / , ndé / le /
the manner / of ruling / themselves / and / of liberty / , but / that /

i bi boña / i nyu / biloñ bi Afrika / bi / bi yé nkabag[19] /
it was made / to put / the countries of Africa / which / are divided /

i kêté / mog / mi ngi pam / i French Communauté, /
in / prison / without coming out / from the French Community,/

ma nhélés / P.D.G.
they (the words) astonish/ the D.P.G.

P.D.G. / i nkal / le / linogog / i nog /
The D.P.G. / it declares / that / the manner / it understands /

libag li mut / lipém[20] / ni / banga / mahoñol / i Afrika /
the state of man / honour / and / the   true / carings / of Africa

li nla be / kiha / lôñni / ba wé / i kété / R.D.A. / i / Président /
can not / go / with / being / in the / D.A.R. / whose / President /

a mpot / nyo to liten[21] / le / Afrika / i konde / ndig / ba / isi /
has said / clearly / that / Africa / continues / only / to be / land /

ane[9],   /   ni hala[22]   /   a nsem[23]   /   libag[8]   /
(of) domination, / (and) therefore / has betrayed / the situation /

---

[13] Note the plural form using *bi*-, cl. 8, genre 7/8 which in most Bantu languages includes most names of material things.
[14] Literally 'ways of speaking'.
[15] Literally, 'road' cf. 'way'.
[16] *bon ba Afrika* 'the children of Africa'; *bot ba Afrika* 'the people of Africa'.
[17] Literally, 'side > direction'.
[18] Traditionally it means 'the condition of not being a slave'.
[19] Literally, 'in a state of division'.
[20] Literally, 'reputation'.
[21] Literally, 'with a mouth without saliva', an excess of saliva being supposed to hinder speaking.
[22] Literally, 'with that'.
[23] Literally, 'has given'.

li Afrika / a yeleg / ki / liyi jam / li Secrétaire
of Africa / (and) rejects[24] / also / science[25] / of the Secretary

Général Séku Turé / , nu / yi yé Politique /
General Sékou Touré / , that one (whose) / knowing of politics /

i bi boñ / le / Guinée / i teb / longe / njel / i téba /
has made / that / Guinea / choose / the good / road / to show /

banga / su / i adna Afrika, / i yônhag[26] /
the true / face / of the union (of) Africa, / (and) corresponds /

ki / mahoñol / ma kunde / ma bôt ba Afrika.[16]
also / (to the) carings / of liberty / of Africans.

Inyu / ngui / kunde / loñ ni i banga /
For / the strength / (of) liberty / (of) the country and of the true /

ane / i Guinée / , P.D.G. / i mbédés / kiñ / i kal / le /
rule / of Guinea / , the D.P.G. / raises / (its) voice / to say / that /

i ta ha bé / Section i R.D.A. / nile / ibôdôl /
it is no longer / a Section of the R.D.A. / and that / beginning from /

hano / i yé / ñadbaga / ki / ligweag / yag / hiki / Section i
now / it is / bound / as / (by) birth / with[27] / each / Section of the

R.D.A. / to i P.R.A. / to / nlôñ / u ane / wo ki wo[28] /
R.D.A. / or / of P.R.A. / or / group / of command / whatever it be /

u / u ga éba wo mede / i kété / sañ / inyu / adna / i Afrika /
which / will show itself[29] / in / the fight / for / the union / of Africa /

, i nla be bagla ni sañ / inyu kunde /
, (fight) which cannot be separated from the fight / for liberty /

loñ, / inyu yônôs / ngôñ / ikeñi / i i yé / iboñ /
(of the) country, / to answer[26] / the desire / big / which is / to make /

adna / biloñ / bi miñindô / mi Afrika.'
union / of countries / of the Blacks / of Africa.'

---

[24] Literally, 'refused'.
[25] Literally, 'the fact of knowing non-material things' (most Bantu languages contrast 'material' with 'non-material' things).
[26] Literally 'to fill', cf. 'fulfil'.
[27] Literally 'among' (French: 'chez').
[28] Literally 'he as he'.

3

On the Mode of Production

of the Hunting Band

CLAUDE MEILLASSOUX[1]

In an earlier paper I tried to build up the model of a self-sustaining agricultural economic system in its progress towards social hierarchisation.[2] The method involved in constructing the above mentioned model was roughly based on the following steps: (1) recognition, through the detection of a set of common articulated features belonging to several samples of social formations, of a type of society; (2) detection of the basic—determinant or critical[3]—traits of the system; (3) examination of the conditions of reproduction of the system within the limits imposed by the interaction of the above traits; (4) effect of the impact of exogenous factors (Meillassoux, 1965). While an analysis of several samples of social formations is necessary to reveal, through comparisons, their common characteristics as well as to formulate the type to which the model is applicable, this does not necessarily demand an exhaustive comparative study. The comprehensiveness of the model (that is, the logical

[1] *Claude Meillassoux* (b. 1925), M.A. (Economics, University of Michigan); Dipl. Political Science (Paris), Ph.D. (Sorbonne). Research Fellow, National Centre for Scientific Research (CNRS). Extensive field research in Mali and the Ivory Coast. Specializing in Economic Anthropology, he can be considered one of the leaders of a neo-marxist trend in France, particularly interested in the development of a united field theory for the Social Sciences. The original French text of this paper was published as 'Recherche d'un niveau de détermination dans la société cynégétique', *L'Homme et la Société*, 6 (1967), 95–105.
[2] Meillassoux, 1960. The drawing up of such a model raises epistemological problems which, at the time of its conception, could not be enlightened by more recent ideas and researches on the subject (Bettelheim, 1966; Althusser and others, 1966). In spite of their quality, however, the fitting of these works to pre-capitalist formations remains to be done.
[3] Traits are determinant when they condition the overall structure of the society which can be logically deduced from them (for instance, our claim in the present paper is that the mode of exploitation of the land is determinant of the social, political, and ideological processes of the hunting band). Traits are critical when, being the product of a given set of conditions, their alteration causes a crisis of the system and the need of adjustment (self-subsistence, for instance, would be a critical trait of the agricultural community).

relations which are set up between its different parts), its internal dialectic (that is, the contradictory process through which the system changes to perpetuate itself), informs us of its verisimilitude, even when constructed on a limited number of cases.

The validity of such a model can be tested in several ways:

by its application to societies which did not provide data for its formulation;

by the uncovering of hidden traits within social formations of the type;

by deducing the characteristics of societies which will result from a development of the model to its predicted limits; and finally

by fitting the model within a set of homogeneous models applicable to other types of societies.

The last test is much the most exacting, since the model must not only fit the actual social formations, it must also involve concepts of a broader application, operative in a larger ensemble.

THE SOCIAL ORGANIZATION OF THE BAND

The analysis of a hunting economy, which is here briefly compared to an agricultural one, aims at attempting an examination of the possibilities of fitting models, applicable here to two economic systems, into an ensemble through the use of a common concept, that of the *mode of exploitation of the land*; an endeavour which, at the same time, should permit a better characterization of both societies.

Logically we should have begun our proceeding with the analysis of an earlier economic system than agricultural economy. Two reasons have so far prevented us from submitting hunting and foraging economy to this kind of analysis. One was the difficulty of finding operative concepts in the least differentiated social formations. For a long time, reference to their own society led anthropologists to consider the primitive societies as an antithesis (*non*-industrial, *non*-literate, *non*-trading, etc.) that is, in negative and irrelevant terms. Positive categories or traits are more difficult to tease out, since the relevant ones are often perceptible only when they have developed in more complex systems, in such a way that our knowledge of these latter societies helps to understand the former, at least as much as it does the other way round.

A second obstacle is of a different order. It concerns the paucity of data on the social organization of the production among the hunters and foragers in Africa. Besides, most of them are in some kind of contact with cultivators with whom they are associated in an exchange of services and goods. It was therefore difficult to undertake such a task without proper information, and to consider them as representatives of an original way of life, subject to strictly endogenous forces, so long as precise studies of these relationships with neighbouring societies had not been done. We now have some good studies on the subject of African Pygmies in reference to this problem, among which the recent work of Colin Turnbull (1965) provides, for the first time, scientific and usable data on the economic and social organization of African hunters in their own environment, contrasted to their behaviour when living in contact with farming communities. Therefore I shall mainly rely, in this analysis, on this author's work on the Mbuti pygmies.[4]

Turnbull first describes the Mbuti in their relations with the sedentary farmers during their seasonal stays near the village. In exchange for game, ivory, skins, or for guarding the villagers' farms, the Mbuti receive food (consumed on the spot), iron arrowheads, used instead of fire-hardened ones[5] and non-productive goods. None of these products are hoarded, nor do they become items in internal exchange among the Mbuti themselves. The capacity of the Mbuti to produce a surplus to exchange with the outside, without being constrained to do it and without giving up other essential activities, shows that we are not dealing with a society arrested at sheer subsistence level.[6] According to Turnbull, the Mbuti admit that scarcity is more frequently due to laziness than to difficulties involved in hunting and gathering (ibid., p. 28).[7] We are not, therefore, dealing with scarcity in the strict material meaning of the notion.[8] While

[4] Examples are limited to African societies in order to remain within a single ethno-cultural framework within which historical contact between different economic systems can eventually be examined. But since the first publication of this paper in French (1966), important material on the hunters' and foragers' economy, using world-wide comparisons, has been provided in Lee and Devore (eds.), 1968.

[5] Although iron offers little technical advantage, since animals are more often killed by the poison than by the impact of the projectile.

[6] The notion of subsistence economy is not to be confused with that of a self-sustaining one. The former is supposedly foredoomed to the inability of producing more and beyond than its basic needs; the latter satisfies its needs through the exploitation of resources within reach of the group without resorting to trade.

[7] Calculation made from the studies of the working hours of hunters shows that the productivity of their labour is greater than that of a farmer. (See Sahlins in Lee and Devore, pp. 85-9.)

[8] We do not hold with the concept of scarcity as introducing the notion of choice, in the way many classical economists have done. If by scarcity is meant insufficient

living in the forest, the Pygmies return easily to their own, original way of life and to their own institutions. Turnbull stresses the fact that contact with the Bantu peoples does not alter the specific way of life of the Mbuti from the moment they retire into the forest for periods of six months or more. He shows that the Mbuti are capable of satisfying their needs without recourse to exchange. Iron, even fire, and all the foodstuffs consumed in the village, are not indispensable to them. In other words, the self-sustaining economy of the Mbuti is here preserved. Since exchanges with cultivators are only episodic, the Pygmy economy remains basically a foraging and hunting one.

Foraging is regularly undertaken by the women who move in bands for reasons of mutual security. It is also done by men during their hunting expeditions. Only rudimentary tools are needed— sticks, wooden blades, baskets—made from basic materials found in the forest.

As far as hunting is concerned, Turnbull distinguishes bands of archers from hunters with nets. Hunting with nets is a collective activity. Each nuclear family—which in fact means each married adult male—owns a net. Turnbull gives a maximum of thirty nets and a minimum of seven to make up a hunting group, that is, bands of seven to thirty families. The archers come in smaller groups of five or six hunters, although the band which undertakes the big annual collective hunt is about the size of a large group of net hunters. Among both there is individual trapping in the immediate neighbourhood of the camp. Hunting implements are therefore restricted to nets, bows and arrows, spears, and traps. Turnbull gives less information about the archers than the net hunters and we shall therefore confine our discussion to the latter.

The *social organization of work* involves age groups rather than kinship groups, since the latter do not coincide with any co-operative productive units.[9] These age groups distinguish between children, celibate youths, married adults, and old people—sex distinctions,

---

production, this would involve the non-reproduction of the group, therefore a dysfunction which cannot be analysed as an organic feature of the system, but as a regressive or accidental phenomenon. If the notion of scarcity means the impossibility of obtaining everything at once, it gives but a confused idea of the limits imposed on any given system of production.

[9] L. Marshall (1960) has described Kung Bushmen bands as being founded on kinship. In fact, while so-called 'kinship' terms are used in reference to other members of the band, kinship is not the principle of social organization involved. As she says elsewhere, (p. 345) membership of a band derives more from choice than from family imperatives.

according to Turnbull, are secondary. The adults participate in the hunting beats, catch and kill animals with spears; the adolescents and some of the women beat up the game; old people trap individually or stay behind in the camp, making tools or cooking. The spoils of hunting and gathering activities are shared out at the end of the expedition, even if it is an individual one. Collective catches are divided among all the members of a band, according to variable rules, the main one being to assure subsistence to all members, active or otherwise. A special share is also kept for him who has lent his net, if game is actually caught with it.

Turnbull describes the social system of the Mbuti as being the antithesis of that of the village farmers. 'Against political centralization it offers complete decentralization and diffusion of authority. Against a sedentary, patrilineal, patrilocal village it matches the nomadic, nonlineal, territorial band. The vertical village kinship system is countered by a horizontal age-level system. Village values are directly opposed to forest values.' (Turnbull (1965), p. 300.)

The Mbuti are organized in unstable bands whose composition is defined by their exploitation of a same territory. The system of kinship is extremely elementary: there are five kinship terms which designate the father, the mother, and (without distinguishing sex) the children, the first-degree collaterals and the grandparents. Marriage involves a preference for 'sister' exchange, without any payment of bridewealth.[10] It is most frequently matrilocal. A partner is traditionally chosen from a different band, and one which is not an immediate neighbour. The nuclear family has but a mediocre existence as a social unit. Although the married man owns the net, his authority over his close kin is queried at all times, both by the band and by the age groups of which all his kinsfolk are members. Children are easily adopted into other families, sometimes into other bands. Sexual intercourse between unmarried young folk within a band as well as extra-marital relations are frowned upon but common. Marital separation is frequent. Incest is forbidden only between siblings, but it is not proscribed between kin of adjacent generations. None of these prohibitions seem to lead to serious sanctions if they are violated. Genealogical memory does not go further back than two generations; there is no ancestor cult. The closest relationships between kin involve the following: the education of very small children by their mothers, continued by the whole band after weaning;

---

[10] 'Sister' applies here to any unmarried girl from the band. The relevance of kinship terminology in the case of the Mbuti is highly questionable.

the prestations owed by a married man to his parents-in-law over a period of several years (apparently as long as they remain in the hunters' group); the gift of an individual hunting net to a married man by his mother or his maternal uncle. Kinship is neither a durable tie, nor the basis of social organization. Not only the band but even the nuclear family itself is unstable.

THE MODE OF EXPLOITATION OF THE LAND AND ITS IMPLICATIONS

In spite of his excellent description of Mbuti economic institutions, and his acute comments, Turnbull tends here often to confuse economics with exchange and ecology. He implicitly recognizes that there is a relationship between economy and social structure, a relationship which he characterizes, however, as a 'cultural' one: 'culturally they are . . . distinguished from their neighbours as a unit, being hunters and gatherers and not cultivators, with a *consequently* totally distinct social structure.' (p. 22, our italics). Having rightly rejected the ecological determinism of Steward (1955) he pays no further attention to the possible impact of the mode of production on the social organization. Curiously, since the excellence of his observations might have permitted a more refined interpretation, he concludes that Mbuti 'values' (!) provide explanatory principles for the differences between them and the village farmers (p. 16).

Yet it is clear that the main differences between these two societies derive from their mode of exploitation of the land. In the terms of Marx (*Capital*, vol. I, p. 178–9) land is a *subject of labour* for the Mbuti and an *instrument of labour* for the farming villagers. The main characteristics of the two economic systems derive from this. Where the land is used as a subject of labour, man accepts nature's bounty without any attempt towards maintenance or reclamation. The low productivity of the land is compensated by a high productivity of labour. The exhaustion of resources drives the group from one area to the next until the exploited flora and fauna have replaced themselves naturally. Here, exploitation of the land does not lead to the construction of a farming ground, to any lasting organization and arrangement of the landscape; exploitation is only defining a territory whose limits are those of the neighbouring groups of hunters.[11]

This mode of exploitation results in a kind of roving within a loose area. For want of investment in the land, labour applied to

[11] We have here a distinction better expressed in French between a 'terroir' and a 'territoire'.

it yields an *instantaneous* return, not a deferred one. This mode of exploitation involves discontinuous undertakings of a limited duration, independent of each other and whose product is obtained immediately at the end of each venture. Supplies are provided through these repeated operations, carried out at brief intervals, usually daily.

Since the results of labour are independent of any previous investment, they are highly aleatory in return. Turnbull rightly points out that an individual hunter's production is too uncertain to provide him with regular food supplies. The formation of large groups and of organized teams of hunters and foragers reduces the risk of food shortage. Indeed, *individual* hunting might be the main cause of the *social* cohesion of the band. Also, because of their mode of exploitation, the hunters and gatherers find themselves in competition with predatory animals: in exploiting the forest outside the camp they are entering their spheres of activity. *Security* is another reason, therefore, to work as groups: the women gather the food in teams, singing or making noises as they go in order to ward off danger; nor do the archers move about except in groups of five or six, individual hunting —by trapping—is done in the vicinity of the camp only.

Collective hunting, with nets, involves a comparatively advanced co-operative technique. It requires a sufficient complement (from seven to thirty hunters) of partners capable of identical efforts and identical labour. The grouping of hunters is done on an *age* basis according to an optimal size of the hunting party. Groups such as these, in composition and number, go beyond the limits of the extended family. Since kinship organization is quantitatively and qualitatively well below the level which permits it to coincide with any co-operative group, it tends to become reduced to a minimal dimension, that of the conjugal nucleus. Turnbull notes in fact that the factors of band cohesion derive more from economic functions than from kinship. He also writes (1965, 111): 'The terminology of the Mbuti stresses their relative age and economic status rather than their kinship.' Relations of production, therefore, are set up between producers of equal status. The possession of a net by each of them means that they are independent of one another (so far as possession of the means of production is concerned) while they remain dependent on the band for actually putting them to work.

The social organization of production which develops around this mode of exploitation presents, as a result, a certain number of features. Co-operation between the group of hunters and gatherers is only

effective and necessary for the duration of an expedition. It ends with
the dividing of the spoils. The partners, if they wish, could immediately leave the group concerned and join another—without being
deprived or depriving the others. In other words co-operation
may be *impromptu* (it brings together each time the partners willing
to participate) and *ad hoc* (it groups members and agents necessary
for an enterprise in a circumstantial fashion). Since co-operation is
sporadic and precarious, the composition of the productive groups is
not definite (although, as far as each producing agent is concerned,
co-operation must be repeated at frequent intervals in order to ensure
a constantly renewed food supply). In other words, the mode of
production does not require a continued membership of the same
group. Nor does it create a dependence between partners since each
one owns his own tools and the sharing of the produce absolves them
of all reciprocal obligations. Relations of production do not therefore result in any long-lasting social cohesion as far as the band is
concerned. Bands are, indeed, reported to be unstable and composite.

The circulation of goods takes place within a limited and diffuse
circuit; within the co-operative group of hunters the collective
produce is divided and handed over to each of the partners individually through the institution of *sharing*. Unlike the situation in
agricultural societies, there is no redistributive system, i.e. no
centralization of the product and *deferred* distribution—the act of
circulation, as of production, is instantaneous.

The shortness and the sporadic repetition of activities lead to a way
of life which is tied *to the present*, without any duration or continuity.
The way of life is 'instantaneous'. Turnbull frequently stresses this
characteristic of Mbuti society: 'The kinship system does not have the
same importance as a focal point of social control as in other African
societies. . . . It is undeniably linked to the *ad hoc* nature of the
society with *almost* complete lack of concern for the past as for the
future.[12] This is something we shall discover in the economic and
political life and even in the religious life of the Mbuti.' The preoccupations of hunters and foragers are directed towards day-to-day
production far more than towards reproduction. Within the band
there are no durable ties binding young people to their elders,
no material dependence obliging them to remain close to them.
Children do not provide a form of insurance in the sense of their
being future providers for non-productive old people; nor are

---

[12] Our italics.

they the future recruits of an ancestral cult.[13] Social control over procreating women is therefore unimportant, if not non-existent, and women, as a result, enjoy a freedom which is apparently only limited by their physical constitution. Moreover, the weak development of any division of labour, the participation of women in most of the men's activities, in particular net-hunting parties, helps to keep the sexes on an almost equal social footing.[14] The mode of production also offers opportunities for individual freedom which is revealed by the sexual attitudes, the weakness of marital ties, individual mobility, the fragility and instability of social institutions, both within the band and the nuclear family.[15]

The social organization of production does not provide the basis for the development of a centralized, lasting political power. Each producer owns his own tools of production and is able to reproduce them, and there is no basis here for dispossessing him of his product. The leadership of a productive activity never lasts any longer than the duration of the enterprise itself; each time it is discussed anew. Since *sharing*—unlike redistribution—is not delayed, goods are neither withheld, accumulated, nor centralized. Sharing as an institution provides no opportunities by means of which power may be asserted or made to endure since, like hunting itself, it is a discontinuous and repetitive process. Power has no chance to take root and to find its justification in a permanent and necessary economic and social function. It cannot rely—*a fortiori*—on what is in other societies, the ideological prolongation of such a function: the ideology of elderhood. The position of the old people among the hunters is significant. When their strength begins to fail, when they leave the hunters' age group which, according to Turnbull, is the most influential, the old ones become materially dependent on the younger adults, that is, on the producers. Some authors mention the case of old people being abandoned (de Ternay, 1949); Althabe, verbal

[13] Infanticide is the rule when a woman conceives during the nursing period (from two to four years) of an elder child. If twins are born, one is always killed at birth for this same reason.

[14] D. E. Leeuwe (1962) believes in a former 'gynaecocracy' among the Mbuti, but his demonstration is based on a disputable technological determinism. Castillo Fiel (1948) records that Bayele women have a high status.

[15] The Mbuti case which we have dwelt on here cannot be generalized in all its implications to other hunting and gathering peoples. Ecological factors—depending on the nearness of the group to their natural resources for example—result in variations. Thus water shortage among the Bushmen leads to the phenomena of storage of water and the ownership of water-points, which cause the strengthening of bonds between members of bands. But even these are not stable (L. Marshall).

communication) and although Turnbull is silent on the subject, this kind of behaviour fits the logic of the system.[16] Power obviously does not come from age, nor does it grow in correlation with the process of ageing. It is only related to adult physical capacity. Neither social control of the elders over artificial knowledge, such as magic, for the purpose of social domination, nor the control over women, arises in such an occurrence. Understandably, genealogical memory only goes back as far as one or two generations; there are no funerals, no cult of the dead, no celebrations relating the living ones to the ancestors.

Religious representations derive from the above. The Mbuti have definite relations with Nature. Because of its proximity and because of its provisioning and protective character, its role as a source of life and comfort, the forest is not an object of superstitious fear as it is with the village farmers. It is not, indeed, an obstacle to the economic activities of the hunters. It is their working place, a privileged locus, and to a certain extent a controlled one: 'There is certainly nothing in the course of natural events in the forest to suggest to the hunters and gatherers any trace of hostility.' (Turnbull, 1965, pp. 16–22.) It is by preserving the forest and not destroying it that it remains exploitable. Turnbull points out that the attitude of the Pygmies to the supernatural is one of doubt and agnosticism. Tales of the world beyond have the qualities of imaginary legends. What may be called the religious representations of the Pygmies are haunted, not by spirits of the surrounding forest, but by those of the unattainable vault of the sky.[17]

HUNTERS AND CULTIVATORS

Many of the points which Turnbull makes for the Mbuti may be cross-checked by references to observations made on the process of change-over from hunting to farming cultures and also, on the persistence of hunting activities in farming communities. Turnbull describes Mbuti behaviour when they come in contact with farmers, showing how they conform to some of the villagers' institutions in order to place themselves in a situation where communication is

---

[16] It is often out of sympathy for the people they study that social anthropologists conceal facts that could bring moral judgements.

[17] Missionaries, who have long been attracted by these people, have no doubt found this direct upward flight towards the firmament an idealization sufficiently close to Christianity to have derived from it their conviction of the universality of their beliefs and also the existence of a genuine religion among the Pygmies.

possible.[18] But this contact is as yet having no effect on the basic
Mbuti way of life. Turnbull, here, is not describing phenomena of
change, but phenomena of conformity.

Althabe (1965), on the contrary, reports on the process whereby the
Mbaka Pygmies, in contact with the Bantu, are becoming farmers.
From an economic point of view, he notes, as the effects of seden-
tarization and agricultural activities, the adoption of farming co-
operative labour, involving some continuity and the consequent
formation of more compact and lasting family units, and the development of circulation of goods, but within restricted spheres of exchange.
Sociologically, he observes an increase in the incidence of polygyny;
the emergence of bridewealth marriage and the acquisition of goods
for the purpose. Politically, men gain new powers, through their
appropriation of the farms and through their participation in councils
of elders issuing from the grouping in a *permanent* settlement of
several kin groups. As a consequence, the position of women declines.
Also, power tends to be related to wealth, a phenomenon which
reveals a rapid adaptation to a profit economy, since it does not meet
with the obstacles of an earlier hierarchy to overcome or ancient
privileges to safeguard. Such changes, as far as the Mbaka are concerned, are not due to imitative processes, but to the requirements of
their new activities. The exploitation of land now, as an 'instrument
of labour'—as we shall briefly demonstrate below—entails new
characteristic forms of social organization.[19] We find proof of this,
a contrario, in some persistence of the social organization of the band
within farming societies which also engage in collective hunts.

I have already discussed, in relation to the Guro (Meillassoux,
1964, pp. 92–100), the kind of oppositions which arise between
hunting and farming activities: the roving of the hunters, the
settling of the villagers; the sporadic and temporary co-operation
between hunters as compared to the sustained and lasting co-operation
among farmers; the large territorial, but socially loose, hunting group
as against the more restricted, more compact kin-based units of the
farmers, etc. Two principles of organization are opposed here: that of
the bush and that of the village; territory *vs.* the 'terroir'; the first
involves geographically defined groups (moities, villages), the second
concerns kin-based domestic groups (households, extended families).[20]

[18] By the nomination of a 'chief', for instance, a man who, in fact, is only a
powerless spokesman chosen from among the buffoons (Turnbull, 1965, pp. 40–5).
[19] See also Meillassoux (1971).
[20] 'In the bush, we were told at Duonefla (Guro), it is *bei* and *bebu* (territorial
groups) and in the village it is the *guniwuo* (household).' (Meillassoux, 1964, p. 98.)

Yet, while hunting activities introduce the social organization of the band within farming societies, it comes up against the hierarchy of age. It operates therefore only outside the limits of the village, in the bush. Since hunting is no longer the dominant mode of production, the hunter vanishes, in the social sense, as soon as he enters the village and falls under the authority of his elders.[21]

As we said before, a farming economy is differentiated by its use of the land, no longer as a subject of labour but as an instrument of labour, that is by the incorporation into the land of a sum of labour whose output is deferred. The duration of the productive process and the delayed acquisition of the product lead to a prolonged and continuous co-operation in carrying out agricultural activities. The distribution of the tasks as well as the durability of the product, its storage and consumption over an extended period—at least equal to a complete farming cycle—the need to resume work while still consuming the previous harvest, this constantly renewed cycle entails an indefinite prolongation of the ties binding together all those people who co-operate in a same farming enterprise. In such societies, where duration, expectation and cyclical repetition—that is, time— are paramount, the future becomes a concern and, along with it, the problem of reproduction: reproduction of the total strength of the productive unit, both in number and in quality, in order to ensure continued supplies for its members; reproduction of the structures of the unit in order to preserve the hierarchy which ensures its functioning. Descent—which provides for group membership and renews the relations of production—and marriage—which renews the hierarchical structures—become major concerns. Children are viewed as the natural dependants of man; procreation as the most direct means of obtaining dependants, and the family as a divine and natural institution. Relations of production assume the appearance of kinship. Women, as producers of the producer, become the most potent of the means of production oriented towards the future and therefore subjected to coercion and restrictions. Women, in farming societies, are subject persons, and the subjection they endure on account of their reproductive capacities leads to an even more complete subjection in the field of production. Preoccupations with the future also imply a return to the past: genealogies become longer and the ancestors emerge as political and religious figures.

[21] This special way of life of the hunters and this differentiation from the village way of life is also found in Bambara, Malinke, and Fulani hunting associations (Youssouf Cissé, 1964) which have their own hierarchy, independent of the village's, as well as their own cults and ceremonies.

Relationships between man and Nature change. The farmer has to toil ceaselessly to keep his land against the invasion of vegetation and the depredation of the animals. He must engrave his life on the soil and prevent its erasure. The wild bush is the never-defeated invader to be fought off. Instead of being a protective force, Nature becomes hostile. Distinctions between the village and the bush become clearly expressed in the topography as well as in the language.[22] The bush is now a strange and dangerous place, peopled by evil spirits (Turnbull (1965), p. 21), supernatural and fearful beings, representations of the overwhelming forces of Nature which have to be vanquished, mastered, or won over.

The oppositions existing between the two systems (from the social organization of production up to their ideological representations) are of a radical nature.

CONCLUSIONS

A methodological problem arises from the fact that we have compared only these two societies. It seems indeed that we can consider the mode of exploitation of the land as the determining factor in a society of hunters and foragers since we have been able to deduce logically from there the economic, social, and political organizations, as well as their religious representations, and show that a transformation in this mode of exploitation carried along a predictable set of transformations. But if a changeover from this mode of exploitation involves a change of the whole social system we also find that land is used as an instrument of labour in subsequent and different types of farming societies, sometimes incompatible with each other; which would indicate that once this mode of exploitation of the land—as an instrument of labour—has been adopted, the level of determination must be sought elsewhere. In Marxist theory we hold that the mode of production is determinant,[23] but this concept is a complex notion which, at a given level of the productive forces, relates already the

[22] The Soninke contrast the 'brightness' of the village with the obscurity of the bush; *gune* is the word used for bush as well as for Paris or Dakar, the foreign, unpredictable places of migration. (Meillassoux (1968).)

[23] From this point of view all social formations (in so far as they are determined by the *mode of production*) could be opposed to the hunting and gathering society (itself determined by the *mode of exploitation* of the land) in the same way that, in consideration of the worker's social condition, the capitalist society could be opposed, with its 'free' worker, to all the other societies where workers are bound by ties of personal dependence, except again in the hunting society where relations of production are set between equals.

means of production to the relations of production. If we set the determination at this level, are we not ignoring the fact that other factors may have already been at work which, at a certain point in the development of early societies, were determinant of the mode of production? This is but one aspect of the problem of the detection of a level of determination. We should also take into consideration the important comments of Bettelheim (1966) on the composite character of the social formations whereby several modes of production may coexist: the dominant character of any one of them and the relations it has with others, give to each social formation its specificity which is not exactly related to a single mode of production. Moreover, the confrontation of several modes of production involves reactions of a contradictory nature which are susceptible of causing the dominance of critical traits which may prevent the positive transformation of the social formation where it occurs, either endogenously or under the impact of outside factors. If we extend our remarks beyond the limited contrasts between hunting and agricultural economies and refer to our previous model (Meillassoux (1960)) we observe that the self-sustaining character of farming communities, for instance, becomes critical once confronted with a trading economy. Such contact leads to the emergence of institutions, legal or otherwise, which aim to preserve self-sustenance as the dominant frame of the economy. But such conservative institutions, although they may save the society from disintegration, do not derive from the market economy the means for an inner development; on the contrary they tend to prevent development by producing various methods of sterilizing the social product.

These critical traits, although they may become dominant, are not determining factors, since they appear within a system determined otherwise, and as obstacles to another determination.

A typology of economic systems should therefore include a more precise inquiry into the levels of determination by taking into consideration:

(1) relations existing between the constituents of the mode of production; and

(2) relations existing between several coexistent modes of production, as noted by Bettelheim.

Having done this it would perhaps be possible to expose, within the composite mode of production, those critical traits which character-ize economic systems that are incompatible one with the other; such traits would provide the means for a more refined typology, which would be able to take into account, not the formal 'synchronic structures' which have little relevance, but those contradictory dynamics in which the systems are involved and from which the critical traits are derived. Such a typology would also make it possible to bring abstract conceptualization closer to the various historical realities.

The radical opposition which exists between hunting societies and farming societies poses the other problem of an eventual changeover from one system to the other. If labour productivity diminishes with the passage from hunting to farming, it is certainly overcompensated by the growth in productivity of the means of production and with this by the possibility of investing a longer period of labour in production, thereby ultimately increasing its output. With this kind of progress, the subsistence of unproductive persons is better assured, life-expectancy increases, practices of abandoning the aged disappear, while the more compact family organization, plus the growth of polygyny, does away with infanticide. Despite the nostalgic effusions of writers who describe the 'free and adventurous' way of life of hunters and gatherers, social progress is real. Still, we do not detect a continuous development from one economic system to another; nor do we find in hunting societies any sign of those internal contradictions which might have led to change. Moreover we know that hunting societies, even when they come into contact with farmers and are provided with more efficient tools, need not necessarily undergo radical change. Finally it is a noteworthy fact that in Africa farming peoples belong to an ethnic stock which is different from that of hunters and foragers. This fact excludes the historical cases of a changeover from one mode of production to another. The instances of change which we have been able to observe result from contacts with farming communities, themselves already involved in a trading circuit; in this way it was commercial exchanges which acted as factors of change and not the simple fact of contact with village communalist society.

This leads us to question the usually assumed notion that, in the successive stages of human evolution, agriculture proceeded from hunting and foraging. Actually hunting may well be unable to develop into any other mode of production and the origins of agriculture should be looked for among other activities, such as fishing, as has already been suggested (Sauer, 1952).

SOURCES CITED OR CONSULTED

Althabe, G. (1965). 'Changements sociaux chez les Pygmées Baka de l'Est-Cameroun', *Cah. Et. Afr.*, V, 4 (20), 561–92.

Althusser, L. *et al.* (1966). 'Lire le Capital', 2 vols. Paris: F. Maspéro.

Bettelheim, C. (1966). 'Problématique de l'économie de transition', *Et. de Plan. Socialiste*, 3 (March) 124–55.

Castillo-Fiel, Conde de, (1948), 'The Bayele, a Pygmy tribe in Spanish Guinea', *Africa* (Madrid), 5, 83/84 (November–December) 402–6.

Cissé, Y. (1964). 'Notes sur les sociétés de chasseurs Malinke', *J. Soc. Afr.*, 34, 2, 175–226.

Gusinde, M. (1955). 'Pygmies and Pygmoids: Twides of Tropical Africa', *Anthrop. Quarterly*, 28, 3 (January) 1, 3–46.

Hauser, A. (1953). 'Les Baginda', *Zaïre*, 7, 2, 146–79.

Howell, C. and Bourlière, F. (1963). *African Ecology and Human Evolution*. London: Methuen.

Lee, R. B. and Devore, I. (1968). (eds.). *Man the Hunter*. Aldine Pub. Co.

Leeuwe, de (1966). 'On former gynaecocracy among African Pygmies', *Acta Ethnographica*, 11, 1/2 (1962), 85–118.

Marshall, L. (1957). 'The kin terminology system of the !Kung Bushmen', *Africa*, 27, 1 (January), 1–24.

——(1960). '!Kung Bushman Bands', *Africa*, 30, 4 (October), 325–55.

——(1961). 'Sharing, talking and giving: relief of social tensions among the !Kung Bushmen', *Africa*, 31, 3 (July), 231–49.

——(1962). '!Kung Bushman religious beliefs', *Africa*, 32, 3 (July), 221–52.

Marx, K. (1859). *Contribution à la Critique de l'Economie Politique.* Paris: Ed. Sociales [1957].

——(1867). *Capital.* London: Lawrence and Wishart [1970].

Meillassoux, C. (1960). 'Essai d'interprétation du phénomène économique dans les sociétés traditionnelles d'auto-subsistance', *Cah. Et. Afr.*, I, 4, (Décembre) 38–67.

——(1964). *Anthropologie économique des Gouro de Côte d'Ivoire.* Paris: Mouton.

——(1965). 'Elaboration d'un modèle socio-économique en ethnologie', *Epistémologie Sociologique*, (2nd ed.), 1–5, (1964–8), 283–308.

——(1972). 'From Reproduction to Production', *Economy and Society*, I, 1 (February) 93–105.

Meillassoux, C., Doucouré, L., and Simagha, D. (1968). *Légende de la dispersion des Kusa*. IFAN, Dakar.

Quatrefages, A. de. (1887). *Les Pygmées*. Paris.

Sahlins, M. (1968). 'La première société d'abondance', *Les Temps Modernes*, 24, 268 (October 1968), 641–80.

Sauer, C. O. (1952). *Agricultural Origins and Dispersals*. Cambridge, Mass.: The M.I.T. Press.

Service, E. R. (1962). *Primitive Social Organization*. New York.

Schebesta, P. (1940). *Les Pygmées*. Gallimard, 1940.

Steward, J. H. (1955). *Theory of Culture Change*. Urbana.

Ternay, A. de (1949). 'I Pigmei Baka', *Missioni Cattoliche*, 78, 8, 118–9; 9 (September), 136–6; 10 (October), 156–7; 11 (November), 169–70.

Trilles, H. (1933). *Les Pygmées de la forêt équatoriale*, Paris: Bloud & Gay.

Turnbull, C. M. (1965). *Wayward Servants*. London: Eyre & Spottiswoode.

Vallois, H. V. (1957). 'The Negrillos of the Cameroun', *Soviet. Ethno.*, 1, 118–26.

Washburn, Sh. L. (ed.) (1961). *Social Life of Early Man*. Chicago: Aldine Pub. Co.

Oral Tradition and Chronology

YVES PERSON[1]

As Jan Vansina has rightly pointed out,[1a] the history of societies lacking written records does not involve a new discipline—ethno-history—but quite simply history, which takes into account, as it ought, all possible sources. The respective roles played by these various sources are nevertheless quite different from the ones used by the historian of societies with a tradition of writing. While the general methods of historical criticism remain the same their application poses some very special problems which merit careful scrutiny. Instead of taking these into account our pioneer historians of the pre-colonial period have sometimes wandered about in a complete fog and the anarchic discordance of their results, which make any kind of synthesis highly difficult, have often led one to doubt whether anything can be gained from these scrappy collections of local folklore.

It is clear that oral tradition, which is not our only source although it is often the most vital, must be handled with great care. It is full of pitfalls for the unwary; nevertheless it is not lacking in materials—on the contrary. A close acquaintance with these traditions enables one to set up some empirical rules which enable them to be used knowledgeably. It is worthwhile undertaking an explanation of these rules if only to rescue oral tradition from the unmerited scorn in which it is held at the present time and along with it the whole history of Africa.

Oral tradition deals primarily with events and is designed to be

[1] *Yves Person* (b. 1925) Dr. es. L (Paris); Brevet, Colonial Service Cadet School (ENFOM). Professor of African History, Panthéon-Sorbonne University (Paris I) since 1970. Trained first in History (L. es L., 1950). Extensive anthropological field-work in Guinea, Mali, Ivory Coast, and Dahomey has led him to defend, against orthodox historians, the view that there can be a history of non-literate societies. Participating in a neo-marxist trend, and a fighter for Breton revival himself, his interests have been centred on African reactions to colonial penetration and on the problems of recovering the history of non-literate societies. The original French text of this paper was published as 'Tradition orale et Chronologie', *Cahiers d'Etudes Africaines*, vii, 11–13 (1962), 462–76.
[1a] J. Vansina, 'Recording the oral history of the Bakuba', *Journal of African History*, i, 1 (1960), 43–51; and i, 2 (1960), 257–70.

edifying. It is however on the level of events that it must be scrutinized with the greatest attention, because of its deep-seated subjectivity. I shall not dwell here on the application to this special case of the general rules of textual criticism, both internal and external, whose main principles remain valid anyway.

There is one aspect, however, which, as far as oral tradition is concerned, appears particularly fallible, and which has led many historians to make some incredible mistakes: this is chronology. This, according to my way of thinking, lies at the root of that contempt in which historians have held oral tradition since, in fact, history is nothing if it is not the study of the development of human societies over time. There is no history without chronology. We should therefore begin with this if we are not to be condemned to building our castles upon the sand.

In fact, apart from Islamic areas, we are dealing with societies which have no astronomical or mathematical concepts of time. Even the idea of eras is unknown to them; they live according to the rhythm of nature, following the regular patterning of wet and dry seasons. The past, as far as they are concerned, has no precise depth, no existence in its own right; it exists only in relation to the present and as a justification for the present. Our problem, then, is to arrange for the transference of this extremely subjective vision of change into our own rigid and objective framework of time.

Here we must not demand too much from oral traditions, which in other respects may be very abundant. And its contribution, as far as quality goes, varies from one society to the next.

In a dissertation presented for a post-graduate diploma, Djibril T. Niane, who has recently studied the oral traditions of certain regions in southern Mande, contrasts popular tradition—which is fluid and lacks definite form—with 'archival tradition'. The latter is the domain of specialists (*dyeli* griots) who often undergo a systematic training in order to preserve a whole body of precise organized traditions, both at the level of the village and at that of the chiefdom (province) in which they live.[2] I myself have also studied the historical traditions of the southern Mande, partly with the same informants as Niane.[3] I obtained results which closely approximate to his own and it is clear

[2] Djibril Tamsir Niane, 'Recherches sur l'Empire du Mali au Moyen Age', *Recherches Africaines*, 1–4 (1959) and 1, (1960). In cases where it is necessary I have used the orthography of the I.A.I. in this article.

[3] Particularly Babu Kŏnde of Fadama (Kouroussa district). I also systematically questioned griots from the two Dyuma, from Kɛnde-Mɛnde, from Narɛna, Sibi, and Kɛla.

that the organic character and the fixity of Malinke historical traditions are quite remarkable. Nevertheless it is quite narrowly limited
and, above all, represents a very exceptional case. And the same
dyɛli keep both types of tradition, the 'archival' one being reserved to
the very ancient Sundiata's cycle, as we shall see below.

The fact that a feeling for the past and the organic character of
tradition varies extremely from one ethnic group to the other should
surprise nobody. However, they also vary to a considerable extent
within the Malinke ethnic group—a quite diversified one—because
of the mere fact of its size. It is true that griots are an integral part of
the social structure: no Malinke province lacks one; there is no chief
of any importance who does not keep his own. However, they are not
always the scrupulous and respectable archivists, of whom Babu
Kõnde is a typical example,[4] that Niane would have us believe.

We should here remark that those excellent griots whose art sometimes takes on an almost sacerdotal character are to be found mainly
towards the Malian (northern) border, particularly in those provinces
which have a predominantly *Kɛɛta* influence; and this is not mere
chance. As one goes further south the profession deteriorates. The
griot is always to be found but his roles as flatterer of the chief, official
praise-singer and public entertainer here gain the upper hand. He
need not always be a native of the province where he lives and very
often he is not the one who knows the traditions best. It is from those
families who are the traditional rulers of the chiefdom or who
possess ritual functions that one receives the best information. Towards Sigiri-Kangaba, on the other hand, the chiefs will send you to
the griots. Among non-Malinke peoples such as the Kisi, the Toma,
or the Senufo, in spite of recent Islamic influences, we are dealing
with 'stateless societies' more or less differentiated from one another.
Griots never were—and still are not—known there and historical
traditions play little part in their life, hardly extending beyond the
family or village group, hardly ever encompassing a province.[5]

The Malinke therefore are more conscious of history than their
neighbours; their social structure lends itself to the preservation of
details from the past. However, we should not imagine their traditions to be in the form of an homogeneous whole.

A whole group of traditions dealing with the ancient Mali should

[4] Babu Kõnde died in 1966 but his traditions were tape-recorded and part of them
are being published in Dakar by the writer Camara Laye.

[5] In using the term province (French 'canton') I am not referring to administrative divisions but the historical *nyamanaa* of the Malinke. H. Labouret analyses their
structure in his fine book, *Les Manding et leur langue* (Paris: Larose, 1934).

be considered separately: they consist of bits and pieces of varying degrees of importance, often curtailed and studded with misinterpretations, all of which have been published time and time again. Niane has collected a complete and exact version from Babu Kõnde of Fadama who is a remarkable griot.[6]

This body of tradition is basically concerned with the person of Sundiata. He is a more or less well-known subject for most griots, particularly in the *Kɛɛta* provinces. It would be interesting to compare their different versions, but it soon becomes clear that there are in fact few divergences. This is not at all surprising since the common source is the famous 'school' of Keyla, where this corpus was probably elaborated. This does indeed form a homogeneous whole, fixed over a long period and which is common to all *Kɛɛta*.[7] The insignificance of the variants is all the more remarkable when we consider the fact that there are no strict forms and that the griot

[6] Djibril Tamsir Niane, 'Soundiata ou l'épopée Mandingue', *Présence Africaine* (Paris, 1960).

[7] It is also known, more or less exactly, in the Kamara and Konde provinces, but only to the north of Kankan and in Sankaran. Among Malinke groups which are found further south (Kuranko, Konianke) the name Sundiata is vaguely known but his legend is practically ignored unless you come across a griot who has spent some time at Keeta. This is rare in this region, however.

In the case of the Keeta, after the old series which go from Sundyata to Ladji Misa (Kankan-Musa) there is certainly a gap in the genealogies, a gap which seems to correspond to the fourteenth and fifteenth centuries in particular. The genealogies begin to correspond again from the end of the sixteenth century. It was this modern period which particularly interested me when I was collecting traditions in Amana, Dyouma and also at Keyla (Kangaba) where I apparently had more luck than Niane. I shall compare his and my results in a later work. I think, therefore, that it will be possible to fill in a large part of the gaps which, as far as the materials are concerned, separate the Mali empire from the modern Malinke period.

I would attribute dates to several events which are later than those suggested by Niane. Thus it seems to me that the descent of the Keeta into Dyuma and Amana should be placed at the beginning of the seventeenth century, that is, after the Koli Tengrela wars and not during the fourteenth. The ascent of the Niger by the Konde and the Dumbuya (Kourouma) which tradition remembers by the name of Kolokolo kulu seems to me to have occurred somewhat earlier and dates from the second half of the fifteenth century. It was this which initiated the Malinke expansion towards the forest. It led to the formation of present-day Sankaran.

I consider the identification of Tabu—during the time of Sundiata—with Labe (Fouta Djallon) to be erroneous. Without a doubt this should be Tabou, situated not far from Sibi in Kamara country on the Siguiri–Bamako road, about 30 kilometres from that town. This was Monteil's opinion when he wrote *Les Empires du Mali* (BCEMS AOF, xii, nos. 3–4 (1929)). I think it would be best to stick to this.

There are no facts which give any indication that Mali hegemony extended to present-day Fouta Djallon; on the contrary it is quite improbable that he should have lost his troops on these high, arid plateaux, far from any gold mines or commercial routes. Statements of this kind derive from the confusions and later interpolations of griots.

improvises on themes and episodes which have been handed down
to him. This is general throughout Mande country and west of the
Niger bend as far as Northern Ghana. The only genuine texts, which
are fixed in their word structure, are certain historical songs and,
quite often, genealogies. Apart from this common 'official legend'
which, after Sundiata's exploits, continues in the form of a dry and
visibly abbreviated genealogy, each province has its own traditions,
more or less well preserved, and which are known only to them. Here,
since we lack a common source, parallels and convergences become
meaningful and historical criticism a possibility.

At this stage the problem of co-ordinating these innumerable local
traditions presents itself: we must begin to set up a chronology. We
should immediately reject any help from Islamic and Koranic dating.
In the southern Sudanic zone, Moslems were to be found scattered
through the populations of Malinke pagans but always remained at
a very low cultural level. Writing served exclusively magical and
religious purposes.[8] Even the idea of writing a Sudanese-type
tarikh had never occurred to them. At the most we find here and
there some bare genealogies, and, very rarely, a more verbose text;
there are none, moreover, which were written at the time of the events
concerned.[9] In the latter case I found dates two or three times but
since they are visibly derived from earlier oral traditions we are really
no better off than we were before.

These documents, in fact, are useful so far as the spread of Islam
is concerned. But the Moslem groups, absorbed by commerce and
thaumaturgics, had no interest in the affairs of pagan rulers or chief-
doms. As for the rare individuals who acquired a higher Islamic
scholarship they devoted themselves exclusively to religion. We cannot rely on Islam, then, at least as far as chronology is concerned.

In the absence of any external check we are therefore reduced to
chief-lists and genealogies. In places where there is a strong monarchi-
cal structure, as among the Akan and Mossi we have king-lists with
few gaps or hesitations.[10] An ideal situation would be one in which

[8] Apart from the 'Sundiata legend' we have a 'corpus' of tradition which is
common to several provinces. This is the case of the Konde of Sankaran and the
Kamara (Diomande) astride the Konyan of Beyla, the Mawu and the Worodougou
(Ivory Coast).

[9] This is the case of the Tarikh of Mankono (Seguela district), a copy of which I
managed to procure.

[10] However, we are still far from any calm certainty, even as far as the eighteenth
century is concerned. Cf. a recent essay: M. Priestley and I. Wilks, 'The Ashanti
Kings in the eighteenth century: a revised chronology', in *Journal of African
History*, i, 1 (1960), 83–96.

tradition provided the lengths of reigns; many researchers imagined they possessed this advantage. Without any precise mnemonic system of the kind which Mrs. Meyerowitz claims to have found for the Bono kings[11] I believe this hope to be an absolutely illusory one, except, at a pinch, for the last half of the nineteenth century. The old chief, Peleforo Sorho, called Gbon Koulibali, who was still living at Korhogo at the beginning of 1961, said he had been reigning for eighty years.[12] However, precise details relative to the Babemba and Samori campaigns make it possible to state that it was in 1894 that a military column from Sikasso installed the chief Zwakɔnyõ, in his father's stead, thereby violating the matrilineal tradition of the Senufo.

In a society which ignores historical eras and writing, where no one is aware of his exact age, we should not be taken aback if a chief who is still alive has no idea how long he has been reigning. Without any proof to the contrary I hold that estimates for the durations of reigns which derive from oral tradition are null and void. The most we can hope for is a description of the reign as either 'long' or 'short'.

Might it not be possible to establish an average length of time which, for a list of a certain length, might give us a chance of approaching the truth? We would have to set up an average period for each dynasty according to the kinship and social structure applicable in each situation. Unfortunately the only data which could help us to establish this average length of time date from the European occupation; were it not so we should never have had a problem of chronology. Moreover, if there is one indigenous situation which has been completely disturbed by the arrival of the Europeans it is chiefship. Cases of the upsetting of traditional methods of succession, depositions, and exile are countless. Our average figure from the European occupation would therefore have no meaning for the precolonial period. Besides it would be arbitrary to postulate that social conditions determining the ruling system had never varied in the past. The reign of a king of France was not the same in the sixteenth century as it was in the seventeenth despite the fact that the laws of succession never changed. Chief-lists, therefore, seem to be useless, at least directly, in so far as an absolute chronology is concerned. They merely provide an outline for a relative chronology. And this also

---

[11] E. Meyerowitz, *Akan Traditions of Origin* (Faber and Faber: London, 1952), pp. 29 ff. The far from serious approach of this author to her materials must make the real value of this chronology suspect. A verification of the facts presented would be at least necessary.

[12] Peleforo Sorho died in 1965.

H

depends on being able to reconstitute these genealogies which is far
from always being the case. In the Malinke provinces it is nearly
always impossible; this is due to extremely straightforward reasons.
The modern Malinke provinces even if we include the Kɛɛta of
Kangaba, cannot be said to be the heirs of the original Mali empire;
they are merely the basic units which made it up, the *kafu* or *nyamanaa*.

Each *kafu* belongs to the family of the first occupant of the land
or one to whom the role has been delegated. Later arrivals recognized
their predominance and the order of the founding of the villages in
in a single province is always known even if it is not admitted without
some reticence. However, the dominant clan usually split into several
balanced segments—say three—and groups made up of members of
these three branches have scattered and founded new villages.

The traditional chiefship of the *kafu* is the indivisible property of
all the lineages of the dominant clan. Sometimes a system of rotation
is established between their villages. More frequently the chiefship is
inherited by the oldest member of the dominant clan, whatever his
position. In this case he does not change his residence; therefore,
before the arrival of the Europeans most of the *kafu* did not have a
permanent capital.

It will be seen that the elders, whose authority was purely moral
in nature, succeeded to office at an advanced age and died after very
short periods of office, leaving but a vague memory. Even if their
names are preserved, the fact that they had no common dwelling and
that each lineage segment confined itself to its own traditions, means
that it is almost impossible to make any estimate, except for the more
recent chiefs, from 1850 onwards or thereabouts. Occasionally a
warrior chief, a man who was theoretically young and powerful, took
over the role of traditional chief, but in this case this new office did
not survive the holder; he was not one of a series. All the same, despite the lack of continuous lists, many names do exist, if only because a special event fixed them in their minds. We occasionally
know such a succession of events and this provides us with the elements of a relative chronology. We can therefore begin to draw an
outline on our empty canvas. But we still have to fill in the details.
We still have to set up an absolute chronology, even if it is only a very
approximate one.

Only genealogies provide the means for doing this. In my opinion
they constitute the only thread by which one can prudently go back

into Africa's past. Unfortunately they have often been cast aside as tedious and useless or they have been used in a surprisingly flippant fashion. Once again the value of the genealogies varies from one society to the next. There are some stateless societies, such as the Tiv of Nigeria, whose genealogies, whether fictive or real, go back surprisingly far into the past. Others, such as the Kisi and certain Senufo hardly reach further back than five or six generations. A fairly general rule, which holds good for oral tradition as a whole, is that memory is only good as far back as the last migration and begins with the settlement of a group in their present territory. It would seem that visual features (tombs, sacred places, or other distinctive spots) are essential if memories are to remain fresh. Anything older is likely to become effaced within the lifetime of one man. On the length of time that the group concerned has been settled in one area depends the depths to which we can plumb the past. Thus the Malinke of Upper Guinea can remember the migrations which led to their settlement in the sixteenth century, while the chiefs of Korhogo have forgotten everything which preceded their expulsion from the Kong region towards the middle of the eighteenth century.

As far as genealogies are concerned kinship structure is obviously a determining factor. Matrilineal societies such as the Senufo will be less favourable to historical research. Matriliny does not imply matriarchy; it is still the men who govern, while the women occupy a relatively subordinate position even though rights are transmitted through them. Their names are easily forgotten and along with them the exact family tie which links two men. 'X was the uterine nephew of Y,' they say without any exact precision. He might be a nephew, a great-nephew, or a cousin; and this immediately ruins any hope of founding a chronology on this genealogy.[13] As for patrilineal genealogies, they are of no interest in societies of this kind and are purely and simply forgotten; it is quite frequent for a Senufo to be unaware of the name of his paternal grandfather.

In patrilineal societies inquiries are much easier. Moreover here, particularly among the Malinke, patrilineal genealogies sometimes constitute—at least in noble families—a genuine text, which must be recited without any variation and in a special tone of voice. I observed over and over again, along with Niane, that if the interrogator interrupts the informant in order to be able to note down his words, the latter will lose the thread, hesitate, and may have to start again from

[13] Among the Akan, where the role played by 'queen mothers' was considerable, matrilineal genealogies are preserved in a much better fashion.

the beginning. The better Malinke griots possess, moreover, amulets which are endowed with strong powers. In case of hesitation they walk away a little, rub the amulets gently until their fluids have reconstituted the lost thread.

Each genealogy, if it is at all ancient, will obviously be in danger of countless corruptions. Nevertheless, except among Islamic peoples who wish to provide themselves with an eastern origin, I do not believe—although I lack proof—that there is any conscious prevarication.

On the other hand, in societies which have a classificatory structure, where the concept of age sets is more important than vertical filiation, the substitution of a father's brother for the father is constantly occurring. If the name of the real father does crop up, it sometimes happens that it is put in afterwards and this means we are blessed with a superfluous generation. It would even appear, among Islamic peoples, that certain groups of brothers have been aligned in a father–son descent line in order to given an older and more venerable look to their family.

On the other hand, quite naturally, several genealogies have been truncated. One is usually given the ancestor, more or less mythical, who led the last migration, along with his sons who founded those lineages which are at the present time found in segmentary opposition. Immediately afterwards, if the events occurred long enough ago, there is often a gap until continuous genealogies are resumed, down to the informant. In such cases it is obviously impossible to propose any absolute chronology, even an approximate one. Fortunately there are almost always continuous genealogies in other branches of the same clan and this permits cross-checking.

Nevertheless attention should be paid to these discontinuities of which some informants are often ignorant; they boldly stick the name of the most ancient of their ancestors whom they are able to recall who follows just after that of the son of the founder from whom they descend. Sometimes this is a form of conscious cheating which is carried out to save an informant's face and hide gaps from the researcher. Fortunately each lineage is usually conversant only with its own genealogy, particularly among the Malinke. One can then rely on the longer genealogies which are supposedly not truncated. If several of them give the same number of generations without there being any collusion between informants then we can admit them as valid.

Let us look at the case of the Kamara or Dyɔmãnde. After an

incursion as far as the sea in Sierra Leone, corresponding, no doubt, to the settlement by the Vai, they left the region of Baleya-Kouroussa under the leadership of a Keeta clan (Mansare), whom they later eliminated, and proceeded to enter the forest. They first made a settlement at Syano, near today's Touba (Ivory Coast), then, after bringing the whole region under their control, they dispersed throughout the conquered territory. Several lineages settled around Syano, forming Mawu. One common embryonic legend allows us to trace the spread of these lineages; yet each one of them has kept a solid and independent genealogical tradition of its own. While the Kɔŋsabasi occupied Gbee (Goy) and Barala, the several lineages of the Ferēŋkamasi spread over Konyan of Beyla. Afterwards a group of Ferēŋkamasi, known by the name of Sakuraka, came back to Mau to help repel the Dan (Yakouba) and established their supremacy.

Of the thirty or so genealogies I collected in Konyan only ten seem to have been shortened. The others, indicating the same number of generations, can be held to be genuine. Moreover they concide exactly with the Syano genealogy. We know from elsewhere the exact stage of the arrival of the Sakuraka in eastern Maana in Konyan. From this stage the various genealogies of Maana and the ten or so genealogies collected among the Sakuraka reveal the same number of generations. We are therefore on solid ground when we state that, by using the genealogies as a basis, we can hope to determine the approximate date of the migration of the Kamara into Mawu, the foundation of Konyan and the settlement of the Sakuraka.

An absolute chronology, then—the main principles of which we shall discuss below—gives the middle of the sixteenth century for the foundation of Konyan and 1700 for the Sakuraka. The first event is linked with traditions of warfare, which are known as far as the coast towards Liberia. This leads us to the present hypothesis that the Kamara, about 1550, played their part in the famous 'Manc' invasion which the Portuguese mention. These events, which were known only from European sources, were previously entirely isolated in nature and known only out of context.[14]

The long task of collecting countless genealogies, most of which lack any historical interest, and then comparing them all meticulously is a tiring business. However, I cannot think of any other

---

[14] For further details, see my article, 'Les Kissi et leurs statuettes de pierre dans le cadre de l'histoire ouest-africaine', *Bulletin de l'IFAN, Sciences Humaines*, 1–2 (1961). In this article, already out of date (1958) I was mistaken in opposing the Mane and Quoja invasions, which are certainly one.

method which produces results which are not fantasies. I fear this
kind of work has been neglected in other regions where the organic
character of oral tradition can probably produce good results. I refer
to the great Voltaic kingdoms such as the Mossi, the Gurma, and the
Dagomba. In almost every case researchers appear to have limited
themselves to collecting only the main genealogy from the chief's
entourage.

Apart from any cross-checking, certain kinds of internal criticism
are possible when we are dealing with a single genealogy. Thus
the genealogy of the Gurma kings provided by Davy[15] is obviously
unacceptable. This genealogy has ramified, as is often the case,
particularly since the eighteenth century with the existence of
three dynastic branches among whom the chiefship rotates. It is
quite improbable that from their origins until King Bahama—that
is for a period of 500 years (according to Davy)—the genealogy
remained strictly linear, each of the kings succeeding as a son of his
father.

Since we are concerned with an old-established kingdom, one
which was powerfully organized and with strong historical traditions
we may well believe that the list of sovereigns has been faithfully preserved; but the exact kinship relations must have been
forgotten for the period earlier than the end of the eighteenth
century.

Because they did not wish to reveal these gaps or simply in order
to please the researcher the tradition-keepers conveniently linked the
names they had preserved in a fictive relationship of direct descent.
As a result the Gurma genealogy in its present form is useless as far
as chronology is concerned. We might perhaps be able to recover it
through systematic cross-checking with the genealogies of the many
vassal chiefs of the Gurma.

Meanwhile we are unable to set any value upon Davy's data, all the
more so since we are not dealing with a computation based on the
number of generations but on the lengths of the reigns told him by
the tradition-keepers.

When we are told that Lobidiedo (1380–95) imported guns from
the coast or that Banidioba (1336–80) fought the Tomba who had
trade guns we know we could be dealing with later interpolations.
But when we are also told that Tenintwodiba (1395–1439) extended
Gurma power as far as Djougou, we should by right turn our atten-

[15] Davy, 'Histoire du pays Gourmantché', *Mémoire du Centres des Hautes Etudes
d'Administration musulmane* (Paris (MS)).

tion to this kingdom in northern Dahomey. Now, the Gurma dynasty of Djougou, whose traditions are quite well preserved, only go back as far as the eighteenth century. As a result Banidioba must be a eighteenth-century chief; then it becomes quite plausible that he met firearms in battle. This lack of agreement of three and a half centuries means that the problem of Gurma chronology is still a very large one. I cannot help thinking that Davy, although he informs us himself that the relations—and these are incontestable—between the foundation of the Gurma kingdom and the expansion of the Mossi–Dagomba kingdoms are not very clearly defined, has allowed himself to be influenced by a chronology which is commonly attributed to the kings of Wagadugu and Ycndi. He has attempted to make a connection between the origins of the Gurma dynasty and the date of the foundation of the Mossi kingdom which he imagined had been definitely settled.

However, once again, failing a systematic study of genealogies we are still completely in the dark. The dates given by Delafosse, and then Tauxier and Dim Delobsom, are arbitrary ones as far as the Mossi are concerned. And those provided by Tamakloe are no less so for the Dagomba. The latter places under Darigoudyemda, whose dates are estimated at 1442–54, the foundation of the kingdom of Bouna (Ivory Coast). But the Bouna genealogy which Labouret collected and which I have personally checked allows the event to be dated only at the beginning of the seventeenth century. This is confirmed by a precious piece of cross-checking since the passing of the Gonja invading army towards Bouna is remembered and tradition places it before the installation of the present dynasty. And the Gonja manuscripts of Jack Goody now allow us to fix the date of the invasion at about 1600. The Gonja chief, Suleyman Ndewura Jakpa, who reigned according to the same source from 1620 to 1680, crushed the Dagomba king Dariziogo. But Tamakloe had proposed 1543–4 as the date for the latter incident. We find therefore that this chronology has no firm foundations and the problem of Mossi–Dagomba origins is still to be solved. The late David Tait began this study shortly before the tragic death which prevented the publication of his findings. According to information kindly given to me by Professor Fage, Tait concluded, after a close analysis of oral traditions, that the origins of the Dagomba and Mossi kingdoms go back as far as 1400, or at the most to the very end of the fourteenth century. I am completely in agreement with this date of 1400. In fact the rare mentions in the Tarikh-es-Sudan only allow us to state that the Mossi

kingdoms were already organized in the mid-fifteenth century and
that they were then in full expansion. We can deduce from this that
they had been founded not long before.

The anarchical situation of Voltaic chronology seems to me to arise
from the fact that in highly organized kingdoms king-lists were preserved in a more faithful manner than genealogies.

As I have pointed out, the situation in Malinke country was exactly the reverse. Here we are not tempted to make up dates to
correspond to king-lists. Genealogies are often linear, which is precisely the fact I held against the proposed Gurma genealogy. Here it is
not an indication of cheating since it is only a matter of tracing a line
of generations and not at all one of defining relations between names
in a known series of rulers.

After having scrupulously checked these genealogies and accepted
some of them as valid it should be possible to suggest an absolute
chronology, although obviously only a very approximate one. If descent is traced back far enough it is legitimate to suggest a mean
length of time for each generation. Most authors, using this method,
have accepted the figure of thirty years, which is in fact often an
acceptable one. However, we must try to be more particular. It is in
fact necessary to calculate the mean figure for each society separately;
the average time-span of a generation is obviously affected by the
social structure.

If we are dealing with matrilineal genealogies the average figure of
thirty years will certainly be too high, given the early age of marriage
and the rapid sterility of wives. Twenty years would be closer to the
truth. In patrilineal societies we should adopt a lower figure for
Islamic peoples than for fetishists since the marriage of youths is
always late.

So that our proposed figure be not too arbitrary we should make
use of censuses and documents registering births, deaths, and marriages which have existed over the past sixty to eighty years. We
should also remember that the colonial period saw some rapid developments which gave young men the opportunity of marrying
earlier than before. In Senufo country, marriages are frequent today
between the ages of 20 and 25; in the last century they were exceptional before the age of 30. African gerontocracy has always mono-
polized a large number of women. In societies where this phenomenon is clearly marked the figure of thirty may possibly be too low.
On the other hand we should remember that we are dealing with

chiefly families and that marriage in these cases was always earlier than for the common people.

For my own part, after making many experiments, I have settled on twenty years for Senufo matrilineal genealogies, and thirty-five for Senufo patrilineal ones. I have kept the figure of thirty for the Malinke pagans but have come down to twenty-five for the Moslems. For the Kisi among whom gerontocracy is well established I have kept the figure of thirty-five, although this may even be too low.

Of course, since we are dealing with traditional descent and not natural descent and since important men often have young wives and children at advanced ages, our methods may prove faulty in special cases. As far as the nineteenth century is concerned they have only a limited worth, but for this period, fortunately, we have other means of cross-checking our data. On the other hand, any exceptions one way may be cancelled out in the other direction so that our methods do enable us to come closer to the true state of affairs as we go further back in time.[16]

By means of this arduous work we have succeeded in constructing a chronological framework without which we could have no valid history. I have already mentioned some of the more glaring errors. Here are some further revisions which can be made as a result of the application of our methods.

The genealogies of the Korhogo Senufo, verified by a great deal of cross-checking, particularly at Kong, allow us to suggest a date for Nage, founder of the Kiembara chiefship, of about 1750. Delafosse placed it in the twelfth century.

Returning to the Malinke, Niane repeats the tradition already recorded by Delafosse and Labouret to the effect that Māsa Dãŋala-tuma, Sundiata's predecessor, chased by Sumanguru Kante took refuge near Kissidougou where we still find his descendants today. It was in this form that Babu Kõnde, who does not know the traditions of Kisi country, recounted the legend to me. However, it would seem to me to be very far from the truth.

The Lɛno (*Māsarɛ* in Malinke) of Farmaya, where we have the present-day town of Kissidougou, say that they are really of Malinke origin and more particularly that they are descendants of Dãŋala-tuma. However, an analysis of their numerous genealogies, which all

[16] For the analysis of genealogies, see A. Deluz, *Organisation sociale et traditions orales des Gouro de Côte d'Ivoire* (Paris, 1971). This author underlines the differentiation of the average length for senior and junior lines.

concide as far as the generations are concerned, would point to a date at about the end of the eighteenth century for their arrival in Kisi country. This is confirmed by the fact that the Kuranko chiefs who are their neighbours to the north preceded them and the most recent of the latter only date back to about 1700.

The Mãsarε who have now been completely assimilated by the Kisi came from Malinke Seradu in the extreme south of the district of Farana, near the border of Sierra Leone. Seradu, until 1958, was ruled by another branch of this Mãsarε or Kεεta family which has remained faithful to the Malinke language and culture. In Seradu, where my information is more exact, the genealogies I managed to write down incline me to date the expulsion of the indigenous Kisi and the installation of the Mãsarε at about 1600. This is verified by the fact that this event is linked with the Kuranko migration of Sosowali Mara which other facts place at this same period.

We still have four hundred years to fill in before we reach Dãŋalatuma and the people of Seradyu cannot help us here. They simply say that they came directly 'from the Mande'. In order to reconstitute the intermediary stages we looked around for another core of the Dãŋalatuma family which settled at some spot between the Mande and the sources of the Niger. In my opinion the Kεεta of the Dãŋalatuma branch, having been eliminated from any political role by the arrival of Sundiata, lived modestly in the shade during the period of Mali's greatness, without actually leaving the region of Sigiri-Kangaba. They then took part in the great migration of the sixteenth century which brought them to Seradu, and then, two hundred years later, into Kisi country.

The migration of Dãŋalatuma to the forest is no more than an incidental detail in the Sundiata legend and has been incorporated, in my opinion, perhaps a century and a half ago, by griots who noted the presence of this family in Kisi country and wished, in all good faith, to explain it. It is, moreover, possible that this interpolation first of all involved the Mãsarε of Seradu and only specifically referred to by the Farmaya in the nineteenth century. Towards 1850, in fact, the installation of a marabout warrior, Mori Suleyman Savane at Mara led to the immigration into Kisi country of a number of Malinke elements including the usual contingent of griots.

These conclusions explain an anomaly in the expansion of the Malinke towards the forest and give some coherence to any hypothesis which might be made as to the southernmost boundaries of the Mali empire.

In the absence of written sources and any external checking, oral tradition provides us with an opportunity—as long as it is meticulously and tirelessly scrutinized—not only of eliminating many false problems and correcting errors in dating, but above all of elaborating a chronological groundwork which has been very much absent from pre-colonial history.

Quite clearly this groundwork is not in itself history. The history of Africa will be built up gradually by the combined use of sociology, linguistics, a study of religions, the analysis of customs and agricultural systems, ethno-botany. Nevertheless all this material cannot acquire life and meaning unless it is organized in a chronological framework, unless it is actualized by names and facts, unless it encompasses a real and passionate sense of humanity which only oral tradition can provide. Without all this we shall be searching desperately for some scant signs of life in a desert, as if we were attempting—for example—to bring Mousterian man back to life.

Oral tradition limits our chronological framework to a period covered by a few centuries. As I have pointed out it only goes back to the beginning of the eighteenth century for the Senufo. In the better examples we can establish a direct line which goes back as far as the sixteenth century. Beyond this period we have some groups of facts, such as the legend of Sundiata, but they are isolated ones since a big gap separates them from more recent times. If we lacked any external means of cross-checking we should be incapable of dating these. Archaeology and modern methods such as carbon 14 dating will one day enable us to extend our framework to cover these more ancient epochs. But we must first of all firmly establish them within possible limits through the help of oral tradition.

But these irreplaceable materials, without which our knowledge of the African past will always remain bare and superficial, are about to disappear before our very eyes. The strength of an oral tradition depends on the strength of the social structure which it explains and justifies. With the great upheavals taking place in modern Africa, the general decline of traditional institutions, which even their accredited defenders never cease to betray, it is impossible for oral traditions to be maintained. It is an historical tragedy that African cultures are not capable of changing over from an oral tradition to that of a written culture before becoming obliterated by the impact of the modern world. It is up to us to salvage what we can from this huge wreck. Oral tradition is essentially of an evanescent nature and since the social substratum is being removed the task is an extremely urgent one.

If I have been able to show that oral tradition is neither negligible nor totally devoid of any interest and that, as a result, we should set about recording it before it is too late, this article will not have been written entirely in vain.

Food and the Strategy Involved in Learning Fraternal Exchange Among Wolof Children

JACQUELINE ZEMPLENI-RABAIN[1]

The subject of the present essay—food and the role it plays in the strategy of exchange learning among Wolof children—forms but one theme in a much wider study of the modes of relationship a Wolof child—between the ages of 2 and 5—has with his kith and kin. A problem posed by the work carried out by medical men and anthropologists was the starting-point of this study. We know that medical and epidemiological data dealing with morbidity and mortality rates among African children (particularly the high mortality during the first year of life but also during later periods, notably at the end of the second year) have been correlated with anthropological descriptions of several African cultures which tend to confirm the idea of a brutal weaning period (at between 18 months and 2 years), followed by a separation from the mother. A relation of cause and effect has been implicitly established between this type of weaning and both the mortality rates and the poor development of the child in the ensuing period. We are also aware of the importance which has been given to such experiences of separation in determining what has been called the 'basic personality type' of a given culture.

Studies made by the culture and personality school have found a difficulty in making sense of this weaning period, since they sought to understand it on the level of the events themselves, which were isolated and described along the lines of Western psychological models hastily transposed to fit the situation. In our opinion results will only be achieved by studying this crucial period *in the light of the child's ulterior relationships*, not only with its mother but with all those

[1] *Jacqueline Zempleni-Rabain* (b. 1940), Ph.D. (Paris). Research Fellow, National Centre for Scientific Research, Assistant Lecturer, Nanterre University (Paris XI). Field-work in Senegal (1963–5) on child psychology and psychopathology. One of the few French psychologists with full appreciation of anthropological approaches. Main theoretical interest: the relevance of European clinical research to studies in non-European milieux. The original French text of this paper was published as 'L'aliment et la stratégic de l'apprentissage avec les frères chez l'enfant wolof', *Psychopathologie africaine*, iv, 2 (1968), 297–312.

people with whom it comes into contact. It seems to us that only in this way will we be able to judge the significance of the fact of separation and the way its supposedly harmful effects are overcome or canalized.

Without wishing to discuss this matter at any length, we should like to point out right away that the weaning of Wolof children does not seem to us[2] to be an isolated moment breaking up established means of communication with adults. From his earliest age the child establishes, with different members of the community, relationships of physical contact, built on the pattern of relationships with the mother, and these are important in assuring continuity of communication. Western society accords much less importance than the rural African society to this kind of exchange which is complementary to the feeding relation. We know the importance of this dual relationship to the mother-as-food and the mother-as-support for the construction of body-image. Particularly during the course of the second year, the suckling relation becomes closely associated, without any temporal discontinuity, to other kinds of kinetic play brought about through global contact with the mother's body. We have an impression of the child's comfort when he manipulates his mother's breast and body, taking refuge in the receptive zone she permanently provides, or moving away from it when prompted by opportunities for exchange further away, and this impression is not modified in later observations. Solid foods are taken before the weaning proper with the same relationship to the mother as support still obtaining; the child is only gradually separated from its mother and chooses the degree of proximity which suits it.

The feeding system is remarkably permissive and remarkably generous. There are three basic feeding situations which involve the child after weaning and assure him a very great freedom as far as initiative and gratification are concerned. Let us stress this point.

1. At the age of 3 he chooses his own place at the family meal, and here he is encouraged to acquire social norms only gradually. These norms include, in particular, the posture to adopt during the meal, the way to help oneself to food, where to look (for example, eating always with the right hand, looking directly ahead, not watching the others eating).

---

[2] Zempleni-Rabain, J. *Le sevrage chez l'enfant wolof, ses antecédents et quelques implications.* Publications du Centre international de l'Enfance; l'enfant en milieu rural en Afrique, Dakar Colloquium, February 1967, Réunions et conférénces, xiv, 212–17.

2. He has the privilege of extra meals until the next child is weaned. These are given to him more or less when he asks for them, and he can also take the food himself. This includes the remains of the main meal which are specially put aside for him (rice, couscous, different *laax*), or curdled milk.

3. Various titbits, frequently pressed on him, fill up any gaps in an alimentary weft which is already very close. According to supplies on hand, and the time of the year, these will include handfuls of groundnuts, various fruits found in the bush by his elder siblings (*dem, gan, darkassou,* mangoes, monkey-bread) and also little packets of biscuits bought from the local shop.

It will be seen that in the provision of food as well as in physical interaction the Wolof group seeks to reduce discontinuities, delays, and privations which have often been mentioned when discussing the subject of the weaned child.

The child's attempts at feeding autonomy as well as his stray impulses for dependence are received and dealt with permissively by his mother. Two variables are important at this stage: one is that between feeding himself or being fed from his mother's hand; and the other is that of being fed in a situation of close physical contact or at a distance.

The unweaned child may begin to acquire a feeling of independence through extra feeding: eating by himself, either with his mother close by—but not from her hands—or on her lap. Whether direct verbal exchanges are involved or not, the orientation of the mother, and the whole group, in the direction of the child, give significance to the satisfactions gained in this manner.

The mother brought Yande (15 months), who was sitting on the sand, a small bowl of rice. She went back to her hut for a moment and then returned to lie down on the sand opposite Yande who had begun to take and eat a handful of rice. With her face lifted towards the child, who was about a yard away from her, the mother uttered a phrase, in a sing-song voice, which the elder children, Nogoye (7 years) and Aida (3 years 1 month) had been saying not far from them: 'Mummy I'm going to Darominan . . .' The other children then came and settled down around Yande in the same position as the mother.

A recently weaned child[3] often demands more intimate contact than that with which it has been content in the preceding period. It may often be seen, for example, sitting on the mother's or father's lap,

---

[3] At weaning a small proportion of Wolof children are totally separated from their mothers and go to live in another village or compound. See article cited above.

holding a little bowl in its hands, sheltered by the protective arms of the adult. In the following example the mother gives solid food to a child tied on her back, in a manner recalling those occasions when she suckled him.

The child concerned (2 years and 2 months) had been weaned for a month and was slightly feverish the day we observed him.

Lying against his mother's back Abdou is whimpering slightly and then clearly asks for something to eat. An elder brother brings him some rice. The mother tries to lift the child on to her lap. But he grumbles, pushes her away and spontaneously presses himself against her back, becoming immediately quiet. She hands him the bowl of rice over her shoulder; the child takes it and begins to eat all by himself, still leaning against her back. The mother lifts her left arm and passes the child a small tin of water; he leans over, grabs the tin which the mother still holds and drinks in the same position.

Close contact—the child pressing against its mother's back; more distant—with the child held in the father's arms; or the mere proximity of the mother or that of an attentive brother; these are the three degrees of association which are frequently observed in post-weaning physical exchanges and feeding relations.

Because of these associations and contrary to certain prevailing notions, changes in the relations between a child and its mother at weaning, do not mean, among the Wolof, the beginning of a brutal rupture. We go further than this. It should be stated quite clearly that feeding relations are not, for them, a privileged and closed locus for the expression of tensions.

1. If we first consider the degree of control exercised over the amount of food consumed by the child, it will be clear that this is only rarely a theme of anxious maternal concern as it is in Europe ('not eating enough', 'eating too much').[4] Food is not allowed to play a direct role in the acceptance or refusal of the mother by the child, or vice versa. Nor are their respective positions allowed to consolidate themselves in a chain mirror-reaction. If there is any kind of regulating it is most commonly through direct or indirect joking (for example; 'someone by the name of Gueye seems to be eating rather a lot'); and in joking throughout the life cycle and throughout the whole social web food is a favourite theme. It seems to us that these

---

[4] In Europe conflicts centred at first on quantity are eventually focused on table manners. As mentioned above, norms of etiquette are only progressively acquired by Wolof children. Absolute conformity to their rules is not demanded before the child is 3.

jokes are used to avoid the discomfort which is felt in restricting children, a discomfort which is not without a connection with the fear of showing, in the eyes of others, a retentive attitude, a lack of generosity.

2. If we now consider the differential qualities of foodstuffs as objects (ripe, edible, eaten with another type of food), it will be seen that limitations and comments concerning them, occur on rare occasions only. Moreover, as the following example illustrates, limiting the child does not consist so much in bringing out the nature of the object, or making the child explicitly aware of a prohibition connected with the object, as in bringing the child's action within the range of a whole network of relationships between siblings. Here we have the underlying theme of sibling exchanges which we shall bring out more fully later.

Gora (4 years and 3 months) tells his mother he is going to look for some bread and disappears into the hut. Returning to the door he says: 'Mother, here's some sugar.' He waves a piece. The mother, from a distance: 'Show me . . .' then, 'Put it back, Cheikh (23 months) is going to eat it.' The child wavers, then the mother says, coaxingly: 'Come, Gora, come here . . .' and again: 'Where did you find it? Why did you bring it out here? . . . I'll give you a slap.' Then, addressing his elder sister Khady (six years) she says: 'Go and find him some bread.' During this time Gora has come closer to his mother, who gently asks him: 'Where's the rest . . . ? Where is it . . . ? Give it to me! El Hadj will look after it.' (This is the elder brother, a boy of 9 years.)

The mother interfered but did not explicitly refer to the fact that the object in question (sugar) was forbidden—she made double references to elder and younger brothers (Cheikh is going to eat it . . . El Hadj is going to look after it). The prohibition was contained in these *references to brothers and the rule of sharing*. The sugar was symbolically shared by them all: in other words it was not consumed.

3. If we now consider temporal intervals which might regulate feeding habits, it becomes clear that they are barely stressed or made explicit for their own sake, and that, most often, they served to organize short-term reciprocal relations between different persons with regard to common food (looking after an absent child's share).

4. Finally, if we consider the ways in which food as such (as opposed to other objects) is put aside and stored, we notice that food is

not regarded as a store of wealth. Putting food aside is a way of keeping it for someone, an ulterior short-term gift. Care is taken not to waste food but it does not lead to a separation of the mother and child during cooking activities, nor to strict proscriptions as to the things the child may handle. Once again limitations or normative suggestions arise when the rules of exchange are involved.

For example, Soda (8 years) gave M'baye (3 years and 7 months), his cross-cousin, a small fruit found on the sand. He chewed at it, then threw it away. His mother remarked to him: 'When a person gives you something, you don't just throw it away, you understand?'

No society can dispense with rules to regulate mother–child relationships and their substitutes. The lack of restraints characterizing the two major modes of exchange at this period in the child's life—physical contact and food—on which we have just commented, should not lead us into error. Relative to Western society the form and scope of restraints and rules are given a different stress. We now hope to show that these are essentially introduced through the siblings, on whom society has conferred the role of partners in a system of exchange and sharing.

The primary value in Wolof society is exchange. This is an exchange in which food plays a privileged part—as compared with objects proper—no matter the partners or the social segments involved. Before studying the strategy by which a child is encouraged, through an apprenticeship of food-giving, towards lateral social exchanges involving 'brothers', it may be best to say a word or two about the social web which makes these food exchanges meaningful; to do this we shall briefly describe the organization and symbolism of food gifts, as it works in this society.

In a caste society like that of the Wolof, the position of an individual is actualized through ritual gifts which he receives or which he makes on the occasion of certain ceremonies (name-giving, the different stages of the marriage process, funerals . . .). It is up to a *gor* (a man who is a noble, free and worthy) to make gifts to those who are 'below' him, and for the *ñeño*, the man of caste, to claim gifts and to rail at all those who fail to show generosity. Food and clothing are the traditional vehicles of exchange, to the exclusion, we might say, of most other objects.

Within the same social stratum, an obligation to show generosity, to compete in gift-giving with one's 'equals-rivals' (*nawle*), so as not to be 'laid open' to attack, is a basic norm. As far as hospitality is concerned, food exchanges are strictly codified, particularly the presents of cooked dishes (*yakal*) which are made to guests by members of the extended family. Custom requires that anybody present at meal times should be invited to share the food and that invitations should be accepted—otherwise the person will be suspected of evil intentions. Gift-giving obligations have the corollary that a person must never show greed. There are innumerable examples of this theme in oral literature where gluttony—as well as meanness—is punished. Village gossip never fails to comment on gifts which are considered too stingy.

Co-wives within the compound, and female neighbours in the ward, show their knowledge of the rules concerning the circulation of goods between *nawle* by making their own distributions; and by the strict balancing of the accounts which precede them. The objects of this sharing and accounting are delicacies and food gifts from visitors which are obligatorily shared among all kinsfolk (that is the women and children).

The child is associated with this sharing-out process from an early age. He interacts with his own group (his mother and father, his real and classificatory kin, visitors . . .) and in his behaviour reproduces in clear terms the themes of exchange we have just mentioned. The child is not only encouraged to share with his equals and behave like a big brother by distributing food to his juniors (siblings and cousins of various degrees) but adults jokingly bring him into exchanges between kinsmen, between a host and his guests, between freemen and men of caste:

The father has just given Nderi, his 2-year-old child, a sweet. He says, referring to a paternal aunt who is paying them a visit: 'You must give some of the sweet to Astou Ndiaye.' This is an invitation to associate himself with the gifts which are due to a guest, to a kinsman who has come to see them.

In the following example encouragement to give is associated with the theme of matrimonial exchange in a frankly playful way.

The mother is talking to Aida (3 years): 'Do you have a fiancé?' Aida: 'Yes.' The mother: 'What's his name?' The child: 'Ablaye Diagne' (her maternal uncle who lives in the compound). The mother: 'What will you give him?' The child: 'Some rice and some *laax u bissap*.' It is very significant that, without prior suggestion, the child mentioned the required type of food prestation.

By an apparent paradox the invitation to give is seen to have the value of a gratification. This is confirmed by the two following examples:

Mareme (2 years and 7 months) is lying close against her mother, wearing a crabby, wooden look. There are many women present and several children of Mareme's age. Biscuits had been given to all the children and Mareme has some in the folds of her cloth. Her mother tries to get her out of her sulky, withdrawn mood, by asking her: 'Where are the biscuits . . . ? Aren't you going to give some to the others?' By bringing up her duty to share (superfluous in this case since all had their own) the mother was trying to re-establish communication.

The second example shows how the child is encouraged to make gifts, not only as an educative tactic aimed at the gradual integration of the child into the social system but also as an opportunity for all the the people present to reaffirm (by the fact that it provides a representation of food exchanges) the permanence of rules of exchange and reciprocity and also to avoid any threat of conflict which may have weighed down on the group for a moment.

A quite violent altercation took place between Yirim (4 years and 6 months) and his grandmother over a small box belonging to the child which the grandmother wanted to give to his small brother. Yirim cried wildly and her mother protested to the grandmother. After the child has remained disconsolate for more than half an hour, the grandmother calls out to her suddenly, in a lively way, saying: 'Come and give me some big mangoes!' Everyone bursts out laughing.

If we look more closely at this example of interaction we shall find more than one meaningful element. In asking for food a person is establishing an indebtedness of others to oneself: the child to an adult, two kinsmen, a host to his guest. By bringing up this due, the payment of which is made through the gift of food, which has a symbolic value—whether it is actually carried out or merely asked for—a person is reinforcing weakened links, evoking satisfactions which are common in all types of exchanges. However, we go further. We should take into consideration the relationship between *nawle*, a relationship which is the touchstone of Wolof social life, if we wish to understand by what kind of detours a grandmother succeeds in consoling her grandson, by asking him to make her a gift instead of giving him something. In the symmetrical relations which exist between *nawle*, giving is an action which is equivalent to an affirmation of superiority over a rival. He who gives receives respect from others and increases his own self-esteem. However, this is but one superficial aspect of the exchange. The psychological benefits seem to derive less from the prestige attached to these acts of giving a gift than from the fact by which the giver deprives himself of an article at his disposition. In other words, the real satisfaction of giving, in the eyes of others, lies more in the fact of no longer having an object, than of having had a lot. If I make a present to someone, I am not only showing that I am rich and generous . . . I am also manifesting a desire not to be superior to others, by renouncing the doubtful advantage of possessing something. The grandmother's gesture in asking the child to give her a present, in order to console him, can now be understood. In giving, one makes oneself, in a way, the 'equal' of one's 'equal', of oneself—or in other words of one's status, like the noble in relation to members of a caste.

It is in this same way that we can understand the decisive role played by the fraternal group. Adults who solicit gifts for themselves, like this grandmother, are in fact prefiguring future social exchanges which will mainly take place within the extended sibling group. If the child is asked—fairly insistently—to show proof of a disposition towards exchange and his capacity for gift-giving, it is with a view towards his concrete position among his peer group. Demands in their direction aim at obtaining an immediate mobilization of the child. Suggestions, requests, pressing demands, tireless repetitions, enticements of all kinds, are all very numerous in our notes. We shall firstly confine ourselves to two typical sequences:

The children are eating mangoes. A baby of 2 has finished his fruit and started to whimper. The mother suggests to M'Baye (3 years and 7 months) that he should give the child his mango stone which has quite a lot of flesh left on it: 'Give it to your little brother (he is in fact a patrilateral, parallel cousin . . .). Won't you give it to your little brother? Give the stone to M'Baye M'Bassel!' This ordinary sequence shows how the child is made aware of its protecting and consoling role with regard to a younger sibling—through the suggestion that he makes a gift of food.

In another sequence, Bamba (3 years and 3 months) holds some bread which I had brought along as a present. The mother took her baby (8 months) off her back and sat down in front of her. It held out its hand and tried to take the bread away from Bamba. The mother: 'Give him some . . .' The child tears off a piece of the soft part, not a very generous piece, and gives it to the mother: 'Here, give it to him!' The mother then asks Bamba again: 'Shall I give it to him?' The child: 'Yes.' Afterwards a neighbour's little daughter (6 years) comes along with her mother and receives a piece, then Bamba's elder sister and other children.

Here we see the mother halting for a moment in the act of sharing the food with the baby in order to solicit renewed acceptance from the elder boy; in this way he was made aware of the value of his role as a distributor of food.

These two sequences serve to provide a glimpse of the remarkable adaptability with which the mother and others around persuade a recently weaned child—one who has just seen himself supplanted by the birth of a younger sibling—to share food, not with adults, but with the world of his elders and young siblings.

The attention which is given to the demands of a child—which seems at first surprising—remains a constant observable fact until about 4 to 5 years. Certainly we have here a recognition of the child's wishes, accompanied by a technique of verbal encouragement which takes time into account in leading a child to make a gift. But nothing is explained by this, any more than by the assumption that the obscure links uniting a child to the world of his ancestors would impose a certain circumspection towards the child. In fact an adult's attention to the wishes of a child seems to us to boil down to a desire, on the part of the former, to avoid a direct authoritarian relation. If we consider the constant encouragement children are given to make gifts to elders and juniors in this light, the position becomes clearer; it is through his 'brothers' that the child's conduct is given a framework of social rules and regulations. It is they who are looking with society's eyes at him.

All this can be found in the little story about Gora who took the sugar from his mother's hut. Instead of chastising him with a categorical 'no!' or 'put it down!', his mother only said: 'Your little brother is going to eat it. Your elder brother is going to look after it.' The law of brothers is a law of exchange, an exchange which quickly frees itself from the supervision of direct adult intervention and comes into force in a complex play of interactions whereby a social pattern is achieved. We glimpsed this pattern in earlier learning strategies. The functioning of this process, almost independent of adults, involving rules of exchange among a group of children, is a remarkable phenomenon which our observations have confirmed unequivocally.

The following long sequence brings out clearly the oscillations of exchange which occur within the sibling group, as well as acquiescence in the rules and the various possibilities of ruptures in the equili-

brium. The interest of this example lies also in the hierarchy which
is set up between the partners. Here we are dealing with three boys,
a 'small brother', a 'middle brother', and a 'big brother': M'Baye
(5 years and 5 months), Sora (3 years) and their paternal uncle Rab
(8 years).

Sora brings *xul* pods, which he has taken from his mother's hut, out into
the courtyard. He swings the fruit up and down beside his immediate
elder, M'Baye, who is lying on the sand. The latter asks for one and gets
one pod. Sora, who has taken hold of the whole armful of *xul*, cries out:
'Rara, I want to put these *xul* in the calabash!' At this moment the children's
young uncle, Rab (8 years) comes in on his way home from school.

Rab also asks for some fruit. After resisting for a while Sora agrees to
share. A little later he asks Rab to help him prepare a pod: 'Peel it!' Rab
takes off the skin carefully and takes out, whole, the long yellow seed:
'Look, Sora,' Sora takes it, contentedly. Rab begins another: 'Look, Sora.'
M'Baye does the same: 'Look, Rab, I've done it.'

The children eat. Rab has taken charge of operations. M'Baye, who is
trying to get a pod from him, asks: 'Rab, give me one.' But Rab makes a
gesture as if to keep it. 'Wait . . . I want to peel it.' Finally when M'Baye
insists Rab lets him have it.

Sora then opens up the empty husks. He is half-lying and half-sitting
on a large calabash (not far from him, Diana [3 years], his *moroom* [com-
panion, equal] is lying by her big sister). From his position Sora says,
touching the fruit: 'You have spoiled it, Rab.' He looks at him and repeats
the phrase.

M'Baye takes it up and in turn says: 'You spoiled it.' Then, showing
Rab two empty pods: 'You ate two of them!' He takes two full pods for
himself. While Sora, in turn, asks for a pod, Rab remarks to M'Baye: 'You
took the biggest ones!' To Sora, who keeps asking for more, M'Baye gives
a piece of peeled fruit.

Soon Sora gets up, goes into the hut and brings back a full pod. M'Baye
then says: 'Pay me!' and holds out his hand. Sora does so, giving him the
pod. M'Baye turns to Rab: 'Rab, he has paid me!' Sora, satisfied, takes up
the phrase: 'I have paid you!'

Let us analyse this sequence:
At the outset Sora occupies a role given him by the adult world.
He has the privilege of helping himself to food from his mother's
hut. As a junior he has a right to food.

With his first confrontation with his elder brother he comes up
against the rule of exchange and submits. He gives to M'Baye,
although the gift seems somewhat capricious. He is apparently
rather keen to keep all the food for himself ('I want to put them in the

calabash'). Rab comes along, holding the position of the adult law-maker *vis-à-vis* M'Baye and Sora, and therefore establishes an equilibrium. His request 'Give me some,' makes the food something which belongs to the group.

After this 'Give me', expressed by M'Baye and Rab, we then have the 'Look at me' of Rab and Sora, from M'Baye to Rab. The calls for the attention of others begin with the phase of collaboration while the object circulates. Rab replies to Sora's gift with another gift. He asks to be looked at—at himself and at his work.

M'Baye wants to do the same. He asks Rab to look at him. In doing so is he rivalling the latter's position, since he is in the middle of the three boys and has no means of making a gift?

After this collaborative phase, the exchange deteriorates: Rab threatens to keep all the pods for himself; and he temporizes when M'Baye makes his request.

An interruption from Sora brings us back to the starting-point and the situation whereby external adult authority guarantees the younger brother's role: 'You spoiled it!' says the child to Rab. The fact that he is speaking in the name of the adults is doubly marked here: on the level of speech—because of the nature of his normative com-ments; and on the postural plane—by the boy's attitude, with his body supported to a large extent by his mother's calabash. (He is lying in the same position as Diana, his equal, who is lying by her elder sister.) Thus the threat of a rupture in the exchange in this way forces one of the members of the sibling group to call symbolically for an external ruling: Sora evokes, fictively, adult intervention.

For a second time Sora goes back to the initial situation and to the support of adults. Let us look at the cause. The exchange has con-tinued to deteriorate. The rule of the strongest has begun to dominate the rule of circulation within the fraternal group. Rab has taken more for himself than he should have done: 'You ate two of them,' says M'Baye. Faced with the stronger law, M'Baye attempts to rival his elder's transgression. He also takes two large pods. The exchange is blocked by this rivalry between the two elder boys. On his side Sora finds himself opposed to his immediate elder. He gets only a small part of M'Baye's booty. He again relies on adult support and goes back into the hut to find further provisions. The youngest, sheltered by adults, puts a stop to the rule of the strongest; now the exchange can begin again. The rules are then reaffirmed; Sora 'reimburses' M'Baye and Rab is no longer brought in as a witness. Rab once again becomes the middle term which he was at the beginning, watching over the respective roles of the persons involved in the exchange. This long sequence illustrates the functioning and regulating of exchange within a fraternal group. Without any external intervention it constantly oscillates between a tendency to break down—which means the adult world has to be called in—and a return to the rules of circulation. A mechanism for self-regulation exists in the fraternal group, due to the power inherent in the word of the adult, whose direct intervention is no longer needed.

CONCLUSION

Western observers like to measure degrees of constraint in a vertical lineal fashion (if we may be permitted to express ourselves in this way) as far as exchanges between parents and children are concerned. They tend to ignore those lateral interventions which exist on all levels. We hold that it is this which leads to conclusions—in many cases at least—that we are dealing with situations of heightened tension or, on the other hand, situations which are prone to considerable permissiveness and *laissez-aller*. Our observations for the Wolof, show almost unequivocally, that it is wrong to restrict our studies even to the seductive image of a chain of classificatory 'mothers' and 'fathers', whose intervention is vital. We should also take into consideration decisive and weighty factors involved in the fraternal group. Here, our observations have brought out an important point, viz. that the Wolof education system aims less at imposing adult rules on the child, than at creating conditions by which a child gains an awareness and a respect for the 'laws of brothers and equals'. From the most tender age, and by the subtlest of means, it is continually impressed upon the child that 'the others' are primarily his 'brothers' and his age companions. While satisfactions which he gains through body contact and play with the mother are gradually transferred to these persons, the verbal comments of the group as a whole suggest to the child gestures of giving and sharing, which punctuate regularly the new types of physical exchanges and allow the child and his brothers to become social partners. Lateral exchanges, thus strengthened through a long, privileged mediation of giving and offering food, progress steadily to the detriment of those vertical exchanges which preceded them. The latter do not entirely disappear of course, but they are refashioned; from now on any confrontation between adult and child will be mediated by the status which membership of the fraternal group has conferred on him.

Index